Once Upon a Two by Four

by

Ann Combs

ENDICOTT AND HUGH BOOKS

Once Upon A Two By Four

Endicott & Hugh Books
P.O. Box 13305, Burton, WA 98013

www.endicottandhughbooks.com

Copyright © 2012 by Ann Combs

All rights reserved, including the right to reproduce this book, or portions thereof, in any form. Published by Endicott and Hugh Books, Burton, Washington. www.endicottandhughbooks.com

Publisher's Cataloging-In-Publication Data
(Prepared by The Donohue Group, Inc.)

Combs, Ann, 1935-
  [Helter shelter. 2012]
  Once upon a two by four / by Ann Combs. -- 1st ed.

    p. ; cm.

  Originally published: Helter Shelter. Philadelphia : Williams & Wilkins, 1979.
  "Portions of chapter 16 have appeared in The Times Magazine ... and in Helter Shelter, Lippincott, Williams and Wilkins ... "--copyright page.
  ISBN: 978-0-9837115-5-1 (trade paperback)

    1. Combs, Ann, 1935- 2. Combs, Ann, 1935---Family. 3. Bainbridge Island (Wash.)--Biography.   4. Dwellings--Remodeling--Washington (State)--Bainbridge Island. I. Title. II. Title: Helter shelter.
CT275.C73 A36 2012
979.7/76/092 Ba

Book design by Masha Shubin, Cover Photos by Amanda Devine

ISBN: 978-0-9837115-5-1 Trade paperback

978-0-9837115-6-8

Printed in the United States of America

10 9 8 7 6 5 4 3 2 1

First Edition

To the late Larry Ashmead, who first gave me a chance at fame and fortune and, since they seem to have eluded me to Jeanie Okimoto who is now giving me another one

Table of Contents

Prologue

Bainbridge Island was discovered in 1792 by Captain George Vancouver, but then so was almost everything else on Puget Sound. Apparently he wasn't overly impressed with what he found, for after he dropped anchor in what is now Blakely Harbor, he chopped down a tree or two to fix his mast, had a few words in sign language with Chief Kitsap, named Restoration Point in honor of Charles II, and sailed blithely on to discover something else.

Some fifty years later Captain Charles Wilkes was sent out this way by the U.S. government to draw up maps and charts. Therefore every rock, island, and inlet that Vancouver hadn't named for his friends or the kings of England, Wilkes named for American war heroes or presidents of the United States.

Between the two of them they were busy, for Puget Sound extends for a hundred miles from the Strait of Juan de Fuca in the north to Olympia in the south, and in between are islands of every shape and size, not to mention spits and reaches and hooks and peninsulas, and except for a few like Nisqually Reach or Skagit Bay, all have names like Madison, Budd, Admiralty, or Pickering.

Wilkes named our island after William Bainbridge, a naval hero of the War of 1812. It's one of the larger islands, approximately twelve miles long and four or five miles wide, and it's shaped, I used to think when I was little and lay in bed staring at the map on my closet door, like the head of a man with a scraggly goatee.

Eight miles due west of Seattle, it sits and watches as tugs tow their barges up the sound, freighters steam in from the Orient and yachts, spinnakers filled and billowing, glide back and forth outrunning the wind.

Port Blakely, Captain Vancouver's stopover and once the site of the world's largest sawmill, is at the south end of the island and looks across at West Seattle.

North of Port Blakely, up the eastern shore, is Eagle Harbor, a wide, twisting bay, with Winslow, our only city, sprawled on its north side. Marinas and public docks cluster along the beaches, and farmhouses sit complacently on the hills and look out over the water.

From Eagle Harbor the coastline winds north, jutting out for a point here, cutting back for a cove there, and the homes up on the bluffs and those down on the beach nudge and shove each other trying to get elbowroom.

On the north end of the Island is Port Madison. In 1854 George A. Meigs built a lumber mill and Bainbridge Island's first town there. The mill is long since gone, but some of the houses remain, and now along the quiet bay are stately homes and private docks and lawns that sweep down to the water.

From here the shore goes up to Agate Point, past the swift, treacherous currents of Agate Pass, past the bridge that is our one link to the Olympic Peninsula. Then it's down the west side of the Island, where harbors are still and calm. There sunsets stream in living-room windows and fishing boats troll up and down the narrow channel in front.

Point White is at the southern end of Bainbridge, on the western side. Here the summer cottages have been shored up, added to, and tucked in at the comers for winter living. Here new houses spring up overnight and fight for space at the water's edge. When the ferry steams through Rich Passage and heads down the channel for Bremerton, children run up and down the beach and wave at the captain.

From Point White the land sweeps around past a cluster of stores at Lynwood, past Pleasant Beach, past the now deserted radio station at Fort Ward, until finally it turns the corner at Restoration Point.

Down the sound to the south of Bainbridge, Vashon Island stretches out and hides Tacoma. To the north is Whidbey Island, and all around us are the mountains.

The Olympics, craggy and snowcapped for most of the year, run down the spine of the Olympic Peninsula and form our western horizon. In winter, storms roll in from the Pacific and spill over them like waterfalls. In summer, seeing their black silhouettes against the pinks and oranges of sunset, one can almost smell the smoke from ancient Indian campfires or hear the lonely cry of the hawk in the days when virgin forests grew down the hills to the water's edge.

The Cascades to the east are lumpier, tamer, and less visible behind the smoke and haze of Seattle. Every now and then, however, after what we call a good rain (the month of November is usually a good rain), the Cascades lift their curtain and reveal Mount Baker, a restless volcano up near the Canadian border, and Mount Rainier, an exquisite 14,408-foot mirage to the south.

Bainbridge, like all the other islands around here, is tied to civilization and the January white sales by the ferries. In the old days passenger steamers of the Mosquito fleet darted in and out of harbors along our shoreline twice a day, then scooted back to Seattle for safety. Now superferries glide across the sound, daring other boats to get in their way, and you can rush into Seattle for a Chinese cooking lesson in the morning, come home in the afternoon, and take the 6:30 back in for dinner and a ball game.

The ferry schedule rules life here. Things amble along slowly and leisurely; then every forty minutes or so the boat pulls into Winslow, the roads clog, cars back up at the two stoplights and tourists rush headlong up the highway and head for the bridge and the Olympic Peninsula. People caught at the intersections trying to cross from west to east swear and fume while their ice-cream cones melt. Then suddenly it's all over and we take a slow, deep breath and meander on our way again.

The boats make finite affairs of dinner parties that include guests from Seattle. For when the Chicken Marengo's gone, the brandy's been poured, the fire's dying down and you don't think you can take another episode of Florence and Henry's trip to Maui, you simply leap up and shout, "Oh, my God, you only have fifteen minutes to make the boat!" and the evening is over.

On the other hand, no Islander has ever seen the last act of Hamlet or heard the choral movement of Beethoven's Ninth, for just as the sopranos are getting warmed up or Hamlet's saying, "Alas, poor Yorick! I knew him, Horatio," the Bainbridge contingent rises en masse and leaves for the 10:30 boat.

Islanders are an eccentric lot too. We have a conglomeration of bankers and fishermen, lawyers and evangelists. We have the residents of The Country Club at Restoration Point, where deeds to the land have been handed down virtually by apostolic succession since 1890, and we have Indians whose ancestors predate recorded history. We have grandchildren of the early pioneers, and families who just moved in from Kansas. We have the young and the earnest who are searching for a meaningful relationship but are content to settle for less if it's organically grown. We have the staid and the conservative who insist Richard Nixon was maligned and think the Russians are the reason May was cold and rainy. We have Sally Madrone, who owns a gift shop and yells, "Don't touch the merchandise!" if you pick up a cup and saucer, and we have the librarian who calls to say, "A book just came in that I think you'd like."

We have surgeons who look like longshoremen, and longshoremen who play Mozart concertos. We have old Mr. Torgeson, who raises chickens so fat they break their legs leaping off their perches, and Grandma Harriot, who carves historic scenes on cubes of butter.

We have the violently healthy who trot up and down the hills and jog to work each morning, and we have the overweight who form fat clubs and confess to each other they eat because they're sexually deprived.

We have artists and lumbermen, psychiatrists and deck-hands, contractors and politicians, teachers and mechanics. And every other person on the Island is in real estate—men who've retired, wives whose husbands fish in Alaska, and mothers whose children are finally in school. They're all out checking property lines and getting earnest money down.

Have a couple to dinner and he'll offer to sell you a two-bedroom cottage on the beach for only $40,000 down. Let your son invite a friend over, and when his mother comes to get him she'll tell you she has people from El Centro who'll give you cash for your home.

And why? Who knows. In summer, living on Bainbridge is like falling in love. The morning tides are low, the breeze is brisk and salty, and the clams squirt up through the sand and tunnel back down almost faster than you can dig. Then everything is new and fresh. The afternoons are hot and lazy and sensual and humming with the sound of bees. And out on the water, sailboats pester the ferries and make them veer off course.

In fall, the love is consummated with maples turning orange, and blackberries fat and succulent waiting to be picked. Then the apples ripen and the plums turn dark and purple, and the poplar trees are golden paintbrushes against the sky.

But the love wears thin in winter. That is when you find out your in-laws are those weeks of rain, and leaky roofs, and days that end at five o'clock. The soft, caressing breezes are replaced by winds that whip out of the south and whine and complain in the night. This is when puddles envelop the driveway, lakes form on the lawn and the weatherman is at a loss for new adjectives to describe the leaden skies that drip down the back of your neck.

Life on Bainbridge is not for the city-bred or for those used to the amenities. The lights go out when storms bluster through in the winter. The septic tank invariably backs up on the Fourth of July. Wells run dry in summer, and basements flood in January.

Repairmen here have unlisted numbers and can only be reached between six and six twenty on alternate Wednesdays, and never during the salmon season.

Public transportation consists of one taxi that comes only when you have a reservation. If your car's in the shop and you have to get to Winslow or the ferry, you have three choices: walk, beg a ride from neighbors, or do as old Mrs. Duncan does —stand by the side of the road and when a car goes by whack it with a stick to make it stop and pick you up.

A trip to Winslow is not something you plan a whole day around, however, for though it's officially a city and has the papers to prove it, like a ten-year-old who wears her mother's panty hose and stuffs her training bra, it somehow doesn't quite pull it off.

The architecture along the one main street is a combination of Frontier Clapboard, California Adobe, Swiss Alpine, and Longhouse Rustic, with a blue-and-orange bowling alley thrown in for gusto. And though we have gift shops and insurance agencies, a bank and a shoe store, though you can buy diamond rings and imported cheese, wicker chairs and crystal goblets, and though the supermarket has dried squid and Italian chestnuts, the drugstore only carries magazines for people who move their lips when they read, the dress shop limits its selection to anything you want—in size 3—and you have to journey into Seattle to find a set of king-sized sheets in anything but white.

Nor can you find a policeman when you need one on Bainbridge. The county sheriff is rarely closer than half an hour away. He's based in Port Orchard, a town thirty-five miles to the south of us, and unless he's out hunting speeders, you might as well ask the burglar who's walking off with your TV set to leave his name and number, and tell him you'll get back to him.

Winslow, of course, has its own police department, but it only serves those within the city limits. If you live twenty feet across the line and a deranged rapist crawls in your bedroom window in the middle of the night, you're out of luck.

We have a crack fire and medic squad, though. They've revived people with cardiac arrest, rescued stranded boaters, and airlifted accident victims to hospitals in Seattle. When there's a fire, however, though they arrive within minutes of the call, the building somehow always burns to the ground.

Night owls and carousers don't fare well over here either, for entertainment is hard to come by. We have one theater at Lynwood. It's open most evenings, most of the time, and offers a sprinkling of box-office hits combined with The Cockroach That Ate Chicago.

Of course there's the drive-in on the main highway across the bridge. It has the latest XXX-rated features. If you can read lips and hips, you can pull over by the side of the road and see Warm, Wondrous, and Wanton for free.

Other than that, nightlife is pretty much limited to Open Gym at the high school, a sixth-grade band concert, or a marijuana bust at the bowling alley.

And yet, where else will the postmaster call you and say, "The letter from your editor finally came. I'll hold it out and if you like you can come get it"? Where else can you stick a note on the parking meter saying, I don't have any change, but I'll pay when I get back from Seattle? Where can you cash a check without having to show your driver's license, your birth certificate, and a Xerox copy of your high-school diploma? And where can you find a city with a bank that's only been held up once in thirty years? Of course, it is rather futile to wave a gun at the teller, grab the loot, leap into the getaway car, and then have to wait down at the dock for the 10:30 boat.

So we stay on—those of us who've had to heat up soup in the fireplace when the power's off and who've always worn the layered look with sweater over sweater over sweater. We stay on and pay the taxes that go with what is called "waterfront property." We fight to keep the ferries when someone suggests a bridge to Seattle, and we discourage any who would join us.

1

How Many Bedrooms?

In 1970 Karl Wallenda inched across the 700-foot-deep Tallu-lah Gorge in Georgia on a tightrope, Thor Heyerdahl pushed off in his papyrus boat for a transatlantic voyage, Dean Caldwell and Warren Harding clawed their way straight up the face of El Capitan in Yosemite National Park, and my husband, Joe, and I bought an old house on Bainbridge Island and set about remodeling it by ourselves.

We weren't pioneers in the field. Ever since the 1850s, in the days of Chief Seattle, when wood-frame mill houses and white picket fences were sprouting up in every cove and harbor on the Island, residents have been building and rebuilding their homes, adding a porch here and an extra room there.

Unlike most Islanders, though, when Joe and I moved to Bainbridge our training in carpentry had been negligible. We weren't overqualified for the job. I'd read a book, Joe had made a few unsteady shelves and together we'd built a toy chest from a Better Homes and Gardens instruction kit.

But we had little choice. Joe, forty-two and a major in the Air Force, was retiring after twenty years, and the time had come to pack away our passports and settle down in a house that would be ours for longer than the average military tour of duty.

Besides, we work well together. I get an inspiration, see it full-blown in my mind, and batter Joe with,

"Wouldn't it be fun to... ?" and "Why don't we... ?" He, on the other hand, considers a project from every angle and then proceeds slowly and carefully.

I envision the back door a bright yellow and campaign to slap a coat on before dinner. Joe takes my word that the color will be "perfect"; then he removes the door, sands it down, and fills all the nail holes before carefully applying the first coat. And when in mid-project my enthusiasm wanes and I'm on to something else, he carries through till the job is done.

If we'd had one or maybe two children, we might have bought a modest three-bedroom home in the suburbs and spent our declining forty or fifty years fighting the crabgrass, papering the den, and vacationing in Tahiti. But we had a tribe —six scrambling, fighting, boisterous, exuberant children— and our aim in life, if not to have an opulent mansion on forty acres with a tennis court and a swimming pool, was at least to find a home in which each child could have his or her own room. It was a matter of survival.

When Joe and I were married in the late fifties, our idea of parenthood consisted of having pudgy babies in Dr. Dentons who grew into bright, industrious schoolchildren, occasionally rebellious teenagers, and, finally, charming adults. I imagined brothers and sisters playing Monopoly together on winter evenings and pooling their allowances to buy me spring bouquets and lacy Mother's Day cards.

Obviously I'd read *The Five Little Peppers* once too often. The last Mother's Day card I got said:

> *Roses are red,*
> *Violets are blue,*
> *I think I smell dog do,*
> *I think you do too.*

So, with retirement staring us in the checkbook and six raving individualists as yet unraised (David was then twelve; Sylvia, ten; Jenny, eight; Geoffrey, seven; and the twins, Robbie and Joan, five), we were in the market for a large, inexpensive piece of land on which stood a large, if weather-beaten, house with six bedrooms far enough from ours to mute the cries of "Let go of my arm or I'll tell what you have in your drawer!" We'd given up on the dormitory idea when there were only four of them, and though we'd tried numerous roommate combinations, none had worked. Inevitably, the vulgar one got in with the prissy one, the neat one with the slob, and the student with the goof-off.

David was given a room of his own early, shortly after he turned seven. It was just as well. David—tall, serious, and a hermit since birth—is our mathematician. He's the type of child whose idea of a good time is spending a Sunday afternoon adding up six years of check stubs. He thrives on new math, old math, algebra, trigonometry, calculus, and astronomy. He can multiply fractions in his head, compute the interest on the national debt, and convert statute miles to nautical miles and back again for anyone who's interested. I haven't understood a thing he's said since he was in the second grade.

When David was eight he decided to see how far he could count. It was a trying time for all of us. He counted during breakfast, counted on the way to school, and lay in bed at night mumbling, "One thousand two hundred seventy-five, one thousand two hundred seventy-six, one thousand two hundred seventy-seven ...

I still haven't recovered from the night I was sleeping peacefully when David burst in the door and shook me awake. "Mom," he said. "Mom, wake up!"

I bolted upright. "What's the matter? Are you sick?"

"No ... no, Mom, nothing's wrong. I want to tell you something."

"Honey, it's late."

"I know. But I was in my room figuring, and—"

"If you can't sleep, David, take an aspirin or a warm bath."

"It's not that. Listen to me for a minute."

"All right, all right, I'm listening. Go ahead."

"Mom," he said, his voice rising with excitement, "I'm positive I've trisected an angle!"

He waited for the news to sink in. Joe, his eyes wild and his dark hair standing on end, reared up next to me. "What's the matter? What the hell's going on?" he bellowed.

"David's trisected an angle."

"Huh?" Joe tried to bring his mind into focus, then gave up and flopped back onto his pillow.

David shrugged. "I'm going up and check the proofs once more."

Sylvia earned her own room when she was eight. It was the natural order of things. She was next in line. Besides, Sylvia was not easy to room with.

She's our volcano. She burst into this world bellowing, "Hello, out there! It's me, Sylvia. What's happening?" and she has yet to slow down. She's a girl of extremes, with a round face, huge blue eyes, and golden hair, cut, for longer than she wished, in a Dutch bob. She either shrieks or whispers. She's a tomboy or a lady, vulgar or sedate, and there's nothing she won't try. When she was three she learned how to ride a bicycle. When she was five she broke her arm roller-skating down a hill. And it was she who vaulted off our roof with a blanket for a parachute.

She and David were roommates as babies and toddlers. At nap time, if he slept, she kangarooed her crib over to his and pelted him with sticky pacifiers and wet diapers.

By the time she was in school we'd put her in with Jenny. Sylvia was in her neat phase by then. Jenny wasn't, and it infuriated her that Jenny couldn't make her bed. So every morning before she left, she made both beds, usually with Jenny still in hers.

The fall Sylvia was seven was our Superman period. She and David spent their spare time draped in bath towels and launching themselves off the couch yelling, "Up, up, and away!"

Jenny ignored them, but Geoffrey watched silently for days, mesmerized by their derring-do. Then one day Sylvia saw her opportunity and took him in hand.

"Now it's your turn," she told him as she tied a towel around his neck. "Don't worry, it's simple. You stand on the couch and flap your arms. When you get going fast enough, jump off, and you'll fly."

Geoffrey held back for a while, but she egged him on, and finally he clambered up on the table. He flapped as hard and as fast as he could. Then he leaped up into the air and crashed to the floor.

As he picked himself up and I checked for broken bones, Sylvia sighed. "Dummy," she said, "you didn't flap hard enough."

Jenny chose a less bombastic route to prominence in the family. Petite and dainty and our only redhead, she let it be known early that climbing trees and shagging balls was not her idea of fun. She preferred more refined activities.

At the age of two she spent her leisure hours tiptoeing around the neighborhood trying to rustle up a tea party. She likes ruffles and lace, bone-china teacups and maidenhair fern. She rescues birds and cats and lame spiders, and grows pots of weeds on her windowsill.

Our pianist, Jenny, gave me a near-perfect rendition of the "Moonlight Sonata" one Christmas. She's also our Broadway producer (I personally have attended fourteen operas, six plays, and a recitation) and our family hostess. She greets guests who come early and delights them by saying, "Mom'll be in when she gets her girdle on."

Jenny is definitely a charmer, but underneath this frothy exterior beats the heart of a despot—and not a benevolent one. I detect it when I won't let her bake cookies at midnight or when she decides to produce her latest opera.

On rainy Sunday afternoons when she's bored but the rest of us aren't, Jenny gets opera fever.

"Today we're going to put on an opera," she announces.

"Not me," Geoffrey calls out.

"Me either."

"I hate opera."

"That's only because you don't know how," Jenny responds. "I'm going to teach you."

"Not me."

"Me either."

"Joan has a crummy voice."

Sensing she's losing control, Jenny resorts to force, and soon pillows are flying, Robbie's being dragged by the scruff of the neck and Geoffrey's charging with the broom or a baseball bat. This is when Joe roars out from watching TV in the bedroom and misses the touchdown of the century.

When it's all over and I've forbidden any more operas for the next three years, I hear Jenny over in the far corner of the living room whispering to Joan. "Here's your part," she says. "You play the ugly stepsister."

Geoffrey's another sort of person entirely. For one thing, he's shy. He doesn't stare at the floor or scuff his feet in the dirt, but he doesn't start conversations with visiting clergy or aging relatives either. When Grandmother comes by and the other children are climbing all over her, filling her with lies about how good they've been and how much better they'd be if they could go outside with a new pair of roller skates, Geoffrey stands off to one side saying nothing. He simply grins. Naturally, he ends up with the skates.

Another thing sets Geoffrey apart from the others. He's neat. He has been ever since I can remember. It's not my fault. I gave him the same meticulous training I gave the others. But he was born in Japan and spent his formative years following Fusako-san, our maid, around. It was she, not I, who taught him to put his toys away, pick up his blocks, and bring his tricycle home, and under her tutelage he learned to wipe up spilled milk and orange-juice stains.

Lately he's getting so he leaves his shoes under the couch and his basketball in the bathroom, but still he never turns in school assignments with footprints in the margin or goes off in the morning wearing one blue sock and one brown sock.

Not only is Geoffrey tidy with his clothes and his belongings, but he thinks neatly too. He never flashes his thought processes around, which is marvelous for him and makes his reports on "The Phases of Venus" clear and concise, but half the time I haven't the faintest idea what he's talking about.

"How much is Texas worth?" he asks me as I sit trying to balance my checkbook. "How much does the sun weigh?" and "How many gallons of water does a tree suck up in a day?"

I prepared myself early with answers to questions such as "Who is God?" and "Why is grass green?" but he's not interested in that.

"How do you make a freeway?" he asks, and though I try to answer, bringing in tar and gravel and cloverleafs, it never suffices. So he goes back to his solitary wondering, and days later, when all thoughts of freeway construction have flown from my mind, he comes at me again.

"Are you sure you don't know how to?"

"How to what?"

"You know. What we were talking about."

"When?"

"The other day."

"Which other day?"

"When I asked you."

"Asked me what?"

"Oh, never mind."

To this day we haven't settled how to make a freeway. What Geoffrey lacks in verbiage, the twins, Robbie and Joan, more than make up for. When they blew on the scene, their brothers and sisters had been at this business of living for a long time. So for about a year they sat back, took notes, and were amenable to being dragged around the house by Sylvia and Jenny (who wanted real babies when they played house), to being ignored by David (who said they were messy and smelled), and to being tolerated by Geoffrey (who roomed with them and had to pick up the toys they tossed out of their cribs).

Once they figured out what was going on, they set about carving their own niches. Robbie, a wide smile under an umbrella of yellow hair, seeing that we had no dedicated slob in the family, rushed to fill that position. Joan, awed by the total pandemonium, decided to worry.

Robbie attained perfection in his chosen field almost immediately. Whereas his coordination is such that he runs faster, jumps farther, and climbs higher than any of the others, he's never mastered the art of closing anything, and he thinks a hanger is only meant for getting marbles out from under the drier. He's the only child I know who keeps his toys in his dresser, his socks in the toy chest or the woodbox, his shoes out by the lawn mower, and his coat on the floor of the car.

Robbie's aim in life, as far as I can tell, is either to be a carpenter, building boats, rafts, go-carts, and doghouses, or a demolition expert, concentrating on tearing apart boats, rafts, go-carts, and doghouses. It all hangs on whether he finds the lost crowbar or the lost hammer first. He built a marvelous doghouse once—but he didn't include a door, and someone had to be on duty at all times to lift it up when the dogs wanted in or out.

Nothing daunts Robbie, and nothing scares him. He'll climb a tree with his leg's in a cast or attack David, who's a good three feet taller than he. When he was nine he had open-heart surgery, and three days after the operation he sat up in bed, with drainage tubes and other paraphernalia drooping all over, and said, "Well, what was so bad about that?"

Joan, on the other hand, takes life seriously. She suffers for the world. If I serve pot roast for dinner and the carrots are crunchy, as they are wont to be at times, while Joe is snarling and asking why I wasn't home to put them in earlier and the rest are gagging and hiding theirs under the plate, Joan chews bravely on and insists they're the best carrots she ever ate. She's the one who brings me bouquets of wild flowers on a rainy day, who offers me tea when I have the flu, and who writes thank- you letters without having to be threatened.

And Joan is a planner. By Easter, she's wondering who her teachers will be in the fall. By the first of May she's figured out her Halloween costume, and Christmas preparations are ever on her mind.

Four years ago she picked out the house she wants to live in when she grows up. Without seeing the inside, she decided on the bedroom arrangement, where she wanted the living- room furniture, and what color she would paint the kitchen.

"The first Thanksgiving I'm in my house," she told me one day, "I'll have you and Daddy over to dinner. We'll have turkey and dressing and mashed potatoes and sweet potatoes and the bean stuff and strawberry salad and three kinds of pies." Then she thought for a minute. "Would you cook it for me, Mom? I don't know how to cook."

In 1970, Joe and I and this group of wild nonconformists lived and churned and stumbled over each other in a house like all the other houses on our street in Colorado Springs, Colorado. We squeezed around the table in the dining area at mealtimes. We struggled through the kitchen, fighting our way to the sink or the refrigerator, and we all ended up in the bathroom at the same time. It was obvious that if anyone grew so much as an inch more we would burst through the walls. So during the week we carried on as usual. On Saturdays and Sundays we looked for a larger house.

There were plenty of houses for sale. The city was growing in all directions, heading up a mountain here, creeping out across a plain there. There were whole settlements springing up with street names like Serendipity Circle and Never Mind Lane. There were ranch houses and town houses, old houses and new houses. We traipsed through each and every one: through daylight basements and rec rooms, through family rooms complete with indoor barbecue pits, and out onto decks that overlooked the patio and a triple garage.

"How many bedrooms?" we asked, and the salesmen showed us two or three tiny rooms with shallow closets and mechanical windows that wound out to let in an inch or two of air.

"But our king-sized bed won't fit," we complained.

The salesmen sneered. "Most people don't have those."

And they left us to find our own way out.

One house we saw was exactly what I had in mind. The stairs were wide and winding, with a landing larger than our living room. There were cozy bedrooms on the third floor, with slanted ceilings and dormer windows. One of the four fireplaces was in the master bedroom, and the dining room had both a crystal chandelier and pocket doors that slid silently out of the wall and latched with a barely audible click.

"How many bedrooms?" we asked, and I felt a surge of excitement when the answer came back: seven.

"And how much are you asking for the house?"

We found our own way out.

One night, after months of peering into closets, measuring kitchens, and asking the eternal question, "How many bedrooms?" Joe and I lay in bed reviewing the places we'd seen that day. Suddenly I sat up.

"What if we moved back to Bainbridge?" I asked. "Maybe we could buy an old farmhouse and fix it up."

We'd both grown up on the island. We'd spent our summers digging clams and swimming in the icy waters of Puget Sound. We'd picked wild blackberries and baked salmon over an alderwood beach fire. We'd been brought up in the rain and laughed at people who carried umbrellas. We'd searched the woods for trilliums and lady's slippers in the spring, sneezed when the Scotch broom came out and itched when we got into the poison oak. I'd even picked strawberries to earn enough money to buy a Mickey Mouse watch. Surely, I thought, there'd be a place for us there.

Joe stared at me. "Do you mean it? Do you really want to?"

"Yes, yes, I do."

The next morning we consulted the children.

"How'd you like to move back to Bainbridge Island when we retire?" Joe asked.

"Hooray!" they shouted.

And it was settled.

So it was as Karl Wallenda headed for Tallulah Gorge, Thor Heyerdahl loaded the Ra II with provisions, and Dean Caldwell and Warren Harding laid out their ropes and pitons that Joe and the children and I brought out the trunks and the suitcases and got ready to head home.

2

Look for Signs of Settling

No one buys a house because it's on an island, has windows that swing out, and has an upstairs door you can't get to that leads nowhere. No one disregards a minuscule septic tank, an inadequate water supply, and a heater of ill repute, seeing only an enormous lawn and a dogwood tree outside the bedroom window. But we did, and one thing's for certain: Repairing and remodeling it in order to make it livable has kept us out of trouble, off the streets, away from bars, and in debt for the last eight years.

In nineteen years of marriage, Joe and I have lived in eight different houses, including this one. They've ranged from a garage apartment in Texas with a three-foot-long bathtub, where we gnawed our knees clean, to a quadruplex in Tokyo, where our bedroom window adjoined that of a little boy named Kenny who threw up every morning at five thirty.

We and the children have experienced every disaster a house has to offer, with the possible exception of having it collapse totally.

We've had water heaters burst in the night and flood the basement. Second-story windows have leaped off their tracks and plummeted to the ground below, shearing off the outside faucet in the process. Kitchen light fixtures have dropped off the ceiling, and furnaces have expired with a final, all-pervading, sooty blast. But not until we bought a house on Bainbridge and started remodeling it by ourselves have disasters lined up expectantly, waiting for their turn at us.

One would think that with our luck we would have left nothing to chance and would have tapped and tested every two-by-four before we bought this house. Come to think of it, we intended to. But then we saw it.

It was one of those rare June days on Puget Sound. The fog had lifted. The drizzle had blown off somewhere south of Mount Rainier, and the sunshine was skating over the blue water and fluffing up the murmuring pines and hemlocks. It was one of those days when both the Olympics and the Cascades had brushed the clouds from their foothills like cake crumbs, and the gulls on the waterfront were screeching and circling and drying out their wings. It was the kind of day we hide from the tourists lest they decide to stay, a time when the natives stand around nodding their heads, saying, "See, aren't we clever to have decided to live here?"

I was doing just that as I stood on the deck of the ferry from Seattle to Bainbridge and inhaled all the clean, familiar smells of salt air and seaweed and watched a sailboat heading into the breeze up near Whidbey and saw the Vashon ferry dog-paddling its way back to the mainland. I was home again, and this time to stay. Traveling, packing, and unpacking with the Air Force was almost over.

The air was fresh, like clear mountain water, and I couldn't seem to get enough of it—perhaps because I'd just made the two-thousand-mile trip from Colorado Springs stuffed in our Volkswagen bus with all the children, three cats, and a large box of rancid Kitty Litter.

Joe, who liberated me way before it was fashionable, and certainly before I was ready, was still in Colorado.

"It's simple," he'd said when we first decided to come back. "Since I don't retire till the end of August, the smart thing to do is have you and the children go up and stay with your parents till you find a house. Then you can move in and get the children settled before school."

I couldn't fault his logic, but somehow visions of his playing golf and sipping martinis down there while I unpacked dishes, set up the beds, and arranged the furniture kept swimming in front of my eyes. I knew he meant it when he professed to get lonely without us. He claimed the silence depressed him after a day or two, and he found himself listening for the sound of a good, honest fight over who's hogging the Sunday funnies. Frankly, I thought he'd been hitting himself over the head with a hammer for so long he'd forgotten it's supposed to feel good when you stop. And I longed for a week or two of his depression. But I had no counterproposal, so here I was, as the ferry churned its way across the sound, watching the Island grow larger and the Olympics, which had loomed in the west when we left Seattle, gradually sink behind the lumpy, green horizon of Bainbridge.

The children raced around the decks, checked the cigarette machines for change, and every now and then stopped to ask, "Can you see the house from here?" "When do we get there?" "Are we going to buy it?"

My reply to everything was, "I don't know. We'll see. Grandmother will show us when we get there."

Mother was my scout. With the impetus of an extended visit at her house, she'd rushed out at the first word of our coming, checked all the available houses for sale, and had come up with one she thought might be what we wanted.

"It has potential, and I think you can afford it," she'd written before we left.

Potential in a house you can't afford, I later found out, means there's room for a tennis court and a gazebo on the back six acres. Potential in a house you can afford means the roof leaks, there's no insulation, and the heating system is as effective as a fire in an ashtray.

But it was June. The sun was warm on my back. Soon I could air out the bus, find the hard-boiled egg we'd lost under the front seat somewhere between Laramie and Rock Springs, rest my driving foot, and sing my last chorus of "When the Ants Go Marching

One by One, Hurrah, Hurrah." So as the ferry slid into the dock we all climbed back in the bus and set off to meet Mother.

She was waiting in her car, and after a brief flurry of greetings when all but David and Sylvia deserted me to ride with her, we headed off through Winslow.

The town hadn't changed much. The Islander Restaurant was a different color, and the Bainbridge Review was in a new location. The old office, down by the dock, had burned to the ground several years before. But the bank and the Thriftway were the same, and business seemed brisk as usual at the liquor store.

I looked to see if I recognized anyone, but aside from George, the town dog, and Martha, his sometime playmate, who were ambling down the street, stopping now and then for a pat on the head, I didn't. So we drove on, following Mother's car as she sped past the gas station and the old Wyatt house and headed down the long hill going south.

As we approached Saint Barnabas Episcopal Church, she signaled left and turned.

I was amazed to see how much the church had changed. There was a new parish house and a lower parking lot, and the trees planted on the hill about the time I was eleven or twelve now rose high above the roof. My father had been vicar there for sixteen years before his retirement in 1961, and as I looked up at the bell tower and the stained-glass windows I thought of all the Sundays I'd spent there, dressed in white shoes, white hat, and white gloves, sitting up in the front pew with Mother. I always wanted to turn around to see who was coming in late or who was coughing, but Mother kept me face forward, paying attention.

When I was fourteen I was volunteered as a baby-sitter during the eleven o'clock service. While the faithful gathered in the church, I sang, read, and played games with howling two-year-olds and tried to keep the Phillips twins from sneaking into the sacristy where they wanted to play chopsticks on the electronic carillon. It was a thankless job, and as soon as I could I turned it over to some other coerced volunteer and promptly joined the choir.

That was much more fun. I sat with the other altos, and during the sermon I surreptitiously scanned the congregation, checking to see who was there.

One Sunday, after I'd graduated from college and come home for the summer, I peered down during a lengthy explanation of the Trinity, and there in the last row, sitting straight and serious and looking ever so handsome in his Air Force uniform, was Joe. I didn't know him at the time. Though we'd both grown up on the Island, he was older than I, and our paths had never crossed. They crossed that day—my, how they crossed—and now here I was fourteen years later back at the crossing.

I hadn't remembered any houses below the church when I was a girl. Perhaps there weren't any, for the house we were headed for had been built in 1950, a couple of years before I left for college. Three more were barged in from Seattle in the sixties, when freeway construction was spitting out old houses like so many watermelon seeds, and they huddled together like gossiping old women in a colony off by themselves. Our house, a native Islander, stood proudly by itself on a knoll overlooking the head of Eagle Harbor.

It wasn't what the local real-estate people would call "choice waterfront property." The beach was mud flats at low tide and a still pond when the tide was full. Unlike the ads in the Sunday papers, it had neither a "magnificent view of sunset over the Olympics" nor a "breathtaking view of sunrise over the Cascades." It did, however, have an unobstructed view of noon.

But when we first came down the road, I wasn't thinking of views. I was rehearsing all the things I'd been told to look for in a house. I'm not overly practical, and as I tend to fall in love with charming but decrepit houses, Joe had given me a list of pitfalls to look for before I left Colorado. He'd found them in an article entitled "So You Think You're Going to Buy a House."

"First," he'd told me, "look for signs of settling."

"How do I do that?" I asked.

He shuffled through pages of notes. "Check the basement walls for cracks or newly repaired cracks."

"But Mother said this house has no basement."

"OK, then check the doors and windows to see if they're plumb."

"If they're what?"

Joe's do-it-yourself vocabulary had previously consisted of three words—hammer, nails, and damn—but now that we were considering a house with potential, new terms sprouted up in his conversation like dandelions on a newly mowed lawn.

"Plumb," he said, writing it out for me. "It means straight."

"Why can't they say straight then?"

"Because it's plumb." He glared at me over his glasses. His round face, usually so genial and cherubic, was stern. He was in no mood for insubordination. Then he went on. "You'll also have to determine whether the floor's level. It says here to drop a marble on the floor and see if it rolls in one direction or the other. Do you have any marbles?"

"I'll see." I got out my purse and emptied it on the table. "Here's a squirt gun I confiscated. Here's the brandy soufflé recipe I've been looking for. Here's the dentist's bill and three gum balls. They're a bit linty." I searched the bottom. "Here we go—two marbles."

Joe didn't appreciate my carefree attitude. He seemed anxious to move on. "Fine," he said, crossing the marble suggestion off his list. "The next thing you have to do is check the roof. For God's sake don't stand out in the middle of the lawn squinting up at it and say, How's the roof? or That's some roof. Borrow a ladder, climb up there, and take a good look at it." Oh, how he loved giving orders. I think the Air Force overtrained him.

Once I was up on the roof, clutching at the shingles to keep from sliding off, he wanted me to check for leaks.

"See if there's been a lot of patching or if the shingles curl."

"Do I crawl to the top and check the other side, or is one side enough?" I asked.

"Good idea." He whipped out his pen and wrote furiously. "Check both sides. Then inspect the chimney for cracks in the mortar and take a look at the flashing."

"The what?"

"The flashing. Now, pay attention. This is important. Before you come off the roof, jounce up and down a bit to be sure it feels solid."

"Oh, come now." I eyed my girth. "What if I jounce right on through? What do I say then—I'm sorry, we can't buy this house. It has a hole in the roof?"

He pretended he didn't hear me. Besides, he was on to plumbing. This was his forte, for once, early in our marriage, somehow we managed to anger the great gods of plumbing. I don't know where it was or when, but we've been paying for it ever since. Pipes have clogged and fallen apart in our hands when we tried to unclog them. Sinks have shot water six feet in the air. Bathtubs have filled up mysteriously and then overflowed. And once the whole front section of the toilet bowl broke off, which delighted Sylvia, then two, who seized the controls and flushed till I overpowered her, because it was fun to watch the water spew around the room in an arc.

"Check all the fixtures for cracks," Joe said. "Then go into the bathroom. Flush the toilet, turn on the faucets in the sink, then the ones in the bathtub, and finally the ones in the kitchen."

"Then what do I do?"

"See how it affects the pressure. We don't want to buy a place without sufficient water pressure."

I had to agree there. I spend more time doing laundry than I do cooking, cleaning, and carousing put together. If the water's off, even for an hour, dirty socks and mud-encrusted jeans start oozing out of the hamper and flowing down to the floor.

"All right, I'll check the pressure."

"Now"—Joe was coming to the end of his notes—"there are a few more things I have here. Check the paint for signs of peeling, the floors for dry rot, the windowsills for wet rot, and for heaven's sake check the heating system. We don't want to get stuck with a floor furnace like the one we had in Tokyo." That was a furnace that could only have been designed by a government committee. It sat in the floor in front of the door and at the bottom of the stairs, so all the heat went to the second floor, with none left over for the living and dining rooms. When we walked over it—and there was no other way to get from the living room to the dining room—flames licked at our shoes, and standing at the front door for long melted the soles.

Joe had finished his lecture and was gathering up his papers. "Well, that about does it," he said, "except, of course, you do know enough to slam every door you go through, don't you?"

"Why?" I asked. "If I've already come through the roof and flooded the bathroom and the kitchen, don't you think the owners will get a bit testy if I wander around whacking doors shut?"

"You have to. To see what rattles."

Not me, I thought. With my luck the ceiling will cave in. But now, as we bounced along the road behind Mother's car and the cats flipped Kitty Litter around for one last time, I wondered. Perhaps I should slam doors. After all, we wanted potential, but not from the ground up.

"I'll check everything," I said out loud. "I'll do it right. I'll evaluate the defects, then make an intelligent, unemotional decision."

Our bus lurched up a small hill and went straight down the driveway on the west side of the property, and I saw the house for the first time.

It was a big square box of a house with a gently sloping roof and faded maroon shakes. The gray siding on the attic was flaked and peeling, and whitewashed windows stood open, letting summer in. It looked like a proud old mother hen, her wings stretched out holding her chicks close to her side. All around, guarding her, were trees. A poplar, its leaves trembling in the breeze, stood by the corner on the left. A huge maple and a walnut shaded the side door, and peering over the roof from the far side I saw a fir and a pine with a dogwood pushing up between them like a child fighting for a chance to see.

The front of the house faced north, and an enormous lawn swept out to the deserted county road. On the lawn were forsythia bushes, apple trees, lilacs, and an umbrella- shaped plum tree with branches that touched the grass.

I pulled into the parking space, and we all piled out of the car. For a moment we stood there. It was warm, still and infinitely green. All I could hear was the sound of the breeze rustling through the poplar, the rising trill of birds, and somewhere off across the bay the distant sound of a car heading for Eagledale.

"I have to have this house," I said to myself.

"Mom." My reverie was broken as Geoffrey tugged at my arm. "What's that door up there?"

I looked up. Halfway up the side of the house was a door. There were no stairs leading to it. It simply stood there, with a narrow window by its side for company, looking out over the bay.

I turned to Mother, who was standing nearby. "Where does that door go?"

"To the attic."

"How do you get to it?"

"Well, three owners back, there were stairs on the outside, but now you go in, pull yourself up through a trapdoor in the utility room ceiling, and then walk over the joists."

"You mean there aren't any stairs inside either?"

"That can be your first project," she said, as she opened the side door and went into the house.

It began to dawn on me what she'd meant when she said the house had potential.

I followed. She was standing in the utility room under the trapdoor. "There it is," she said.

I glanced up. "Oh," I said, wondering if I was up to hoisting myself through it. "Well, I'll tackle it later."

The utility room was large and sunny, about the size of our kitchen in Colorado Springs, and outside the window that looked out over the backyard, climbing pink roses grew up and scratched against the pane.

"This'll be the laundry room," I told Mother, who was yelling at the children, warning them not to touch anything.

"This'll be a great laundry room," I said again. And I remembered all the years I'd spent in dark basements folding diapers and towels and waiting for the summer when a single shaft of sunlight ventured in through one tiny window.

"Now, here's the bathroom." Mother was back. She'd given up trying to corral the children, and she opened the door to our left and stood aside so I could go in.

"Good Lord," I gasped, when I saw it. "This is the biggest bathroom I've ever seen."

"True, but there isn't any shower," she warned," and I know how Joe likes his morning shower."

"Oh, that's no trouble. We can put one in. Besides, look how big and deep the bathtub is."

"And this cabinet around the sink isn't very fancy."

"Who cares? I've never had a cabinet around a sink. Look over here." I opened a cupboard door. "A linen closet in the bathroom itself—not down the hall and two doors to the right!"

"But the floor's going to need work. It sort of buckles over here."

"So what? Can you imagine how many kids will be able to brush their teeth at the same time?" I whirled around. "I think it's bigger than Joe's and my bedroom in Colorado Springs."

"Well, enough of the bathroom." Mother led the way out. "Come on. Look at the kitchen."

I followed her back through the utility room and into the kitchen. It too was huge. To the left of the door was a counter and a cabinet and an old refrigerator. In the corner stood a water heater, and on the north wall was a high pass-through and a doorway into the living room. Below the pass-through an ancient stove huddled between two cabinets. Across the room I saw another door, and next to it was a broken window.

I peered through the hole. A long, dark hall with a row of four little windows on the south wall led to a low doorway.

"Where does that go?" I asked.

"That leads to the chicken house." Mother shrugged. "Of course, you don't have to raise chickens. I think the hall was once a porch and one of the owners closed it in. Otherwise, I can't explain this window here." She turned back around. "Now look at the view you'll have out here on the south side."

There were two windows next to a small dining table, and another one over to the right above the sink. I went over to the sink.

"Let me check it from here," I said. "After all, this is where I'll be most of the time."

I looked out. A mass of trees—bright green and cool and so tall and dense I could barely see the sky or tell where one stopped and another began—stood at the bottom of a little slope at the edge of the lawn. Directly in front of me, they dipped and melted into bushes and blackberry vines and clumps of Scotch broom, and I could see the bay and the hint of a narrow path leading to the beach. The bay was full and still, reflecting the hills and trees on the other side. A single house down by the water on the far shore peeked out from behind a willow tree, and as I watched, a couple of sea gulls circled lazily and then dove into the water after a fish.

I turned to Mother. "I could look out of this window forever," I said. "I never realized it was so peaceful down here. It's hard to believe it's part of Eagle Harbor. It looks just like a lake or a millpond."

"Well, don't forget, when the tide goes out it's mud flats. Of course, that's when you'll see the blue herons. They stand there and wait for the tide to change and the fish to come back."

The children had finished their inspection of the house and they circled around me.

"Isn't it neat, Mom?"

"Don't you love it?"

"Can we have it?"

"Come on, come look at the living room."

"All right, all right," I said. "I'm coming. Don't push."

"I warn you," Mother called after me as I followed them out of the kitchen, "the living room's dark."

She was right. It was dark. Whoever had built the house had laid things out in the shape of a U. The kitchen, the bathroom, and the back hall were on the south side. The library, with a pair of French doors between it and the living room and a narrow bedroom were on the west, and three bedrooms, lined up like rooms at the YWCA, were on the east. In the middle was the living room, with two windows at the north that looked out on the front porch and the lawn. To the right of the windows around a corner was the front door, and though the top half of it was glass, it didn't let in much light.

I glanced around, visualizing a couch here, a couple of chairs there, maybe a desk in that corner. This room could hold forty people, I thought, probably more. Imagine the luxury of not having to sweep a couple of kids off the couch in order to find a place to sit down.

"We'll get lamps," I called out to Mother. "We'll get lots of them. That'll make it light enough."

Mother didn't answer, and Sylvia was pulling at my sleeve.

"Look here, Mom." She pointed over to the corner at a fireplace that nestled up against the living-room side of the pass-through wall. "We can have big fires in the winter and make popcorn and toast marshmallows."

I looked at it closely. Most of it was painted white, but apparently the last owner didn't approve, for there were signs of scratching and scraping, and the original brick showed through in some places.

"We'll finish the job and take the rest of the paint off," I said.

Sylvia looked at me hopefully. "Does that mean we're going to buy it?"

"I'm not sure. Daddy has to see it first," I answered, knowing full well that this was my house and no one could take it away.

"Come look over here." Sylvia led me to the library doors. "See, we can put the Christmas tree in there, and then we can spray some of that snow stuff on these windows. Won't that be perfect?"

"Mom, Mom!" Jenny rushed over and grabbed my other arm. "Come here. I found yours and Daddy's room." She dragged me across the room and threw open the door in the comer. "Isn't it neat?"

I went in. This room was big too. Apparently it had once been two small rooms, for half of it was painted pink with a white ceiling and the other half was blue and dirty yellow. I assumed it was a recent, perhaps spur-of-the-moment, remodeling job, for there was a rut down the center of the floor and down the middle of the ceiling was a two-by-four with bent nails still hanging out of it.

It looked as if someone had stormed in one day, pounded his hairy chest, and said, "Me want bigger room." Then, I imagine, he'd reached out with one hand, grabbed the wall as one would grab an unruly drunk, and ripped it out.

I must say, though, I agreed with him. It was lovely, spacious and airy, and when I saw the windows I was sold. I don't know if they were plumb or not, but it didn't matter. They swung out. I'd had my fill of modern construction and tight aluminum windows that had to be pried open with a crowbar. These were windows I could fling open. I could lean out of them. I could sit on the windowsill and watch the moon rise through the trees.

I opened one window and reached out, almost touching the dogwood. The smell of pine was heady, and I listened to the sound of sea gulls screeching and heard the ferry's booming answer echoing down the bay.

"It's mine," I whispered to myself. "Mine, mine, all mine."

I tried to find flaws, really I did. I dropped the marbles and a gum ball on the floor and watched them go off in all directions. "That must mean it's all settling at once," I said.

I also tried to be depressed when Mother took me into the unfinished and windowless room off the kitchen, a room she called the pantry. It was dank in there, cobwebs hung from the ceiling, and spikes jutted out from the two-by-fours.

"It's a perfect place to store the mops and brooms," I mumbled. "Besides, we can put up shelves and stick canned goods in here."

And I tried to let the long hall to the chicken house discourage me. There was even a chicken in there pecking at something I assured myself wasn't a termite. But all I could think was, we won't have chickens and Joe can easily make a door to cover that opening and keep out the cold.

Sylvia and Jenny showed me the long, skinny bedroom next to ours. They giggled and poked each other as they pointed out messages that had been written on the wall to Betty, who, it seems, led a fascinating, if not altogether proper, life. I pretended not to understand and told them we'd paint there first.

We looked at the bedroom next to the skinny one. It was about the size of the master bedroom.

"This one'll be ours!" Sylvia shrieked.

"Yeah," Jenny agreed. "Yours, mine, and Joan's. Hey, Joan, come and look at your room!"

I didn't have to check the plumbing. The children did this for me—several times. They even sat in the tub to measure how long it was.

I verified the existence of a heating system and was happy to note it wasn't a floor furnace. Instead, a charming old circulating oil heater stood in one corner of the living room, looking ready and anxious for winter. Later we discovered charm was all it intended to give off, certainly not heat.

I was so exuberant I only glanced at the roof. It was a bit tacky, I figured, with whole areas of different-colored shingles. But I was sure it was fixable. I completely forgot to slam the doors to see what rattled—which was a good thing, I found out. Slamming the kitchen door made the windows in the back hall fall out.

As our tour ended, I stood on the owner's antique hutch and peered into the attic. With the help of a flashlight, I could see that it too was enormous. With a little work, I thought, Joe and I can easily put six bedrooms up here. As I played the light around, I found an added bonus left by a former owner. There, sitting on one of the joists, were his and hers bedpans. This was a warning from the ever-menacing gods of plumbing, but in my enthusiasm I failed to recognize it.

That night, still in a trance, I called Joe.

"Did you check everything?" he asked as soon as I'd said hello.

"You'll love it," I answered. "It's so quiet and green. It sits all by itself with no houses in sight except those across the bay. There are at least twenty trees on the property and the windows swing out and even the bathroom is bigger than our master bedroom in Colorado Springs." I stopped for breath.

"Is it settling?"

"I don't think so, and there's more than enough room in the attic for the children's bedrooms. There's a door up there leading to nowhere. It's magic, I know, and if I step out, I'll be whisked away to Never-Never Land, or at least Over the Rainbow."

He didn't comment. Though he's tolerant of my romantic enthusiasms, he doesn't like to encourage excesses.

"What about the roof?"

"Well, it might need some patching, but Mother says everyone on Bainbridge has leaky roofs."

He snorted and I went on.

"The children will be able to build forts, climb trees, and go rowing. There's access to the beach. You won't believe how much room there is, and the morning sun will come right in our bedroom."

"What about the plumbing? Did you check that?"

"It seems fine, and David says the tub is at least eight feet long."

The children gathered around, impatient to talk too, so I turned the phone over to them. By the time I got back on the line, Joe was worn down a bit.

"Tell you what," he said. "I'll try to get a flight up this weekend, if you think it's that great."

"I do," I said. "So will you."

The following Saturday, Joe saw the house, we signed the papers, and it was ours. We've never regretted it, except for the time...

3

I Don't Look Well in Basic Albatross

Having a well run dry in the middle of summer is a little like having an eight-year-old tell you her dreams. It seems to last forever, and you can be a brick and pretend to enjoy it only so long.

I know. Our well ran dry in July, three weeks after we moved into the house.

It was a Saturday morning. Joe had come up for the weekend the night before. He'd walked around the property in the late dusk, memorizing each bush and tree so that when he went back to Colorado Springs he could remember every detail. And before he came to bed, he'd stood for a long time in front of the open window, breathing in the cool night air.

When I woke up in the morning, around seven, the sun was streaming into the room, and I watched lazily as the shadows of the dogwood leaves danced on the far wall. A breeze blustered in the open window, nosed around the room for a bit, and left.

I turned to Joe, who was already awake. "See?" I said. "Isn't this a lovely place? Aren't you glad we bought it?" He'd been staring at the ceiling, but now he looked at me. "Does the pump always run that long?"

"What pump?"

"The water pump. Listen."

I listened. I could hear the 7:10 ferry whistling its departure from Winslow, but no pump.

"I don't hear anything."

"It's a humming noise."

I listened again. He was right. I could hear a faint humming coming from out near the chicken house.

"I don't know. I never noticed it before."

"I did, and it's been going for over an hour."

"Maybe it does that," I said. Machines baffle me, so I simply accept the fact that they have their own reasons for making the sounds they do.

Joe started to get out of bed. "I'm going to check it."

"Now? Why don't you wait till after breakfast?"

But he had his shirt and his pants on and was looking under the bed for his shoes. "Don't worry, it'll only take a minute."

Since my puritan ethic allows me to stay in bed only if I can convince everyone else to do the same, I staggered to my feet and went into the kitchen to start the coffee. The water pressure was low, but finally I filled the pot. I put it on the stove as Joe came back in.

"My God," he said. "It's a wonder the house didn't bum down. Do you know what kind of a jerry rig they have out there? I think the whole thing's wired with lamp cord. When I opened the door it was smoking. Another half hour and it would have burst into flames."

"What'd you do?" I held my breath.

"I turned it off for now."

"Can you fix it?" I eyed the pile of dirty laundry in the corner of the utility room. Even as we talked it was swelling and pulsating.

"I think so, when I get some decent wire. But till then the water will be off."

And so it began. Joe got the wire, turned off all the electricity, and crawled under the house among old beer bottles, two-by-fours, and chicken droppings.

Meanwhile the children got up. They were not pleased to find the water off. Sylvia wanted to wash her hair. She claimed Jenny had taken all the hot water the night before. Jenny said, "I did not," and asked if I'd washed her shorts yet. Joan ate a peach and wanted to rinse off her hands. David decided he had to clean the spokes on his bike. Geoffrey was thirsty and the orange juice was gone. Only Robbie was happy. He has an aversion to any water not specified for swimming.

I tried to settle things down while I waited, with a growing sense of panic, for Joe's triumphant "It's fixed—you can use the water now."

The call never came. I heard muffled curses, and a bellow or two came through loud and clear, but no triumph.

When I could stand it no longer, I went out to look. Joe was sitting under the house guru fashion in the tiny space next to the pump. His knees were caked with dirt, his hands were greasy, there were cobwebs dripping around his ears, and he'd cut his finger.

"How's it going?" I asked.

"Nothing, absolutely nothing." He whacked the pump with a wrench. "This damn thing. I changed the wires and primed the pump. It didn't do any good. Then I checked it again and primed it again. Still nothing. Hell. With my luck we've probably run out of water."

"Oh, not that!"

"Can't think what else it would be. We might as well take a look."

He crawled out, and we walked down to the well. It was a large concrete monster about three feet high and three feet across, with a cover that had a hunk of iron embedded in it for a handle. Joe hefted the cover aside and looked down.

"Just what I thought."

"No water?" My back began to itch and perspiration trickled down the back of my legs.

"Look for yourself."

I peered into the darkness. I could see water about twenty feet down.

"What do you mean, no water?"

"Oh, there's water down there all right, but see the pipe coming out of the wall?"

"Yes."

"The water has to be higher than the pipe for the pump to pick it up."

The water wasn't much lower, and I tried an optimistic view. "Maybe it'll rise if we leave it for a day or two."

"It might, but I doubt it."

"What are we going to do?" I could hear Sylvia inside screaming at Jenny that she had too used all the hot water last night.

"I guess we'll have to dig a new well."

"Dig a new well?"

"You want water, don't you?"

"Yes, but how are we going to dig a new well?" I dreaded the answer to this question because we might mean me. Joe still had a month and a half till retirement and was only home for the weekend. In fact, he was going back the next day. I pictured myself out in the yard with a pick and shovel while Sylvia stood behind me prodding. "Hurry up, Mother. I have to wash my hair."

"We aren't going to do it, silly," he said. "We'll have to find a well digger."

He gave me the look he gives me when the children knock over their milk in a restaurant or the dog jumps up on his mother and leaves footprints on her new linen chemise. The look is one of frustration, but it always seems to blame me. Just then, as if on cue, a truck lumbered up our driveway.

I thought a passing well digger had intercepted my unspoken scream for help and had come to rescue us. One hadn't, but it was the next best thing—the garbage man.

This garbage man was Bainbridge Island's version of the Yellow Pages. While electricians and plumbers may hide out and travel incognito—lest they have to wire a lamp or clear a drain—the garbage man was always available, and he could tell you where to buy a good used truck, where to get your sump pump fixed, and where to find a man to spray your trees.

"Sure, I know a good well driller—Harry Barker. He's the best in the county. That man could find water in the Sahara."

A torrent of words poured from inside the house as Jenny swore "on a stack of Bibles" she hadn't used all the hot water. I pretended not to hear, and Joe gave me the look that blames again.

The garbage man was unperturbed. "Don't worry. Give Harry a call. He'll have you fixed up in no time." He got in his truck, backed over one of our cans, and left.

We called Harry Barker and found him home. We didn't know it then, but this would be the last time we'd find him home. At least the last time he'd admit it. He came right away. This too was a first and a last.

I wasn't sure what to expect in a well driller. The closest I'd ever come to one was Femandel in the old French movie The Well-Digger's Daughter. As a matter of fact, Fernandel didn't even drill wells. He dug them and, as I recall, spent most of his time climbing in and out of them while rapidly delivering long speeches in a French I couldn't understand. The subtitles insisted he said, "Good morning, Madame Picard. I have come to dig for you a well." I didn't believe those subtitles and, from the look on her face, neither did Madame Picard.

So when Harry came, jumped out of his old truck, and flashed a toothy smile, I was apprehensive. Femandel never did, as I recall, finish a well or find water. But Harry exuded confidence, so I pushed Madame Picard and her dry well out of my mind.

"Sure, I can drill a well for you," he said after Joe had given him a tour of the pump and the old well. "If you lived in Eagledale, I couldn't promise much. It's hell to find water there, but it shouldn't be any problem here."

I was ecstatic and Joe looked pleased.

"Fine," he said. "Can you start today, or do you work on Saturdays?"

"Oh, I can't start till—let's see—next Thursday at the earliest."

"Next Thursday?" My palms began to sweat and I could hear my voice rising hysterically. I grabbed Joe's arm. He was calm—but then he was going to desert us.

"Why can't you start sooner?" he asked.

Harry scratched his head, and mine began to itch too.

"I have to finish a couple of wells I'm drilling now. One's for a guy at the north end of the Island. He and his wife just had a new baby. They had to move in with his mother-in-law, and he can't take it much longer. The other's for a guy in Port Madison. We've gone down three hundred feet and still nothing."

"Could that happen here?" Only sheer willpower kept me from grabbing him by his plaid shirt and shaking him.

"It could, but I doubt it. We should hit water here at about forty feet."

"How long after you start will it take to drill, say, forty feet?"

"Can't say for sure. It all depends if we hit hardpan or not. If we don't, it shouldn't take too long. But if we do, I can't say."

The lack of specifics was too much for my nervous system. I mumbled something, went inside, and left Joe to work out the details.

When he came in he was smiling. Why not? I thought. Every bone in his body was yelling, Hooray, hooray, I'm going away!

He came over and put his arm around me. "Don't worry, honey," he said. "We've got three five-gallon containers. You can fill them up at the church or at your mother's, and there's a Laundromat on the Island. It won't be too bad."

I glared at him. I was hot and smelly and not about to be consoled.

"Tell you what," he added. "I'll go get you some water right now." And he escaped out the back door.

The next day Joe left early. I begged him to stay, but he pointed out this was impossible. I knew he was right, but it didn't help.

Right after breakfast I drove him to the ferry. I watched as he walked down the ramp, his back ramrod straight, and I'm not positive, but I'm pretty sure I saw him jump in the air and click his heels as he stepped onto the boat.

The days were long, waiting for Thursday and Harry. Mornings and evenings we hauled water. In between we went to the Laundromat.

I learned some basic truths in those five days. I learned that sitting makes the back of your thighs sweat, sleeping makes your head sweat, standing makes your feet sweat, walking makes everything else sweat, and bourbon tastes rotten with orange juice.

I also discovered something I'd never known. My mother, the vicar's wife, the proper grandmother, and the charter member of the "always wear your girdle, dear, so you won't pooch" club, is also a water witcher. She picked up the technique from one of the Island's foremost witchers, and though she was modest about her talent and claimed her arthritic hip threw her gait off, she decided that as long as we were waiting we might as well see what water was available. So every afternoon she stalked around the yard, divining rod in hand. I tried it a few times and nothing happened, but for her the old branch shivered and bent as if possessed. By Wednesday she'd located three places.

"Tell Mr. Barker to drill at any of these locations," she ordered. "He'll hit water about thirty to thirty-five feet down."

"Yes, Mother." I don't argue with a witcher.

Finally Thursday came. It was a clear, hot day. I rose at dawn. I wanted to be ready. By seven thirty we'd had breakfast. By eight I'd hauled water from the church's spigot and had done up the breakfast dishes.

"Today he's coming," I told the children when they begged to be taken swimming. "Today he starts our well."

Eight thirty came. No Harry. Nine, ten thirty, eleven. I called his wife.

"He's coming," she said. "He told me so before he left." I heard a deep voice laughing in the background. "He should be there any time now."

By three thirty in the afternoon, I'd given up hope. I was about to call Mrs. Barker again when I heard a rumbling, spluttering, and coughing in the front yard. I ran to the window. Sure enough, a big rigging truck that looked as if it could drill to the bowels of the earth was bouncing across the lawn. Right behind was a white Lincoln Continental. I rushed outside.

"Boy, am I glad to see you," I said. "I was afraid you weren't coming."

Gone was his radiant smile of the week before. "I said I'd come today," he snapped, and went around to the other side of his truck. His assistant leaped out of the Continental, brushed past me, and began undoing chains and ropes. Obviously they didn't want me around. I'd planned to show them where to dig, as per Mother's instructions. Instead, I slunk back into the house and waited for whatever noise it is a drill makes as it digs happily down to water. There was no sound, so I ventured outside again. The Lincoln was leaving. I chased after it.

"Where are you going?"

The car stopped. Harry stuck his head out. "We'll be back," he called. "We're going to lunch."

They drove off.

True to his word, he came back—at five. He spent twenty minutes banging and clattering. Then he informed me he'd hit hardpan, turned off the motor, and went home.

For the next seven days I was up early every day hoping Harry would take pity on me and come early. He never did. If he arrived by ten he took two hours for lunch. If he didn't come till one thirty, lunch only lasted an hour and a half. Saturday and Monday he didn't come at all. On Tuesday he explained his parents had come for a visit, the first in three years. One day he left early to go home and shoot his cat. By now I didn't press for details. I listened to the grind—thump...grind— thump, and every now and then I peered out the window or ventured out to offer a cold beer.

"How's it going?"

"OK."

"Any sign of water?"

"Nope."

A hill of clay built up by the well outside our bedroom window, and a mountain of laundry built up in the utility room. Every time I went to Winslow, I dropped by the gas-station rest room for a sponge bath. The children made friends with the office staff up at the church and filed in and out all day, paper cups in hand and washcloths slung over their shoulders.

Finally, after a week of drilling and thumping, of sweating and flushing the toilet by standing on a chair with the five- gallon jug, Harry hit water.

He was casual about it—so casual, in fact, that once he made sure it wasn't a false alarm he went home to rest for a day or two. Finally, however, he came back, hooked the whole system up, and put in a pressure tank. For three days the bathtub was never empty. Even Robbie indulged.

Harry's bill arrived promptly, and to this day we haven't figured out whether the extra $1.50 was a mistake in addition or a charge for what it cost him to go home and shoot his cat. I advised Joe not to ask for details.

4

Pardon Me, Boys, Is This the 7:10 From Winslow?

Joe's retirement was the retirement of any man with six children still at home drinking milk by the half-gallon six-pack and growing out of their school clothes on the way to the bus stop. It ended eight days after it began, and he joined the hordes of commuters on the morning ferry into Seattle and the same group on the 6:30 boat home at night.

Commuting by ferry is not a pastime to be entered into lightly. It takes dedication, an acute sense of timing, and a good pair of legs.

It starts at dawn. Ten minutes before the 6:30 or the 7:10 or the 7:50 is scheduled to pull away from the dock in Winslow, cars all over the island start up, careen down the driveway, and head for the boat.

A man from Port Madison, speeding out onto the highway, takes a gulp of coffee, then sticks the cup up on the dashboard and prays he won't have to make a sudden stop. A woman from Point White, with an old army jacket thrown over her nightgown, navigates onto the main road, complaining all the time that what she'd like is another car so her husband could drive himself to the boat.

A University of Washington sophomore, heading for an early class, realizes as he skims through Island Center that he left his chemistry book on the kitchen table. And a bright and eager girl, in her first week on the job as a bank teller, steers her car with one hand and searches through her purse for her earrings with the other.

They all converge at the stoplight in Winslow, and when it turns green they spring forward and either turn down to drive onto the boat or they head for the last few places in the parking lot. By this time there are about two minutes left, and the race is on.

Men, their briefcases flying out behind them, vault over the chain around the lot, and women clump along on their wedgies and clutch their purses to their sides as they whip through the ticket booth and gallop down the long ramp trying to get there before the gangplank is taken away.

"Come on!" they yell back to each other. "You can make it!"

"They wouldn't dare leave us now."

The ferry captain, entering into the conviviality of it all, gives a blast of the whistle and chuckles to himself as everyone leaps in the air, then speeds up.

Once on the boat, the camaraderie is gone, and it's every man for himself, for the commuter is a creature of habit and is territorial about his place to sit. He doesn't take change well, and should his seat be taken by a housewife who's going in early for jury duty or by a couple from Oklahoma City who have to catch the morning flight, he stands there glaring, his newspaper clutched in his hand, and fumes till they either move or he's forced to sit in the coffee shop next to someone having breakfast who eats his egg yolks whole.

Some people play bridge on the thirty-five-minute trip in. Some settle down in the smoking section and read the morning news. Women who rushed on board, their faces still in their cosmetic kits, crowd around the mirrors in the ladies' room to glue on their eyelashes and comb out their hair. And groups of men sit around the tables in the coffee shop and relive last night's ball game. But no matter where it is, they sit there every day.

As the boat gets under way the captain comes on the inter-com and mumbles something unintelligible about no smoking in the nonsmoking section and beer must be kept in the dining area only. No one listens.

Every now and then, about halfway across the sound, he comes on again. "Attention, please. We are now passing a pod of killer whales on the port—that's the left—side of the vessel."

Those who understand his message pass the word along, and everyone rushes to the port—that's the left—side.

"Where are they?"

"Oh, there they are. My, they're big."

"Look at that one. It looks just like a log."

"That is a log."

"I'm going back to sit down. If I look at the water too long I get sick."

The later boats—the shoppers' specials—are more leisurely. They're the ones the lawyers and the bank executives take. Matrons on their way to a sale at Frederick's, housewives heading for asser-tiveness classes, and retired businessmen scheduled for a morning game at the tennis club all converge on the 9:10 or the 10:30.

Once or twice a month you meet up with a busload of fifth- or sixth-graders on a class outing to the aquarium or the zoo. They cover the boat like ants, feeding the candy machine, spin-ning around in the coffee-shop chairs, and thundering back and forth on the open top deck. When the ferry pulls into Seattle, teachers herd them back downstairs, and the rest of the passen-gers take a deep breath, gather up their coats and shopping bags, and line up to get off.

Joe became a regular on the 7:50. His father, who owns a home wine supply business and was heading into his seventies, had persuaded him to join the firm as manager, head salesman, truck driver, mail clerk, janitor, and bottle washer. So every morn-ing as the children left for school I drove him to the boat, and he journeyed into the world of sacchrometers, champagne corks, and zinfandel concentrate.

He came home on the 6:30 boat, and he came home in the dark. In winter, of course, it's dark in Seattle from four thirty on. In June, when the sun sets at nine and the wind is warm and soft, the commuters stretch out on the top deck or fly kites from the stern. But in winter they huddle inside, sipping their beers and reading the paper while the wind and rain lash against the windows.

Joe carried a transistor radio, and with a plug in his ear, like Walter Cronkite checking on the latest from the Middle East, he read the sports section and listened to the Seattle SuperSonics as they battled somewhere across the country against the Detroit Pistons or the Phoenix Suns.

I waited in the parking lot on the Bainbridge side. I do that a lot. In December and January I try to time my arrival to coincide with that of the ferry. I'm not often successful, so I sit in the cold car and count the flashes from the Alki Point light over in West Seattle, and I watch the ferry as it slowly rounds the corner out by the bell buoy and heads into Eagle Harbor.

In the spring and summer, however, I leave the house early, sometimes before the boat has even left Seattle. I drive down to the dock, pull into the lot, turn off the engine, get out my book, and read. It's quiet there. No one's asking how long till dinner. No one's complaining about a report on the Aztec ruins that's due Wednesday or badgering me to explain dangling participles. It's one of the few times I can read in peace.

Of course, sometimes I get distracted, for others come to the dock early, too, and not all have come to read. One lady I've seen a lot does her nails—her toenails. She must paint them three times a week. She pushes back the seat, sticks her foot up on the steering wheel, and slaps on a coat or two of polish.

Once in a while her foot slips and honks the horn, and the quiet evening air is shattered as she bellows, "Jeeesus Keerist!"

Another woman, a summer resident, I think, brings her four children and reads to them to keep them amused.

"And what do you know," I hear just as Robert Benchley is describing how he got John Greenleaf Whittier's hat, "before he realized it, Mr. Bunny had eaten all the marshmallows. He'd eaten the green ones. He'd eaten the pink ones. He'd eaten the white ones. He'd eaten the red ones. And now he felt sick, very, very sick."

One hot August afternoon, when I was deep into Peeling Pounds Permanently, I happened to glance up to see if the ferry was coming and noticed a truck parked up the hill from me. It was facing the other way, but through the back window I could see a couple entwined in an enthusiastic embrace. I looked back down at my book. I was up to the section that tells how suppressed anger can make you fat. I looked up again. Arms were groping, hands clutching and massaging. I averted my gaze and tried to concentrate on nonfattening ways to handle rage. When I peered up again, both heads had disappeared. They bobbed up when the boat whistled its arrival, and after much collar straightening and hair combing, a middle- aged woman jumped out of the truck. Her balding partner got out the other side and together they waited, scanning the passengers as they streamed off the boat. I watched breathlessly. Finally the woman's face brightened, and she walked down the hill to meet a tall, skinny man.

"Hi, honey," I heard her say as they strode past my car. "Guess who just came in from California? Your brother Chuck."

While I watch people swarming off the boat, hot and tired after a long day's work, I also see ladies in long gowns heading in for the opera and families going in to a ball game at the Kingdome. And every once in a while when domesticity and the wonderful world of motherhood cloys, Joe puts on his good suit and I get out my beaded bag and we go into Seattle to kick up our heels. We don't kick very high as a rule, so we're usually safely back on the 10:30 boat with the rest of the early-to-bed, early-to-rise Islanders. But now and then, when the company's scintillating and the wine is mulled, we throw moderation to the winds and say, "Oh, what the hell, let's make the one twenty."

Now, heading for the 1:20 is a dangerous practice. For one thing, if you miss it there's nothing till four thirty in the morning. For another thing, a railroad track runs along the Seattle waterfront between the ferry terminal and almost everything else except the Holy Mackerel Bar and Grill. At that time of night the engineers on the Burlington Northern are bored. They're upset because they were taken off the day shift, and they feel hauling boxcars back and forth in the middle of the night is an insult after thirty years on the Seattle-to-Chicago run. So, to liven things up they crawl along the waterfront just as Islanders are heading for the boat to Winslow.

By ten after one they have all the streets blocked. At quarter after, when drivers are saying, "I see the caboose, Maude. I think we're going to make it," they grind to a halt with much clattering and banging.

At one eighteen they shift into reverse and back up for a block or two, then just as the boat whistles and pulls away from the dock they go forward again, speed up, and disappear into the night. Sometimes if the wind's right you can hear the engineer laughing and slapping his thigh.

Missing the 1:20 leaves one with three choices. You can stay at the dock and argue over who flirted with whom and who could have made the damn boat if he'd had the brains to remember where he put his coat. You can take the 1:30 to Bremerton, an hour's ride, and drive home from there by way of the Agate Pass bridge. Or you can drive thirty miles south to Tacoma, across the Narrows bridge, and up the peninsula through Gig Harbor, Gorst, Bremerton, Chico, Silverdale, and Poulsbo. No matter which choice you make, you get home about an hour before you have to get up and go to work again.

As Joe struggles out of bed and stumbles off in the general direction of the shower, he shakes his head and says, "Commuting is definitely not for the weak and the cowardly."

5

The Three-Month Itch

With blackberries ripening on the vine and plums, fat and golden, dropping off the branches onto the ground, wine makers rushed into the wine store to replenish their dwindling supplies of siphons, steamers, and crocks, and Joe worked six days a week. So, for a while we limited our remodeling projects to things we could do inside in the evenings or outside on Sundays.

One week we tackled Robbie's and Geoffrey's bedroom. It was the long, narrow one next to ours. We painted the walls, obliterating forever the messages the long-gone Betty had written about Jim and the gang at Mac's Tavern, and I glued carpet samples I'd collected over the years onto the floor.

The next week we crawled around on our hands and knees installing acres of shag over the red-and-brown linoleum in the living room and library. It was a glorious color, green and yellow with flecks of orange. When the late afternoon poured in through the library windows, it lit up like an alpine meadow. Unfortunately, dogs—and there were many, not all ours— noticed the resemblance to all outdoors too. Some evenings and Sundays were spent swabbing shag.

When October came, however, and we found ourselves wearing two sweaters and wool socks to bed, we realized it was time to tackle something major—namely, insulating the attic rafters. The charming circulating heater was not going to do its part toward keeping us warm, and though the fireplace tried, it had to combat the breeze that roared under the back door and seeped in through the wall plugs in the kitchen. It also lost considerable ground every time a gale out of the south blew out the windows in the back hall.

At dawn one October morning, Joe was awakened for the third day in a row by the sound of those windows crashing to the floor. It was all he could take. He leaped out of bed, grabbed a hammer and some nails, stormed into the back hall, and nailed them into their frames.

Later, at breakfast, as he tried to warm his hands over his toast, he announced in a voice reminiscent of a town crier, "This Sunday we're going to insulate the attic. Maybe that'll keep in some of the heat."

Muffled shouts of joy burst from the bedrooms where the children huddled under mounds of blankets trying to keep warm as long as possible before leaping out into the cold to get ready for school. I let go of the hot coffee cup I was embracing and cheered.

Immediately Joe started making plans. "I'll take the car into Seattle when I go to work," he said. "Then I'll pick up the insulation and we can start early Sunday morning."

I snuggled up to my cup again. "Can we do it all in one day?" I asked. I didn't see why not. It seemed fairly simple, but I needed confirmation.

Joe thought a minute. "Sure. All we have to do is staple the stuff to the rafters."

We were wrong, and would be time and time again. Jobs we thought we could do in a weekend took three months, and the ones programmed to take three months still aren't finished. But that day we were full of energy and hope. So I went to force the children out of bed, and Joe climbed into the attic to take measurements.

That night he brought home thirty-seven batts of insulation, and the next day, as I dropped him off at the boat, he turned back for a minute. "Leave the insulation where it is," he said. "I'll get it tomorrow."

He said that sort of thing a lot when we first began remodeling. "Wait till I get home," he'd insist." "Don't worry about it. I'll take care of it." But then when he found I took him at his word and waited and didn't worry, he began to get nervous.

Joe was raised with the idea that God created daylight as a signal it's time to get up and work. As a child, when he wasn't sawing and chopping wood on the beach or hauling it up to the woodshed, he was washing walls, buffing the kitchen floor, or cleaning the windows. So when he married me it came as a shock to him to find that I take coffee breaks after I've made the bed. With the monstrous remodeling project ahead of us, it further depressed him to realize that our children, now that they'd grown into the age of usefulness, had inherited my dilatory attitude toward work.

So, slowly, as we progressed in our remodeling, his parting words as he left for work changed from, "Wait till I get home," to, "If you want to haul in the plasterboard or spackle a wall, fine." When this brought minimal progress, he reached back into his Air Force training and issued orders. "I want the plywood unloaded and put in the living room. Have the children help you."

In October of 1970, however, we were still in the first flush of excitement about our new home, so with little encouragement the children and I decided it would be fun to surprise Joe and have all the insulation up in the attic when he came home.

It wasn't a difficult chore. The rolls were light. But it did present a few tactical problems. There were, of course, still no stairs to the attic, only a ladder to the magic door, and once we got the batts up we had to stack them in the section of the attic that was floored. It wasn't the part near the door. It was at the other end. In between were open joists with only a plank or two here and there for a path.

Threading the path was precarious. Miss an intersection or lose your balance and you went right through the living room ceiling or the library ceiling, or you dropped into David's room, the skinny bedroom next to the library. With you, you took a pound and a half of grit and dirt. Behind you, you left several layers of skin.

Everyone except Geoffrey and Robbie went through at one time or another. Sylvia stepped between the joists the first day. She and Joe and the rest were inspecting the attic. I was downstairs making beds. I'd barely finished and was on my way into the kitchen when I heard a crash and a scream. Dirt rained on my head, and a battered leg popped through and dangled in front of my face.

Each person blasted through in his own way. Joe, on his knees working in a far comer, kicked out a few ceiling tiles with his feet. I pushed out two with my hands when I was trying to balance myself and reach a pair of scissors at the same time. My nephew, Burry, fell across the joists and knocked out ten at once.

Some people went all the way through. Joan did, one night as I was leaving to pick up Joe at the boat. Thoughtfully she landed in her own closet, and though she walked funny for a couple of weeks, the doctors could find nothing wrong and eventually she straightened up.

The main drawback about all this falling, kicking, and scattering ceiling tiles wasn't the loss of tiles. They were in the great master plan as something to be replaced. It wasn't even the injuries, which for the most part were negligible. It was the gaping holes they left. They contributed substantially to the condemned appearance of the house. Some first-time visitors glanced up at them, then averted their eyes. Others stared in amazement and asked, "Who won the fight?"

But that Saturday we weren't concerned with looks. It was the blasts of cold air that bothered us. So with the idea that insulating the rafters would solve our problems, the children and I put up the ladder to the outside door and formed an insulation brigade.

David took the rolls out of the bus and handed them to Sylvia. She gave them to Jenny halfway up the ladder. Jenny handed them to me in the doorway. I tossed them to Geoffrey, and he wended his way along the planks to the far side. Joan and Robbie, only five at the time, rummaged around in the bus, kicking out a roll or two and unraveling a couple more. But even with their help we managed to finish the job.

Joe was properly impressed. He oohed and aahed and hugged the children as they crowded around him. Then he climbed up to the attic to see how it looked, and we clambered up after him.

"Well," he said, patting the rolls of pink fiberglass. "By this time tomorrow it should be all in. That'll warm us up a bit."

And the next morning we began our first major endeavor.

We were methodical about it. First we gathered the equipment. I located the stapler, under Robbie's bed. He'd been using it as a hammer. Then I unearthed the only pair of scissors that hadn't been used to cut cloth, paper, hair, twigs, or rug samples. They were in a bottom kitchen drawer. Joe finally found a flashlight. Then he threaded an extension cord through the trapdoor in the utility room and carried a floor lamp up the ladder to the attic.

While he did this I assembled old sweat shirts and gloves for us to wear. Then I made masks. They weren't fancy. In fact, they looked like something the Lone Ranger would wear to muck out Silver's stall, but they kept us from inhaling fiberglass.

If you believe what you read, putting in insulation is a simple process. Both the directions on the batts and all the magazine articles I've ever read give it a difficulty rating of about two in a scale of one to five hundred. They lie. Magazines lull you with pictures of women in tight slacks and ruffled blouses insulating rec room walls and basement game rooms. Their husbands, only in the picture to show that their wives begged to let them do it, stand by smiling and munching a com dog.

I wish those photographers had been at our house that day. They would have seen Joe flat on his stomach stuffed in a comer where the eaves meet the floor. I would have been the lump in the baggy sweat shirt holding a batt out of the way with one hand and clutching a flashlight with the other. The article would have had to include Joe's brief but forceful speech when I inadvertently shone the flashlight the other way and he almost stapled his nose to the rafter.

As he worked his way up the roof line, the photographers could have taken a series of shots of Joe wobbling back and forth on top of a small stool on top of a larger stool on top of a rickety table as he tried to reach the peak in the roof.

When we ran out of flooring, Joe lay on a couple of boards that barely reached from one joist to another. That would have made some fine action shots. And the authors could have interspersed their narrative with poignant descriptions of Robbie climbing up the ladder, peering in the attic, and bellowing, "Who'll take me down to Grandmother's to play?"

At the end of a long obscene Sunday, the magazine would have had to report: "As darkness fell, the Combses stood back to admire their work. Five rafters fully insulated. Only thirty- two left to go."

That was how it was, but no one would dare print it. As we stumbled down the ladder in the blackness that Sunday, trying not to scratch the red welts made by contact with the fiberglass, Joe tried to console me. "Once we get the hang of it, it'll go a lot faster," he said.

It didn't, and each Sunday we were less and less anxious to jump out of bed and seal ourselves in the attic. We suddenly remembered other chores that needed doing. One week Joe sat on the roof of the chicken house in the rain with a bucket of tar, trying to patch the shingles. Another time, I was so desperate I washed all the windows inside and out.

In between we had guests, hundreds of them. People I hadn't seen in years, who'd never left their home states before, drove thousands of miles to visit us. They came with children, without children, with dogs, without dogs. Some brought picnic lunches. Others worked up an appetite on the way. But all came with plans to stay longer than they did. For after the first deluge or two frittered away our precious Sunday, we made everyone who came don a mask and help.

Most agreed, reluctantly. Only Jan Renner refused.

"God, kid!" she roared as she watched Joe balance a board across the joists and lower himself onto his stomach. "You're nuts if you think I'm going to get on my hands and knees and wallow around in the fiberglass." She paused. "I'll come up and talk to you if you'll give me a cup of coffee, but that's all."

We agreed. Jan's an Italian with Sicilian tendencies, and it's best not to cross her.

I first met Jan in early September at a kindergarten open house. As I recall I'd already been to two other school programs, one for the sixth-and eighth-graders and another for the third and fourth, and I'd pretty much had my fill of squeezing into tiny chairs and staring at pictures of the Mayflower landing at Plymouth Rock.

Joe, for some marvelously inventive reason, had refused to accompany me, and as I was new to the Island—at least I felt new after having been gone for thirteen years—I stood at the back of the room and watched as Robbie and Joan and all the other children wove in and out among the parents like mice going through a maze.

Some of the parents I recognized as being older copies of kids with whom I'd gone to school twenty years before. There was John Akahito standing with his wife next to the door. He was still incredibly handsome, and I remembered how I'd had a crush on him in the eighth grade. Valerie Morgan and her husband, Clint something-or-other, were leaning against the radiators over by the window. She had always come to school with her hair in curlers and then spent half an hour in the girls' bathroom combing it out. Alex Paine and his wife, Carole, were talking to the teacher. Alex's sister Judy had been in my class. She played the cornet in the school band about the same time I was faking it on the clarinet. The only piece I ever mastered was a watered-down version of "The World Is Waiting for the Sunrise," but Judy was "first chair" and always had the solo parts. Mother had told me earlier that Alex and Carole had put money down on our house a couple of weeks before we bought it, then decided on a place in Eagledale, and I wondered if I should go over and reintroduce myself.

Then, over in the comer with another couple, I saw Martin Renner. He'd been a senior when I was a fat, gawky eighth- grader, and I remembered thinking of him as one of the untouchables. Standing next to him was a short, dark-haired woman I assumed was his wife, Jan. She was in the middle of what appeared to be a marvelous story of considerable length and obvious hilarity, and her arms sawed and chopped at the air as she held the other couple enthralled. Martin seemed to have heard it before, and he had the look of someone who's decided it's time to go home. As he scanned the room nervously, he caught my eye, and I could see he recognized me. He then tried, with repeated nudges that were emphatically repelled, to interrupt Jan and get her to look over too. Finally, after a whispered, behind-the-hand conclusion that sent her audience into gales of raucous laughter, she gathered her dignity about her and glanced my way.

They both came over. Martin, with one arm breaking the path and the other urging her on, shielded her from what appeared to be the danger of further conversations. And Jan, with the feisty stride of someone used to having crowds part for her, swept across the room.

"I was invited to your bridal shower," she said after the formalities had been dispensed with. "I used to live next door to Joe, when the Combses had a house on Woodlawn Avenue in Seattle, and I knew his Aunt Patty. Remember she gave a luncheon for you at Rossellini's and asked me to come too. I can't think why I couldn't make it." She paused, then chortled. "I was probably being ravaged in the back room at McCloskey, McCrusky, and Barnard where I worked."

Martin rolled his eyes, and Jan continued. "Say, where's Joe tonight?"

"Home," I told her. "He said he couldn't take another open house."

"God, kid, isn't that the truth? Except I kind of like them. This is Bobbie's, our baby's, first year, and I think it's fun to see what the little monsters do for that brief hour and a half they're gone every day." She pointed to a small boy with deep-red hair, standing by the teacher's desk. "That's Bobbie, over there," she said. "He's the adorable redhead. Say, which kid is yours?"

"I have two somewhere around here," I answered. "They're twins—our grand finale. Joe and I decided when they started coming in litters it was time to stop."

I located Robbie. His shirttail was already out, and he was plucking at the feathers of a monstrous Big Bird in the middle of the room. Then I searched the room for Joan. I finally found her hiding behind me, and I brought her around and introduced her.

Jan gave Joan a fierce squeeze, and Joan squirmed but said nothing.

"Mrs. Renner used to live next door to Daddy," I explained. Then I had an idea. "Say," I said, "why don't you all come down to the house and see Joe? Frankly, I think he stayed home to watch the football game, but he'd be delighted to see you two."

"Why not?"

So we gathered up our children and fought our way through the crowd out to our cars, and they followed me home.

As I suspected, Joe was stretched out in his underwear on our bed. But it was halftime, and he leaped up and struggled into his pants when he saw we had guests.

"My God, Jan Jacobucci!" he yelled. "How the hell are you?" He gave her a bear hug. "And Martin! I haven't seen you since I graduated from old BHS."

Martin took off his coat. "Yeah. Weren't we on the same baseball team?"

"Right. I was center field and you were second base. How about a glass of wine? I've got some ten-year-old loganberry my dad made that's pretty good."

"Well"—Jan poked him in the ribs—"I'm a champagne girl myself, but if you've got loganberry, that's what I'll drink." We sat till after midnight that night, Martin and Jan and Joe all interrupting each other and fighting for the airways.

I heard about Angelo J. Manousus who taught civics up at the high school. "He was a pretty good egg," Martin said. "He used to kibitz when we played chess in the back of the room during class."

I heard about life on Woodlawn Avenue, "down by the gasworks," when Joe was fourteen or fifteen.

"He used to do the dishes every night, about the same time I took out the garbage," Jan told me. "And since it was summer and hot, I went out in my slip." She cackled. "Boy, Joe's mother would catch him peering out at me and she'd yank him away from that window and not let him back till I was inside again."

I heard stories about his maternal grandmother, who predicted earthquakes, saying they always came during "earthquake weather," and used to baby-sit with a little girl named Jill. "The trouble is," Jan recounted with glee, "Mrs. Wood didn't like the name Jill. She said it wasn't a name, so she called her Suzanne."

I heard about Dolly, the voluptuous blonde neighbor whose husband was with the Coast Guard in Alaska.

"Remember, Joe," Jan said, "how Dolly would come out to sunbathe and within minutes all the men on the block were trimming their hedges and cutting their grass?"

"Yeah," he said. "And then there was the time Dolly's husband was coming home so she decided to cook a goose as a special dinner." He turned to me to explain. "Dolly was not a cook, but she was determined to make this a big affair and everything went fine till Ralph—wasn't that his name?—till Ralph started to carve." Joe savored the moment, chuckling to himself at what was coming. "Dolly didn't realize she was supposed to clean the goose out before she cooked it, so with that first cut a horrible smell of steaming entrails exploded into the room." He laughed. "Hell, we could even smell it over at our place."

At quarter to one Martin looked at his watch and jumped up. "Come on, Jan, finish your wine," he said. "We've got to get home." He picked up Bobbie, who was sound asleep on the couch, and headed out the door. After a few "Come on, Jans" shouted from the car, she got up too.

"Come back again," I called after them.

"Yeah," yelled Joe. "You can help us remodel this house."

"The hell you say," Jan answered as they drove off into the night.

But they did come back. Martin even helped with a couple of rows of insulation. And sometimes when she was out taking her other son, Nicky, to Cub Scouts, or driving her daughter, Maria, to her piano lesson, she'd stop by, roaring up the driveway, the dust billowing out behind her.

Jan drives a car the same way she does everything else, with fervor and a certain wonderful flair all her own. She has an aversion to backing up and sees no reason why driveways and parking lots shouldn't be laid out so she can always go forward. And when it happens that she drives up onto the sidewalk or backs over someone's mailbox, she merely shifts gears and drives off, totally unaware of the wreckage she's left behind.

In her driving career she's knocked down barns, battered chicken houses, and once sent her mother-in-law's car careening down the driveway into the bushes. It took them ten minutes before they found it cowering in a laurel bush.

"I thought I felt something," she told Martin when he asked her why. "But when I got out to look, nothing was there."

So when I'd hear her dented Pontiac rattling down the driveway, I'd hold my breath and wait for the crash.

"Come on down out of there," she'd call if I was still up in the attic. "It's time for a coffee break."

Sometimes, however, we made her come up the ladder, complaining all the way, and while I held the flashlight and kept the insulation out of Joe's way, she regaled us with tales of her years as a student at Holy Angels, where the nuns outlawed patent-leather shoes because they were afraid of what they might reflect.

The work was more fun when Jan was there, but still it went slowly.

By Thanksgiving, we'd finished seventeen rafters, and as Christmas approached we still had ten to go. In honor of exhaustion, Joe ordered work to cease till January. By then he hoped to have a five-day week. We all agreed gratefully, but then, in a burst of Christmas spirit, the children and I and assorted children living close by decided to surprise Joe and finish it surreptitiously.

We worked every day. I took the shift under the eaves. David was tall and did the part at the peak, and the rest took turns in between. On New Year's Eve we stapled our last staple.

When Joe came home we said nothing. The girls giggled, and the boys poked each other, but we sat down to dinner as if it were any ordinary evening. After dinner when the dishes were done, following an intricate master plan Jenny had devised, I pretended I needed the scissors.

"Joe," I said, "are those scissors still in the attic?" Sylvia snickered and hid behind her hands.

Joe didn't seem to notice. "I don't know, I'll see," he said, and went out the door.

We waited till we heard him at the top of the ladder unlocking the door. Then we all rushed out to hear his reaction.

"You finished it!" he shouted. "My God, you finished it!"

"Surprise!" We climbed up into the attic.

The foil ceiling glistened from one end to the other. If we'd had a floor we could have danced. Everyone chattered at once.

"Did you suspect, Daddy?"

"We've been doing it for days now."

"We even let Robbie and Joan do some."

"And I put in the last staple." David likes to put in the last of things, including the last word.

Late that night, after everyone had gone to bed after Guy Lombardo had ushered in the New Year and played his last chorus of "Auld Lang Syne," Joe and I lay in bed listening to the heater complain. The ice was forming on the inside of the window a little later than usual, or so it seemed, and Joe was still exclaiming about our work.

"That insulation sure makes a difference, doesn't it?" he said.

I pulled the blankets up around my ears. "Sure does."

"That finishes project one. Next we'll put stairs into the attic."

I scratched my nose and grunted.

"Annie." He poked me. "You know I'll bet we can do the stairs in two weeks at the most."

6

The Rabbet Fits Into
the Dado Groove

If necessity is the mother of invention, poverty is surely the
father—at least in the world of remodeling.

Joe and I had great plans for our house when we moved in. It
was going to be a mansion, but we didn't quite know where to start.
So even before we battened up the attic hatches with insulation, we
decided a small cry for professional help was in order. Luckily Paul
Stewart, an Island architect and our neighbor, heard it.

Paul lives over the hill from us—over the hill and through the
nettles and across a board that spans the creek. When we first
came his house wasn't there. His land was a meadow with gnarled
old apple trees and a tangle of blackberry bushes. Then one day,
floating in on the full tide, came a little white house. It was like
a dollhouse with a veranda that encircled it completely and tiny
dormer windows that peered out from the second floor.

"Hey, Joe," I called out. "Come here. Come look at this."

Huge flags from Canada, Saudi Arabia, Great Britain, and
Brazil were draped from the eaves on each of the four sides and
billowed in the breeze. And flying higher than the rest, from a
pole that had been lashed to the chimney, was the American flag.
It looked like a Mississippi riverboat, and I wouldn't have been

surprised if I'd seen a paddle wheel churning behind the back door. Even as it sailed toward shore, I could almost hear voices singing, "Way down on the levee, in old Alabamy."

"Whose house is that?" asked Joe.

"Paul Stewart's. Remember? You met him the other day when he was down checking his property lines."

"Isn't he an architect?"

"Yes."

"Well then, there you are. Let's get him to draw up some plans for our remodeling."

So we did, and with a stroke or two of the pen Paul changed our house from the world's largest single-unit tenement dwelling into a country estate.

The mammoth empty attic was to be transformed into a second floor with six bedrooms and a bath. Four bedrooms would be lined up along the north side, with a long hall going straight down the center. For the south side, Paul drew in a bedroom on the east comer, then the stairs, then another large bedroom, and finally a bathroom. At either end of the house, in place of the magic door on the west and instead of two tiny windows on the east, would be balconies. Three bedrooms and the hall were to open up onto these. For light, Paul suggested we cut out a center portion of the roof and raise it a foot or two.

Downstairs he planned a dining room instead of the back hall and half the girls' bedroom, a den with the other half of their room, and the stairwell in the pantry. I didn't mind. With six children the food goes so fast I rarely have time to store it anyway.

Paul also decided that Geoffrey and Robbie's room, the narrow one next to ours, should be cut in half sideways. The front half we'd turn into a closet opening into the master bedroom, and the back half would eventually be a third bathroom. The thought of it was beyond my ken. A bathroom of my very own. No sneakers in the hamper, no basketball on the floor, not even garlands of dental floss hanging from the towel rack.

Finally, Paul's plans specified that David's room, the one next to the library in the northwest comer of the house, would one day be my study. I was ecstatic. Treatises on the state of mankind churned within me, and it seemed inconceivable that one day I'd have a place of my own where I could put them down on paper.

For weeks we pored over Paul's drawings, visualizing each change. For weeks the children fought over who was going to get which bedroom. The more we studied them, the more impatient we got.

I was all for getting started by knocking out a wall or two, but Joe, as usual, was more cautious.

"There are structural alterations you and I may not be able to handle," he told me. "Why don't we contact some of the local contractors and get bids on the major stuff? Then you and I can do the finishing."

It seemed like cheating, but I had to agree. Basically Joe and I were shelf-makers, and raising a roof was not a shelf- maker's job. So I restrained my urge to get on with it, and Joe arranged for three contractors to come, survey the scene, and then submit bids. They arrived together. They knocked on walls and figured stress factors. They crawled up into the attic and burrowed under the house. They noted load-bearing walls and tapped at foundations. Then they went away.

The bids came in the mail a week or so later. We opened the envelopes slowly. All I could see were unending columns of figures, and each total had more commas between the numbers than the last. Joe turned a sickly gray.

"Good Lord," he said. "The cost of the labor alone would send David and Sylvia to college and on to graduate school."

I nodded.

"And look here. It says, 'The above costs do not include Washington state tax, or our 12% fee which will be added to the billing.' "

I sighed. The dream of each child in his or her own room, and me in my study, flickered and began to fade. "Isn't there anything we can do?" I asked.

Joe didn't answer. He had the plans spread out on the kitchen table. He studied them for a long time, making notes, adding figures. Then slowly, deliberately, he rolled them up.

"Annie," he said, smacking the roll down on the counter so hard I jumped. "We're going to do it ourselves. You and I. We learned to make shelves and that toy chest. We'll learn how to do this, even if we have to take carpentry classes at night. It may take longer, but we're going to have the best damn house on Bainbridge Island."

"Right!" I shouted. But mentally I was biting my fingernails.

Fortunately, the same God that looks after children and drunks had seen some of our handiwork, and he brought us Hal. He even arranged for the meeting to be at church—the following Sunday.

It was after the services were over, when the faithful indulged in a cup of coffee and a cookie or two. I was monitoring the children's cookie intake, and Joe, not one to stand around making small talk, was mumbling about having to leave or he wouldn't get any work done before the day was over, when Hal, seeing we were new, came over and introduced himself. He and Joe exchanged pleasantries and I glared at Geoffrey, who was on his fourth brownie, when Hal made his fatal mistake.

"Did you buy a house around here?" he asked innocently.

He never should have opened his mouth, for we were bursting with the bliss that makes ignorance so delightful, and in a matter of minutes we'd overwhelmed him with every detail, including how we were going to do the work ourselves. Strangely enough he listened, not nodding off or looking glazed as others had done. In fact, he seemed interested, and as we were leaving he took Joe aside.

"When you start," he said, "if you need any help or advice, let me know. I've done a lot of remodeling myself."

We nodded and thanked him for his offer, but, as with most significant moments in life, we didn't realize then that this man was going to make our whole implausible scheme possible. Under his tutelage we would learn to move walls, build dormers, mix cement, install plumbing, hang doors, reroof, put up paneling, cut plasterboard, frame in windows, glue on Formica, and countersink nails.

For Hal, as we were to discover little by little, is an expert, a master craftsman, at everything he does—and he does everything. In his seventy-five years he's been a carpenter, a plumber, a real-estate salesman, even a barber. He's built homes, laid bricks, constructed bulkheads, and poured concrete without having the forms buckle. He's mended lacquer tables, built church pulpits, tooled leather, made kitchen cabinets, and reroofed houses without once having his shingle hammer slide down the roof and over the edge.

He's a gardener who can prune a tree without killing it, who actually plants his peas on Washington's birthday, and whose autumnalis really bloom in autumn.

His workshop is neater and more organized than an interplanetary space capsule. His saws and chisels are all sharp, and I think it's safe to say he's never used his level for a hammer.

But we didn't know this when we first met. We knew he knew more than we did. That was all, and that was enough.

All that fall we'd puttered around, painting the walls, stapling the insulation, slapping on the roofing tar, and gluing down the shag. We were building up our confidence. Then as January and 1971 dawned, we decided to move on to something grander, more impressive—namely, opening up the stairwell and putting in the stairs.

We called Hal, and he agreed to come.

It wasn't the opportune time to open a hole into the large, drafty attic. It was bitter cold that year. We'd had several inches of snow on the ground for a week, and long silver icicles hung from the eaves and splintered the lukewarm sunlight. The heater belched and roared but gave out little heat, and the only time any of us could get warm was when we were in bed or chin deep in a hot bath.

We would have been wiser to tackle weather-stripping or furnace repair, but we were more anxious than wise. So when Joe finally got a week off, the stairs it was going to be. The shelf-makers were moving on—to treads and risers and cleat supports.

On the morning Hal was to come, Joe was as nervous as an intern at his first tonsillectomy. He was convinced that cutting into the attic would cause the whole roof to collapse, and as he paced back and forth drinking cup after cup of coffee he had me convinced too.

"That beam worries me," he kept saying. "I know it has to come out, but it looks as if it supports the whole attic."

Only the knowledge that Hal wouldn't do anything rash kept him from canceling the whole venture.

Hal arrived promptly at eight thirty. I saw him flinch slightly as he surveyed the atmosphere in which he was going to have to work. It was an ordinary Saturday morning as far as we were concerned, but to a man whose children are grown it must have been like a hermit stumbling onto the freeway at rush hour. Cartoons blasted from the TV in the living room. David and Geoffrey wrestled over the comics at the table. The girls dashed by in their pajamas and flew into the bathroom, where we could hear them giggling and shrieking. I tried to look calm.

Joe motioned me to quiet everyone, then took Hal into the pantry. It was gloomy and dark. Here and there spikes protruded out of the studs. Cobwebs dripped from the ceiling as if leaking through the attic floor. Suddenly I wished I'd vacuumed before he came. But Hal didn't seem to notice. He studied the beam and pounded on the wall a couple of times. Then he came back in the kitchen and surveyed the wall from that side. He stared at the door jamb and took a few measurements. We waited anxiously.

Finally he took off his hat and rubbed his bald head. I was certain he was going to say it couldn't be done. So was Joe. I could tell by the way he clenched his teeth and his lower lip jutted out. Finally Hal spoke.

"How come you didn't start yet?" he said. "You don't need me to show you how to rip all this junk out."

Relief exploded on Joe's face. "I… I didn't know where to begin."

"About anywhere'll do. We have to take out this window" —it was the broken window between the kitchen and the back hall—"then the door comes out, and the wall between the kitchen and the pantry—except for the studs, of course—then the pantry ceiling. That ought to open it up enough for a good-sized stairwell."

He put his coat on the living-room couch and picked up his hammer and his crowbar.

"Let's go to work," he said.

So began a day of bashing walls, ripping shiplap, pulling nails, tearing window frames apart, and unhanging doors.

By noon Joe looked tired. I know I was, and I'd only helped pull nails and haul the old boards out of the way. He'd been swinging the hammer, wrenching the shiplap with the crowbar, and climbing up and down the ladder. When I heated up steaming bowls of borscht for lunch, I saw him slump over his beets a bit.

"Are you OK?" I asked when Hal went into the other room for his pipe.

"No, I'm exhausted." His face was grimy. The lock of hair assigned to cover up his bald spot was hanging down over his ear, and cobwebs clung to the back of his sweat shirt.

"Why don't you quit for today?"

"I can't. Hal's still going strong. Besides, we have to get this done."

"But Joe—"

Hal came back in, and I said no more.

"Come on, Joe," he said as he lit his pipe. "We won't get anything done sitting around."

I watched Joe ease himself to a standing position and shuffle into the pantry. The time had come to tackle the beam, and he didn't look enthusiastic. But Hal assured him everything was sufficiently braced, and they began sawing.

The beam, six inches by eight inches and solid fir, didn't come out easily. First Joe went at it from above, kneeling on a board slung across the open joists. Then Hal took a turn from below, standing, wedged up against the wall on a stepladder. Then Joe went at it again. Perspiration mixed with grime ran down his face in rivulets. Even Hal seemed a bit weary, but finally they made it through the old, hard fir. It was so heavy they both held it till the last stroke of the saw broke through. Then they lifted it down gently.

The roof didn't cave in, but with the cold rush of air tumbling down from the attic, it felt as if it had. I put another sweater on over the two I was wearing and wondered how many fingers and toes I'd lose before spring.

By the time five thirty crawled around and Hal got ready to go home, the window was gone, the door was gone, the ceiling was no more, and where a wall had been stood a row of bare studs. The wind whistled around the kitchen and I got out a pair of mittens. Joe looked as if he were on the verge of total collapse.

After Hal left, I gave Joe a martini, but it did little more than liquefy him. He flowed to the nearest chair, where he sat sipping and staring while I got dinner. The children, rested and energetic, took turns climbing the ladder into the attic.

After we'd chipped our way through dinner, which had turned to ice the instant it hit the plates, I asked Joe if we should clean up the debris in our new stairwell, but he shook his head slowly. "It'll only get dirty again tomorrow," he said. Then he got up and stumbled off toward the bedroom.

By seven thirty he'd had a hot bath and was in bed, a prostrate mass of aching, twitching muscles. He couldn't have moved if the house had caught fire. Not long after, the rest of us followed suit. It was the only way to get warm.

The next morning, Joe rose slowly and carefully. Breakfast revived him slightly, but when Hal came he was still nursing his coffee.

Hal walked into the kitchen, yawning. "Boy, I'm tired today," he said, putting down his saw and other tools.

Joe straightened and smiled for the first time. "You are?" he said. "So am I. I ache in every bone in my body."

Hal looked up, surprised. "Oh, I'm not sore from the work we did. I'm sleepy. When I got home last night, Helen and I had dinner, then went out to a dance. We didn't get home till after midnight."

Joe slumped back against his chair.

"Hey, Joe," Hal called from the stairwell, "you're going to have to learn one thing about carpentry right now. When you finish a job, clean up the mess." He got out a broom and swept up a pile of sawdust. "That's the way it's done. Now let's see. What do we do today?"

The days following were a mixture of clouds of sawdust, the high shriek of the power saw, and dirt flying around the house then settling everywhere.

Joe and Hal framed in a new doorway, moved plugs and switches, and brought in, cut, and nailed up plasterboard. Finally they started on the stairs.

I stayed out of the way, fetching new saw blades and bags of nails from the hardware store, making coffee when necessary, and holding the dog so he wouldn't attack the delivery men from the lumberyard.

Hal and Joe measured, marked, sawed and nailed, all the while speaking a foreign tongue I couldn't comprehend. I got the gist of things when Hal told of the nocturnal habits of the French nobleman's wife, but they lost me when he called out, "Keep it flush, Joe, keep it flush," or, "See, over here, Joe. The rabbet fits into the dado groove, and the tread dadoes fit over the risers."

The children, in school most of the time, rushed home every afternoon to check on the progress. They slammed in the front door, threw their books on the couch, checked the refrigerator, the cupboards, and the oven for food, and then came to see what had been done. Invariably they stood a moment, chewing and looking, then said, "Is that all?" and left.

Mother inspected too. I think the county had her on retainer. Her visits were frequent, and she missed nothing— at least nothing remotely dangerous. "It's nice," she'd say as Hal and Joe pointed out a major alteration, "but shouldn't you sweep up those nails? The children might step on them," or, "Is it safe to use the power saw? You might cut one of your fingers off." The peril of slivers haunted her. She'd read somewhere of a child who, as a result of a sliver that turned gangrenous, had to have his leg cut off, and she cited it often.

Jan swept in every now and then, but the mean temperature in the house, which hovered around 52 degrees, was too frigid for her hot Italian blood, so she never stayed for long.

On the Sunday before Valentine's Day, Joe and Hal finished constructing the stairs. They needed to be stained, they hadn't been pushed up against the wall, and they had no railing as yet, but they were grand, every bit as elegant as any we'd seen, and we raced up and down them, commenting on their sturdiness and their width.

Hal grumbled at our antics. Being the perfectionist he is, it was like desecrating the flag to consider using them before the last coat of stain had dried and the last nail had been countersunk.

Mother agreed with him. But whereas he complained about soiling the risers, she saw children falling to their death in the open stairwell. It didn't help matters when Sylvia and Jenny pushed past her, pillows and blankets in hand, and informed her they were moving upstairs, and she grumbled like a dormant volcano for a month or more till the stairs were safely pushed against the wall and a makeshift railing was up.

Then, one evening late in March, Joe installed a large, wrought-iron chandelier in the stairwell, and all was complete.

"You know, Annie," he said as he patted the freshly painted walls, "that's one magnificent stairway—and we did it."

"Right," I said. "And now we can rest for a while, and I can vacuum some of the dust and grime out of the rugs."

He didn't hear me, and I saw a faraway look come into his eyes. He was planning.

"Tell you what," he said after a considerable pause. "On my next day off, let's bash in the wall over there. It's on the plans and will extend the hall into the living room and make the living room lighter."

I shrugged. "Oh, why not? The rug will only get dirty again, and I love bashing. It gets rid of my aggressions. Besides, it's cheap fun."

7

Mix With Drinkable Water

It's my own fault. If I hadn't been so eager to avoid cleaning out the large patch of baked-on lasagna in my oven, I might never have been suckered into doing the world's most detestable job—that of taping and spackling walls.

There is an occupation with nothing to recommend it. It's the type of project that turns teetotalers into certified alcoholics and disintegrates thirty-year-old marriages. And almost everyone who's tried it has one thing to say on the subject. "Leave it to the professionals. It's cheaper in the long run."

I say "almost everyone" because there is one stubborn soul who's never called up his local Sheetrock man saying, "My walls are yours," and he, naturally, is Joe. The reason is simple. He bribed me to do the job.

He first brought up the subject when he and Hal were working on the stairs. They'd finished the new wall against which the stairs were to be pushed, but it had to be taped, spackled, and painted before they could slide them over. Somehow they decided it was a natural occupation for me.

"You see," Joe explained, "it's something you can do on the days when I'm at work. With all the children in school you have lots of time."

I bristled. "What do you mean, lots of time? I still have to do the laundry and the cooking and the cleaning—not to mention the after-school chauffeuring. Why, it's going to take me two hours just to scrape out the oven you've been yelling about. I'll have to spray on the junk, then let it sit, then rinse it twenty or thirty times. See this scar?" I held up my left hand. "That's where the lye ate into me the last time—"

"All right, all right," he broke in. "I'll make a bargain with you. If you do the wall, I won't mention the oven till you're through. In fact, if I get the time, I'll do it myself."

Talk about everyone having his price. Joe had just met mine.

"You mean you won't make snide remarks and flap at the air when it gets a little smoky in here?"

"Right."

"And you won't tell me how clean your sister keeps her oven even though she has six children too?"

"I promise."

Hal, standing close by, sucked on his pipe. Being a tidy person by nature, it had taken concessions on his part to tolerate my housekeeping at its best, and here Joe was fostering my sloth.

"OK, I'll do it," I said. "Hal, you know how to do everything. Will you show me how?"

"Sure, it's simple."

The way he did it, it was simple. A little compound, a little stirring, the right amount of spackle on the putty knife, a few deft strokes, and he'd done three nail holes and a seam.

I could hardly wait to start. This'll be a cinch, I thought, and with all the walls we'll be putting up, I won't have to face the oven for years.

The next day, as soon as Joe and the children left, I began. I had all the ingredients, and Joe had picked up a pamphlet outlining the various steps to putting up a professional-looking wall. I studied the instructions over a second cup of coffee.

"Step 1: Combine powder with drinkable water and mix until wet." I checked that again. Why were they specifying drinkable water? Was this one of those strange mixes pregnant women crave, like laundry starch, or had the Food and Drug Administration discovered that 40 percent of the babies in Paducah, Kentucky, got sick from licking walls finished with undrinkable water? I couldn't think of an explanation, and though I asked, I never got a satisfactory answer. A neighbor said if you mix the compound with water from stagnant ponds (undrinkable to be sure), your walls will mildew or grow moss on their north side or something, but that seemed a bit farfetched. Anyway, I vowed to use drinkable water.

The next stumbling block was how much water to how much dry compound. The directions were exact. "For a 25-lb. sack of compound, use 16 1/2 pints of water." That, however, would mean mixing it in the bathtub. I needed to work out smaller proportions. Unfortunately, this meant using mathematics, and my ability in math is so rudimentary that David balances my checkbook and adds up my gin rummy score.

Since David was in school, I tried the "if Johnny has three apples and Mary has two oranges" method. It didn't work. The compound was too thick. I couldn't stir it. I think Johnny had more apples than he let on.

Next I tried the procedure I use in whipping up pancakes: a little compound, then a little water, then a little more compound. I arrived at a consistency perfect for pancakes but not for taping a wall seam.

Finally I called the school and had David paged. He gave me the right proportions.

I put the compound into a plastic bucket and added the water a bit at a time. Then I stirred. I stirred and stirred and stirred, mashing the lumps against the side with a stick. Eventually I had a thoroughly mixed mass of gray mud. It smelled like badly rendered kangaroo, and I stuck my head out the door several times to quell my nausea. Then I went on to Step 2.

"Step 2: Apply sufficient putty to the wall seams to allow tape to adhere." I slopped on a mass of the mixture and swore ever so softly as globs dripped off onto the floor. The swearing got louder as I progressed to Step 3.

"Step 3: Now that the tape is centered ..." Now that what tape is centered? I measured out a six-foot strip of tape and cut it off. It flipped around and stuck to the wall. I pulled it loose, climbed the ladder, and centered one end at the top of the seam near the ceiling. Then I worked my way down, centering, straightening, pressing lightly with my fingers, which by now were caked with putty. To keep the end from sticking to the wall before I could center it, I draped it over my shoulder. This coated my shoulder and my back with putty, but by then I didn't care.

I checked the directions again. "Now that the tape is centered, press firmly, but not hard, with your putty knife at a 45-degree angle. Some of the excess will squeeze out."

I held my knife at a 45-degree angle and pressed firmly, making a downward stroke as Hal had done. The tape came along with me, bunching up as the mound of putty grew. The excess squeezed out and splattered onto my shoes. I scraped off what I could and went back to Step 2. This time I held the top of the tape with one hand, scraped with the other, and kept my balance by wrapping one leg around the ladder.

After forty minutes of struggling, I finished the first seam. There was no resemblance between my seam and Hal's. There were bumps and ruts and globs of putty hardening on the floor. But it was the best I could do. I'd improve, I was sure.

In the meantime, I tried a couple of nail holes. They were fun—a simple X motion and they were done. I was tempted to do nothing but nail holes and leave the seams for another day when I was stronger. But my Protestant background allows reward only after work, so I rationed them. After each seam, I allowed myself ten nail holes.

By the time the children came home from school, I'd finished one coat on my assigned wall. Of course, I'd forgotten to take anything out of the freezer for dinner, the beds were unmade, and the breakfast dishes sat curdling on the counter, but I didn't care. I was proud of my work.

"Come and see what I've done," I called to David and Sylvia when they walked in the door.

"Yuck," said David. "To make this you called me out of Algebra?"

Sylvia reached over and pulled some hardened spackle out of my eyebrows. "You got more on yourself than you did on the wall," she said. "Are there any cookies left?"

"It's my first try," I yelled after them. "Once I get the hang of it, I'll be able to do a whole room in a couple of hours."

It was the same old "once I get the hang of it" story, and I believed it then as I had with the insulation. I'm not what you'd call a quick study.

I covered the still half-full bucket and sped around the house, cleaning, washing, straightening.

When Joe came home he was impressed, at least he pretended he was. He ignored the imperfections and lavished more praise on me than he had since he taught me how to change a tire. He knew instinctively it was a rotten job, and he was determined not to do it himself.

The next day I let the walls dry, and the day after I was on to Step 4.

"Step 4: Wrap sandpaper around a wood block and sand lightly." That seemed simple enough. No doubt it would have been if I hadn't put too much spackle on in the first coat. I sanded lightly. Some large bumps broke away and the wall began to look like a bas-relief of the moon. I sanded lightly again. A little better, but by no means smooth. Hal had told me, "You have to have it smooth." I sanded heavily. Nothing.

Then, in a burst of genius, I got out Joe's electric sander.

It smoothed things out all right, and I considered using it for the lasagna on the oven. Then I noticed it had shredded the tape and filled the air with a fine white dust. I glanced in a mirror. My hair had turned white, my eyebrows had turned white, and each wrinkle was etched in white. I looked as if I'd crossed the border on the last yak out of Shangri La

I coughed, choked a couple of times, wondered if there was a white-lung disease, and went back to the block and sandpaper.

By three in the afternoon, I'd decided I'd sanded enough. The walls were still pocked, but I figured a second coat of spackle would fill in the rough spots.

That night Joe was effusive in his compliments. "It looks fantastic," he said. "You seem to have the touch."

I sensed I had a permanent position.

The next day was spackle time again. The compound (or taping mud, as the professionals call it) had by this time been sitting for three days. It had matured. In fact it had matured to the point where I cleaned out the litter box three times and checked the soles of my shoes before I narrowed the stench down to the bucket. When I located the smell, I found it was nothing compared to what had built up under the cover. I took the lid off, and waves of the most horrible aroma since a neighbor gave me a bowl of stewed bear heart overtook me. I slapped the lid back on and went to clean the oven.

As I chipped at the lasagna, I tried to figure out what to do. It was snowy outside, too cold for me to spackle with the door open, and if I put the bucket outside, the putty would freeze. Suddenly I remembered the masks we'd used when insulating. I slammed the oven door shut and dug them out. With two on the smell was only strong, not overpowering. I pried off the lid again and started the second coat.

It was, if anything, harder than the first. "Apply the second coat and feather the edges about 1 1/2 inches beyond the first coat," Step 5 instructed. "Feather the edges" was the key phrase.

"You want it to blend in with the surrounding wall," Hal had explained. "Then when it's painted the seam doesn't show."

It sounded easy, but every time I got an almost-perfect feathered edge, I pressed either too hard or not hard enough, and ridges, bumps, and streaks formed. That night I had only two seams and twenty nail holes finished. The oven began to look more and more appealing, and I offered to trade back. But Joe was having none of it.

"We made a deal," he said. "Besides, how much do you think Hal and I are going to get done if we have to stop every day or so and spackle?"

I tried to enlist the children's help.

"David, you have long artistic fingers," I said. "I bet you'd be a natural at this."

But David is swifter than I, and he knew what would happen if he agreed. He knew his father's modus operandi: Get someone to do a job once, then make it his for life. So he declined.

"No way, Mom."

I then approached Sylvia. She was amenable, but she had conditions. I had to let her bring home another kitten. She wanted a new pair of shoes and a hair drier, and she thought it would be fun to host a weekend slumber party up in the attic. I declined.

"No way, Sylv."

The rest were willing but unskilled. Had I been smart, and had I had the patience to stick with it through the apprentice period, I might have trained several talented successors. But I could see gobs of spackle splattered on the windows, clinging to the draperies, and matted in the dog's fur, and I abandoned the idea.

In the end I did it myself, and I did our bedroom wall, so Joe and Hal could build in bookcases and a dresser and two window seats. Then I did the hall and the dining room and the den and our closet. Our closet had the added attraction of a new ceiling. Spackling it left me with a crick in my neck, bursitis in my arm and shoulder, and putty in my eyes.

By the time the children's bedrooms upstairs started to materialize, Joe was hauling spackle home by the seventy- pound tub. I tried to improve my working conditions with numerous coffee and cigarette breaks, and I put a TV on a chair in the middle of the room so I could keep track of Bill and Laura and old Doc Horton on "Days of Our Lives," but even with rape and incest and an occasional murder or two to keep me amused, my affection for the chore at hand remained at zero and I gradually found other things to do.

I took up sewing and learned to bake sourdough bread. I volunteered to help with the eighth-grade language arts class up at the middle school, and I enrolled in a writer's workshop in Seattle. Jan went with me. In fact she talked Carole Paine (the woman who almost bought my house) into going too, and together we journeyed up to the YWCA every Thursday morning and spent two hours hearing and writing about rape, incest, and an occasional murder or two.

Joe fumed. Then he snarled. Then he nagged. Finally he learned to do the job himself. He didn't mind too much. It was football season and it gave him a chance to combine the two things he likes to do best—work and watch a tight end go out for a short pass.

Eventually I cleaned the oven.

8

A Table for Nine by the Window

The winter of 1971 was not a winter littered with dinner parties and evenings carousing in Seattle. When your dining table is plunked in the middle of the kitchen, your living room ceiling is pockmarked with holes where people have fallen through, and it's so cold you're wearing long johns under your panty hose, you don't readily invite two or three couples over for a candlelight supper and a game of charades.

Conversely, if Saturday night is traditionally the time for rinsing off your putty knives and pulling the slivers out of the palms of your hand, you tend to put the idea of dinner for two at the Space Needle out of your mind. So most of the time Joe and I stayed home and slapped on another coat of spackle or rubbed Ben-Gay into our aching muscles.

Once in a while, however, we treated ourselves and dined out in Winslow, at the Islander. It was about the only restaurant in town then, and though its menu hadn't changed visibly since the doors first opened, and though the cook occasionally imbibed overly in Old Grandad and sent out a frozen scallop or two, it was an evening away from the stove and a chance to wear an outfit not built around thermal underwear.

Since then, of course, progress has washed up on the shores of Bainbridge, and now restaurants are everywhere. The Islander tries to keep up. They've expanded, added a salad bar and now feature live music and dancing on Saturday nights. And while the serious drinkers congregate at the bar and pass the pretzels, energetic couples stomp and shuffle to the electric strains of "You Can Take Your Job and Shove It."

Back then, however, it was a simple table for two by the window, with a view of the ferry traffic, a couple of martinis, and a steak with a side order of onion rings. Sometimes Jan and Martin joined us. Sometimes we talked Carole and Alex Paine into coming along. Why not? It gave them such pleasure, as they listened to our tales of icy winds sweeping down out of the attic, to know that they'd passed up the opportunity to revel in the same experience.

Of course, we celebrated birthdays at the Islander too. In a family with six children, birthday parties are like baby books. After going all out for the first one or two, you lose interest.

I lost interest after Sylvia's third birthday. We held the party a day early, on a Sunday afternoon. I baked a green rabbit cake with floppy ears and all. We had games and prizes and a trip to the park. We invited eight and twenty came, and Cindy Barstead fell off the swing and went home with a bloody nose. That night, after the last crumbs were wiped away and the last balloon had popped, I went into labor. Sylvia still considers Geoffrey her birthday present.

After that, I issued a proclamation: "Birthdays and the related festivities will take place at the restaurant of your choice with you, your parents, and one guest. Cake and ice cream will be served after dinner at home."

Since I'd cleverly managed to have six children with only four birthdays, this meant only four outings a year in the company of diners who slide under the table, stand on their chairs, and make numerous trips to the bathroom to play with the hand drier. It still, however, meant six cakes, which was a considerable sacrifice on my part, for I am not a cake baker. I can whip up wild-blackberry pies with crusts so flaky you'd kill for a piece, and my Mandarin Orange Mousse is known all over the Island, but when I bake a cake, the layers sag and slant. I've never mastered the art of making roses and delicate green leaves, and the frosting invariably runs out before I've covered the sides. This leaves outcroppings of chocolate cake that look like rocks on a snow-covered mountain.

Still, I never managed to persuade any of my children to opt for pie or Mandarin Mousse on their birthdays, so on a cold, dismal Saturday in 1971, February 8, when the twins turned six, I woke up with the sinking knowledge that today was to be a two-cake day.

Robbie and Joan had been up for hours. Ribbon and wrapping paper were strewn all over the living room. Joan was on her third batch of popcorn made in her new toy popper, and Robbie had set up long sections of track and was shooting cars down off the couch, around a lamp, and into the library.

"Hi, Mom," Robbie yelled as I stumbled out of my room heading for the kitchen. "Look at what we got."

I admired everything, watched a test run of a baby-blue Corvette, and told Joan I'd try some popcorn after breakfast. As I left to go make some coffee, Robbie stopped me.

"Mom?" he said in a small voice.

"What."

"I have to tell you something."

"What."

"I accidentally invited two people to my party tonight."

"You mean someone besides Eric?"

"Yeah...Brian."

"How'd you do that?"

"I don't know." He looked down at the floor. "I asked Eric first, but he didn't know if he could come, so I asked Brian. Is it all right?"

He seemed so miserable I bent down and gave him a hug.

"Sure it's OK."

Joan had been listening intently, and now she bounded forward.

"Can I ask someone else too? Please, Mom. Linda already said she could come, but Chris invited me to her party next week, and she said she's going to buy me a present. Can I ask her too?"

The thought of taking six six-year-olds out to dinner was depressing, but what could I do?

"All right, all right. We'll call her after breakfast," I said, and I retreated.

The rest of the morning went fairly smoothly. Joe was at work and he called to say happy birthday. Jenny made a couple of cards out of construction paper and aluminum foil, and everyone had some popcorn.

Shortly after lunch, I started the cakes. Sylvia and Jenny volunteered to help. I agreed.

"Sure. You two can do Robbie's. His is chocolate. I'll make the white one."

They were delighted. Sylvia and Jenny love nothing better than to be able to cook. They produce batches of cookies at the drop of a chocolate chip, and I think they've stirred up more loaves of zucchini bread than any other living human. Within minutes, beaters were whirring, Jenny was greasing the pans, and Sylvia had the oven preheating.

I should have let them make both cakes. They were better at it than I. But by the time they had theirs in the oven, the kitchen was littered with debris, and they vanished when I suggested cleaning up. So I proceeded alone, rinsing bowls out as I needed them and clearing off a small space on the counter to give me room to work. It didn't take long—mixes rarely do —and except for the fact that one layer was slightly thinner than the other, they looked fairly good.

I hauled them out of the oven when they were done, flipped them onto a cake rack, and set them down to cool on top of the stove. It was the only clear surface left. Then I turned my attention to loading the dishwasher.

Meanwhile the girls, sensing it was safe to return, had wandered back into the kitchen.

"Can we make the frosting now?" Sylvia asked.

"No. Wait till I finish cleaning up."

"But our cake's all cool."

"There isn't any room," I protested, about to launch into my usual, "finish one thing before you start another" speech. But the phone cut me short.

"Hello, Mrs. Combs, this is Madeline Marchand, Walter's mother."

"Oh, yes," Sylvia had the frosting mix out, and Jenny was searching in the refrigerator for a cube of butter. I waved at them to wait, but they ignored me.

"I have a little problem. My Walter says he's invited to go out to dinner with your Robbie tonight, and I thought I'd better check with you, just to be sure."

Jenny put the double boiler on the stove and turned on the burner. I reached out to grab her, but she eluded me, and I gave up.

"Oh." I tried not to sound surprised. "Oh, yes." I turned my back in an attempt to muffle the banging and clattering behind me. "Of course. It's Robbie's and Joan's birthday and we're taking them out to dinner."

"Well, I know Walter doesn't tell lies, but as I hadn't heard from you, I thought perhaps he was fooling me."

"Oh, no, no, no." My voice was electric with enthusiasm. My mind was planning Robbie's imminent demise. "You tell Walter we'll pick him up shortly after five o'clock." I waited while she told Walter. It sounded as if she had him by the scruff of the neck. Apparently I'd just saved his truthful little life. Then she gave me directions on how to find her house, and after more of her assurances that Walter never lies, I hung up the phone and turned around.

Things were the same as they had been—with one major exception. One layer of Joan's cake was on fire.

"Oh, my God!" I shrieked, flapping at the flames with a dish towel.

Jenny and Sylvia, who'd been engrossed in trying to force the beaters into the mixer, whipped around.

"I didn't do it."

"You did too. You turned on the burner."

"You told me to."

"I did not."

"Stop fighting!" I screamed as the flames rose higher. "Help me put this out."

Jenny grabbed another dish towel, and Sylvia reached out with a long barbecue fork and pulled the rack onto the floor. Finally we smothered the flames. But the commotion had drawn a crowd, and when Joan saw the charred remains she burst into tears.

"What'd you do to my cake?" she sobbed.

"Nobody did anything. It was an accident."

"But now I don't have a cake."

"Don't get so upset. One layer's still good, and I'll run down to Winslow and get another mix. Then you'll have three layers/'

"I will?" She brightened. "Three?"

"I want three layers too," Robbie yelled from the living room.

"You can't." Joan's defeat had turned into a surprising victory. "Yours didn't get burned."

"I can too, can't I, Mom?"

"No, you can't. I'm not going to spend all afternoon making cakes. Besides"—I suddenly remembered Mrs. Marchand—"what's this about your inviting Walter Marchand to come tonight?"

"I didn't invite him."

"His mother said you did."

"He was there when I asked Eric, but I didn't ask him."

"Oh, well, never mind." I decided not to pursue it any further. "Now help clean up this mess, while I go get another mix.

By four thirty the cakes were done. Joan's tilted slightly, like a fat Tower of Pisa, and Robbie's, to make up for one less layer, was smothered in blue and yellow roses.

I changed my clothes quickly, herded the birthday children into the car, and we set off to gather up the guests.

Naturally they all lived eight or ten miles from each other. I picked them up one by one, and while the girls, neat and trim with ribbons in their hair, sat quietly together, the boys rolled around and wrestled with each other. We picked Brian up first.

He brought a bag of M&Ms with him. As I drove around the back roads searching in the rain and the dark for hidden driveways, he and Robbie threw them at each other and tried to stuff them down the back of Joan's dress.

I was relieved when they ran out before we picked up Walter. Walter, however, had amusements of his own. His sister, Judy, had recently taught him how to belch, and he volunteered to share his new talent. By the time I pulled back into our driveway, all the boys were sucking in great amounts of air, then rumbling it back out again. The girls egged them on by squealing "Uck" and "Gross" and "Mom, make them stop."

I stayed out of it. I parked the car and got out.

"All right, now," I said. "I'm going to pick up Daddy at the boat. Then we'll go to dinner. Keep clean and behave yourselves till I get back."

An M&M fell off my shoulder onto the ground, and I heard Walter erupt with one final blast as he disappeared into the house. I got back into the car and headed off again.

I was late. The cars were already streaming off the boat when I came to the stoplight in Winslow. I looked in the rearview mirror. There was a police car behind me, so I didn't creep forward as usual when the light turned yellow the other way. Up ahead I could see commuters heading for their cars in the lot.

Oh, damn, I said to myself. Joe's probably started up the hill already.

I looked to see if I could pick out his silhouette against the glare of approaching headlights.

Behind me a siren suddenly blared out of the night. I jumped, then glanced back. The police car had his lights flashing, and I pulled over to the side of the road. He pulled up behind me, and the officer got out and came over. He was young with bright red hair and a luxurious mustache.

"Did you know your back lights are out, Ma'am?" he asked.

"They are?" I ran my hands through my hair. "That's all I need."

"I'm afraid you're going to have to take this car to a gas station and leave it there till they can be fixed."

"But I can't," I wailed. "Do you realize what kind of a day I've had?"

I gave him a detailed account of the cake disaster and the flying M&Ms and Walter's new trick.

"And now," I said, "I have to pick up my husband, and we're taking seven six-year-olds out to dinner at the Islander."

He stood up and thought a moment. "I tell you what," he said. "Keep your foot slightly on the brake when you're driving. That way you'll at least have some tail lights. Then tomorrow for sure get this fixed."

I could have kissed him, mustache and all. "Oh, thank you! You're the first nice thing that's happened today."

He laughed. "That's OK. Good luck." He got back into his car and I went on down to where Joe was waiting. "What kept you so long?"

"Don't ask."

We hurried home, gathered up the group, and were off again. I laid down the ground rules on the way.

"This is how it's going to be," I said. "You can order either a hamburger and fries or fish and chips."

"I'm allergic to fish," Walter declared.

"Then have a hamburger."

"I don't like onions."

"You don't have to have onions."

"Can I have ketchup with my fries?"

"Yes. Now hush. I don't want any running around when we get there. You stay in your seat or you sit in the car. Is that understood?"

The girls nodded silently and the boys sat still for once. Obviously I was not a jolly mother.

The table was ready when we got there, and they swarmed ahead of us.

"I dibs to sit here."

"I get to be by the window."

"No, you don't, Joan does. It's her birthday."

The other diners glanced up, startled, and Joe quickly took over the seating arrangement. "OK. Boys on this side, girls on that."

They scrambled to their places and made a dive for the basket of crackers. Joe and I eased into our chairs opposite each other at the end of the table, and the waitress—who looked as if she didn't want us there any longer than necessary—came over immediately.

"Would you like to order a cocktail?"

Joe sighed. "Let's see, how about three Shirley Temples, and four Roy Rogers, and a couple of double martinis on the rocks."

"I'll have a couple too," I mumbled. "No, no, I'm just kidding."

Once the food came things settled down slightly. Of course Walter insisted he wasn't hungry any more, and the ketchup ran out by the time it got to Chris, but things actually went fairly smoothly, and I was beginning to believe this day was finally going to end after all.

The waitress brought over another bottle of ketchup. She gave it to Chris, then came down to our end of the table.

"A lady who was having dinner here just left," she said, "and—"

"On our account?" It would be a perfect ending, I thought, to be asked to leave because we were annoying the rest of the patrons.

"No, she said she was so impressed with you all she's paid your check."

Joe put his fork down. "She what?"

"She paid your check."

"Why?"

"I don't know. She just said she thought you looked like a neat family."

"But they're not all ours," I protested. "Heaven help me, they're not all ours."

"I told her that. I said I thought it was a birthday party."

"Who was it?"

"I don't know. She comes in every once in a while, but I don't know her name."

I couldn't believe it. Everyone knows that when things are going badly they continue to do so. It's an extension of Murphy's Law.

Joe drained the last of his martini. "Well, what do you know." He shook his head. "I'm flabbergasted." Then with new life in his voice he turned to me. "Eat up, honey. There's only cake and ice cream at our house left, then I'll take them all home."

"I'm allergic to ice cream," Walter protested.

"Then eat cake."

9

Life Among the Chicken Lice

As a carpenter's apprentice, I've never had to fight for equality. It came unbidden.

"Grab the other end of those two-by-fours," Joe will say, or, "Move that stack of lumber so I can plug the saw in the wall socket."

Sometimes when my knees shake as I stagger backward up the stairs—trying not to drop my end of a sheet of plywood— or my arms ache from ripping out shiplap, I wonder how it would be not to be liberated. But then I know I'd never be able to stand it. I grew up with a brother three years older than I whose favorite words were "Bet you can't," and as far back as I can remember I've been proving " I can too." I guess I still am.

Which explains how I got talked into spending my thirty-sixth birthday under the house, digging a hole for a furnace. I can't remember why I had to dig it on my birthday. It was probably one of those instances where Joe, who has more parting speeches than MacArthur, said to me before he left for work that day, "We could have the furnace brought in this week and I could start putting in the ductwork, if you'd dig the hole for it today."

Anyway, as I recall, I was more than willing. As far as I could tell, the space heater was on its last legs. It had consumed great quantities of oil, spit flames, and made a horrible racket that rattled doors and windows, but the only thing it ever warmed was a batch of sourdough starter resting nearby. That it killed.

Every morning we dressed as if for an expedition up Mount Rainier, and by spring I was convinced our lips were permanently blue. Heat became an obsession. When Joe and I went to someone else's house and their furnace clicked on softly, our eyes met across the room. They were playing our song.

The children kept warm by taking interminable hot baths. Moments after the dinner dishes were done, they lined up outside the bathroom door.

"I get the first bath."

"You had it last night. It's my turn."

"OK, but leave in the water."

And they lay in bed under mounds of blankets and coats till the last moment before getting ready for school.

Then in late April, with spring behind schedule and the daffodils spending the better part of each morning frozen to the ground, we investigated the ramifications of having a furnace installed. We followed the same old pattern.

Joe said, "Bud"—the man from the oil company—"will put the furnace in. Then we'll get someone to do the ductwork."

Then I said, "How much will that cost?"

Then he said, "I'll get an estimate."

Then I said, "How much did he say it would be?"

Then he said, "Too much. Bud will still put in the furnace. You and I will install the ductwork."

So there I was on my birthday, in a sweat shirt and sweat pants, crawling through the chicken leavings, around some old lumber, and past a former owner's collection of bourbon bottles over to where the furnace would sit.

"The hole has to be deep enough so the furnace can be put on blocks and still clear the joists by a good foot or so," Joe had told me. "Don't worry, the dirt isn't packed down, so it should be easy to dig, even for you."

For all his faith in my abilities, he was a realist. He'd seen me dig before. I'm not proficient. I jump on the shovel, wobble it back and forth, beat on the handle with a rock, and still manage only to dent the soil. But he was right. Under the house was easy—if you like to dig sitting down.

There wasn't enough room to stand up, even hunched over, and I tried a time or two on my knees, but I kept pitching face forward in the dirt. Finally I sat like a toddler on a beach and scooped up shovelfuls. Then I flung them to my left and right as hard as I could. Bud had told me to scatter the dirt and not let it build up in piles or he wouldn't be able to get the furnace in.

Digging in a sitting position is hard, but flinging dirt fifteen feet to this side or that is impossible, so finally I let the mounds build up around me, like a minor mountain range. Later, I crawled around on my hands and knees and grabbed fistfuls of dirt and threw them here and there. All the time I kept a sharp eye out for partially decayed gopher and mouse remains. Our dogs had turned hunters, but the hunt was all they enjoyed, so they left the carcasses under the house to rot at leisure.

The digging and scattering took only three hours. If I'd known Sylvia and Geoffrey (one with an idea, one with money) were upstairs tying a ribbon around my birthday present—a pregnant cat—I would have stayed down longer.

When Joe came home, I took him out to look at my work. He crawled in behind me, along the path of old boards I'd laid out. "Great," he said when I turned on the light I'd hung from one of the floor joists. "It looks great. Did you have any trouble?"

"Not really."

"Well then, now we'll have Bud set in the heater, and I'll call Chester Gleason."

Chester Gleason was the metal man. He was going to tell us how many ducts we needed and where they were to go. Then, according to our arrangement, he'd make them, we'd assemble them and hook them together, and he'd show us how to install them.

I'd heard of him before. He's known all over the Island as the best ductwork man there is, and Bud assured us we had the finest.

He forgot to mention, however, that though Chester Gleason has no equal when it comes to installing an efficient heating system, he hates his life's work, every elbow joint and cold-air return of it. He's been scrambling under Bainbridge homes for thirty-five years and has yet to say a single kind word about any basement, crawl space, or understructure on the Island. I found this out the first day he came to look things over.

Hal and Joe had been waiting for him. He was to figure out where the registers would go, and they'd cut the holes in the floor. It was around noon when he came. He drove up in an old battered station wagon, and got out of the car. He was tall and skinny, and everything about him was gray. His shoes were gray, covered with a fine clay dust. His clothes were gray. His face had the sickly pallor of someone not used to daylight. Even the stubble on his bald head was gray. He looked like a heating duct personified.

"Is this the Combs house?" he snarled.

"Sure is."

He stared at the house for a minute. "And I suppose you don't have a basement."

"No, we don't."

"Just my luck." He shook his head. "I don't need this kind of work."

I was at a loss for a reply. Luckily Hal and Joe came out at this point, and I stood back while they all went over to the little door below the kitchen window to peer under the house.

"Jeez, I hate to have to crawl around in all that muck," I heard Chester complain. "You know, it's not healthy spending your life under people's houses. If this weren't my last job, and you weren't doing the installation, I'd chuck it."

When they had gone through the rooms figuring out where to put the registers, he groaned again.

"My God, you're going to have to have so much pipe I may not live long enough to make it all."

Even when he disappeared under the house to estimate the amount of pipe and the number of elbow joints needed, the sound of his muffled curses traveled from one comer to the other, as if an enraged troll were down there kicking and fuming in the dirt. Once he had all his measurements, he left, and Hal and Joe began cutting holes in the floor for the registers. As each hole was cut, a blast of cold air shot up through it like a fountain, and with it came a musty, dank odor that rivaled six-week-old spackle. I stuffed rags in as fast as I could, but the stench leaked through and soaked into everything. We all smelled as if we'd spent six weeks in the Catacombs.

When Chester delivered the first set of ducts, he and Joe went under the house for Joe's one and only lesson in how to install a heating system and jump a joist.

It was a typical June day. The sky was a brilliant gray. The temperature hovered around 50 degrees, and the gaps between the intermittent showers were filled with torrential downpours. We'd had rain for so long that the lakes in the front yard were seeding clams. Under the house was now cold as well as smelly and dirty. Chester snarled at the prospect of one more trip down there. He grumbled as he stepped into his coveralls, muttered as he gathered up the tools, and went out the door in a cloud of curses. Joe followed carrying the ducts.

Two hours later, they surfaced. Joe looked dazed. He was holding a pad of paper with arrows and lines and all sorts of scribblings, and he traced over them again and again.

"Now, let me see if I have this straight," I heard him say as he followed Chester out the door. "You attach the wire to the joist, then—" The door slammed behind him.

"How'd it go?" I asked when he came back in.

"I'm not sure."

"What do you mean?"

"Well, he snapped those things together so fast sparks flew, but I'm damned if I know how he did it."

"Do you think you can figure it out?"

"I'll try." He shrugged. "I guess if you assemble them as he brings them, I'll get them in somehow."

So we set to work. Chester delivered the pieces as he made them, I put them together, and Joe installed them. I loved my part. I had ducts strewn all over the lawn and I scooted around the grass snapping one section to another. As I fitted each piece into place, I hammered the edge over to seal it. The resounding crash of metal against metal was exhilarating. Like bashing walls it relieved tensions.

Wham! Here's to the garbage man who took away three wastebaskets and left the can with no bottom.

Bang! Here's to the septic tank that backed up this morning.

Whap! Here's to a lifetime of dieting.

Joe complained about the noise. "You needn't hit it so hard," he explained. "A gentle tap will do."

Wham again! Here's to Joe.

As I finished each set, Joe dragged it under the house and put it in. It was a little like installing the Los Angeles freeway. Starting at the furnace, each piece had to be fit in, suspended from the joists by a piece of baling wire, then snapped to the next piece. Fit-hang-snap, fit-hang-snap, due south for three lengths of pipe, then a left turn to the den, a double back to the bedroom, and a cloverleaf at the living room intersection. Then back to the furnace again and a southeast spur to the kitchen.

The work went slowly. Joe had labor problems. No one would labor.

I couldn't for some marvelously inventive reason I can't recall, and the girls suddenly became indispensable, folding laundry, doing dishes, and dusting the leaves on the Christmas cactus. This left David, Geoffrey, and the twins. Joe exempted the twins, and David and Geoffrey tried every excuse they could think of to avoid helping.

"I can't, Dad. I've got a stomachache."

"We're having finals in Science tomorrow. I have to study."

It didn't work. It only prolonged the agony and frustrated Joe, who had never had the luxury of excuses when he was a boy.

"You might as well face it," he roared. "If you want heat the work has to be done. I can't do it alone, so come on."

And they followed, shuffling and stumbling and griping all the way.

I can't say I blamed them. It was a grubby job. Cobwebs hung from the joists, and bits of broken glass hid in the dirt. They had to crawl from one place to another, dragging the tools, the ducts, and the extension cord with the light socket. Once there, they sat hunched over like arthritic gurus while Joe fit, hung, and snapped. They creased their skulls on the joists, knelt on rusty nails, and as the weather got warmer spent time dodging champagne corks. Joe had stored some homemade champagne, leftovers from a wine course he'd taught in the winter. They were near the entrance, and every now and then a bottle would explode. David was wounded twice.

The dogs were no help either—Golly and Sheba, big dogs, friendly, loyal, and kind. Unfortunately, they're not too swift. They licked faces, panted hot, steamy breath in ears, and rolled in the dirt. Golly kept trying to bury the hammer. Sheba ate light bulbs. She must have gone through thirty of them. She didn't chew them, just bit them. Joe would be hammering in a nail when *pop*! they'd be plunged into darkness. He and the boys started taking extra bulbs down, but she ate those too. Eventually we worked out a system. When the lights went out, Joe bellowed at the dog. I stamped on the floor to let him know I understood the situation, and one of the twins took a new bulb down.

I think Joe's itch was the final straw. Whether it was chicken lice, mildew, or a fungus I don't know, but one day, after he'd been at it for a week or two, he started to itch—a little bit at first—along his back. As the day warmed up it spread. By night his arms and chest were blotchy.

"You'd better have the doctor take a look at that," I said.

"Don't worry. It'll go away."

But it didn't. The next day his legs itched, then his hands. Even the bottoms of his feet were red and swollen. Finally he agreed to go down to the clinic, and the doctor prescribed a salve. It didn't work, and he squirmed and scratched and rubbed up against doorways like a horse rubbing against the side of his stall.

Back to the doctor. A different salve, then an oatmeal bath, then a couple of ointments, then a spray. Finally, after days of agony and six weeks of the warmest weather we were to have all summer, he finished the ductwork, crawled out from under the house, and the itch went away.

On July 1, Jenny's birthday (we have a birthday fetish with our projects), Bud did the last of the wiring and we turned on the heat. We heard the click, then a whirring and a blowing. It was a glorious sound. I ran to each register. Sure enough, warm air was puffing up through the vents. I took off my sweater.

The furnace hummed contentedly under the house and Bud set the thermostat at 62 degrees. The room seemed a little stuffy, so I changed to shorts and a sleeveless blouse. Perspiration still broke out on my forehead.

Oh, Lord, I thought, I'm not going to be able to stand the heat.

10

The Great Wallendas Train

Iknow it's un-American, but decks make me nervous. I prefer balconies. There's something about a deck that makes me feel as if I should be keeping it company all the time— either barbecuing on it, adorning it with pots of geraniums and calendulas, or sitting with it on hot summer days when I'd rather be under a tree.

But a balcony is another thing entirely. It doesn't require companionship. It likes being alone, and yet it's also content to have me stand on it and gaze at the moon or wish on the first star or strain to see who's getting a speeding ticket across the bay.

We have two balconies—one on the west side, the other on the east. Hal and Joe built them in May of 1971. Jenny's room opens out onto the west one, and she uses it all the time. She keeps potted plants out there. She sunbathes there, peering through the slats to see who's coming and who's leaving. And it's her public-address platform. If Joe and I go out to dinner or take the late boat home, she rushes out on it as soon as she hears the car come up the driveway. Before the engine is still, we know that Geoffrey made cookies and used up all the sugar... Robbie ate ten of them... Joan cut her lip... David won't come out of his room ... and Sylvia has Jenny's leotard.

I'd always thought of balconies, before we built ours, as either being wrought-iron cages large enough for one senorita and her rose, or else small half-moons of ivy-covered stone designed for a papal message or the announcement of a royal birth. Ours fall into neither category. They're more reminiscent of Moscow on May Day when the Soviet hierarchy gathers to view the arsenal parade. They're substantial—four feet wide and sixteen feet long. The railing is high with notched balusters an inch apart all the way around, and like the rest of the house they're comfortable and unassuming.

Joe and Hal put them up during the time when Joe's nights were spent mucking around under the house with the heating ducts. That May, the days were clear and warm, not the kind you waste consorting with mildew and chicken lice, so they decided to make the balconies before the June rains forced us all indoors again.

Balconies aren't complicated once you have the scaffolding up. You put up supports and anchor them to the side of the house, then nail on a platform and enclose it with a railing and balusters, and that's about it. It wasn't the balconies that gave them the problem. It was the scaffolding, or rather the children on the scaffolding.

All six took one look at the poles and planks and suspended walkways and went mad. They climbed on them, swung hand over hand, dropped to the ground, jumped off them, played tag, and made parachutes out of their bedding and leaped off the top boards. Robbie even managed to climb the poplar tree close by, work his way out on a limb, and leap to the scaffolding.

Hal and Joe had been patient during the construction in the stairwell when the children crawled up and down the ladder and swarmed over the half-finished stairs. They'd tolerated the decibels of hard rock assaulting them as they worked on interior walls. Hal had threatened to leave and never come back only twice—once when Robbie's boomerang boomeranged into the windshield of his car and once when a yelling match broke out in the kitchen over who ate the last of the peanut butter.

But when, as they were tearing out the Never-Never Land door, a small body wrapped in ropes and a blanket crept to the top comer of the scaffolding and catapulted off into space with a bloodcurdling yell, and Hal hit his thumb with a hammer, the law was laid down. The Great Wallendas would train no more, at least not during working hours.

With the children creating mayhem somewhere else, Hal's and Joe's dispositions improved and the work speeded up —that is, till Sven came on the scene.

Sven Jorgenson is a big man, slow and sardonic with a propensity for lifting up rocks and finding maggots underneath. He's what you'd call a professional harbinger of gloom, the type of fellow you don't ask to visit you in the hospital. He always knows someone who died of whatever you have.

Joe met him on the ferry one day when we first moved to Bainbridge. We were in the first flush of homesteading, and Joe made the mistake of telling him our plans to remodel the house by ourselves. At the time he didn't know Sven had taken a correspondence course in architecture. Also, he didn't realize Sven's a self-proclaimed expert on everything and he shares his expertise. He even makes house calls.

Because we were neophytes, he generously put us on his lecture tour, and his visits were soon as regular as the tide. That is to say, he arrived when we were finishing a project and he carefully pointed out all the things we'd done wrong.

It was he who predicted the roof would sag and eventually collapse when we cut a hole into the attic for the stairs. He also insisted, after the stair treads were cut, that they were too short.

"A friend of mine cut his treads about the size of yours," he told us, "and that poor guy couldn't stand them. His kids kept tripping over each other. He finally ripped them out and redid them. Cost him a bundle."

The day Sven came to evaluate the balconies, Hal and Joe were working on the railings. I heard his truck coming up the driveway and knew who it was even before I saw him. Joe swore under his breath, and Hal flailed at a swallow with his hammer. She wanted to build a nest under the eaves.

Sven clambered out of his truck. "Hi, Joe," he said. "What you working on now?"

Joe angled a nail into the railing. "Just finishing up on the balcony."

Sven leaned against his truck, shielding his eyes from the sun, then he walked over to get a closer look.

"That balcony's going to fall down, you know."

Joe coughed, and Hal bit down on his pipe stem.

"Brackets aren't strong enough. In fact, if my guess is right, it may pull half the west wall down with it when it goes." He paused. "A guy I know, lives in Yreka now, built a balcony like yours—same kind of supports. I told him it wouldn't work, but he didn't listen, and the whole thing pulled away one day when his wife was out there sunbathing in the nude." He laughed and slapped at the side of the house. "Boy, it laid her up for months."

Joe swung his hammer, missed the nail completely, and swore.

Sven chuckled. "You're really new at this, aren't you? I admire your guts."

I saw Joe's fists clench and he turned white around the mouth. I had the feeling he was going to leap off the balcony like a frenzied musketeer and go for Sven's jugular vein.

I knew how he felt. Sven, who'd worked for a time promoting geoduck burgers till he felt "unfriendly vibes" and quit, dropped by almost every day and lectured me on everything from macrobiotic cooking to the Big Bang theory of creation. Because he considered himself an authority on every possible subject, he was easily diverted to a new topic, and so, like a sacrificial lamb, I distracted him from the subject of the balcony.

"Hey, Sven," I said, starting around the side of the house. "Could you take a look at our peonies? Something's the matter with them."

Sven followed, delighted to have new land to plow, and as we went around to the south side of the house, I heard Joe sigh with relief.

The peonies were in a clump under the kitchen window and next to the back steps. They, like everything else in the garden, were on their own as far as growing and blooming was concerned, and to my untrained eye they seemed to be doing a good job of it. Sven felt otherwise.

"Those things have earwigs," he told me. "You ought to do something about that."

The irises, flourishing close by, were too crowded and should have been separated months before. They probably wouldn't bloom in another year. Around the next corner, Sven spotted a spindly rhododendron the dogs had chewed on as pups. It should be transplanted, fertilized, and watered regularly.

Next Sven considered our thirty-foot fir. "See those ants?" he said, pointing to a line of large red ants climbing up the trunk. "You'd better get rid of them or they'll kill it."

After that he spied dry rot on the windowsills and then a loose hinge. He predicted the window would fall off the next time I opened it. I considered giving him back to Joe and Hal, but decided against it.

As we worked our way to the front lawn, he advised rust remover, a thorough sanding, and new brakes for David's bike. Then he stared at the lawn for a while. I dreaded his suggestions here. We love our lawn—crabgrass, dandelions, moss, and all. It's enormous, and we use it for baseball games, football skirmishes, Frisbee throws, and assorted horsings around. I could tell Sven disapproved.

"You know what you ought to do?" he said. I readied myself for his master plan. "You ought to plow up this lawn and plant a garden—spinach, chard, turnips, and greens."

"But Sven. The children play on the lawn all the time. It's the only really big one we've had."

"Let them play somewhere else. They'll thank you when they taste fresh spinach and chard out of their own garden."

I had trouble keeping my eyes off his jugular vein. Finally, after an hour, we worked our way back to the west side of the house, and Sven jumped in his truck, told Joe he should have come to him for a safer balcony design, and drove off.

I went inside to get a cup of coffee. I would have laced it with brandy if we'd had any.

In spite of his predictions, the balconies remain, though I must admit I stepped on them with some trepidation for a while, and I still can't bring myself to sunbathe on them, even clothed. Joe, I notice, mentally tabulates the combined weight of any group of visitors before he joins them out there taking in the scenery.

Once the last nail was in, the scaffolding dismantled, and the balconies declared open for use, the children began the christening ceremonies. I don't mean they stood there admiring nature or had tea parties or did brief scenes from Romeo and Juliet. No, they decided it was time to sleep out on them. Sylvia and Jenny went first, then Geoffrey, Robbie, and Joan. David elected to remain in the warmth and comfort of his room. After Geoffrey and the twins had had a turn, Sylvia and her cousin Laura tried it.

Then Jenny and cousin Louisa. When we ran out of cousins the neighbor children came. Then children from the other end of the Island. It went on for weeks.

They dragged out the sleeping bags, pillows, extra blankets, and the Japanese futon we'd brought back from Tokyo. After they arranged the bedding, they carted out magazines, flashlights, radios, and enough food to see them through the night.

Naturally, since June is monsoon month, it usually rained at about two in the morning. This meant bringing everything inside and down to the living room floor. They left a trail of cracker crumbs that would have led Hansel and Gretel right out of the forest to McDonald's.

After six or eight weeks, the fascination with sleeping out abated considerably. By then Robbie had invented a balcony game. He discovered that if he put the ladder up to the bathroom window, he could not only spy on his sisters in the shower but also step over to one of the balcony supports. From there he scrambled up to the balcony proper, flipped over the railing, and came in the door.

One day, for an hour or two, he went out the back door, then minutes later came bounding down the stairs. I wasn't paying any attention to him at the time. I was experimenting with a recipe of pocket bread, and my pockets weren't puffing.

Slowly, however, in the back of my brain, it began to register. Robbie was going through the kitchen every three minutes, and always in the same direction.

"What are you doing?" I finally asked as he trotted by for the twenty-fifth time.

"Doing? Where? What?" He's an expert at innocence.

"Why do you keep going through the kitchen, out the back door, then through the kitchen again?" I pulled a set of deflated pockets out of the oven.

"Am I doing that?" He was barely able to control his glee.

"Come on now, Robbie, you know you are. What's going on?"

He grabbed my hand and hauled me to the back door. "Watch, Mom."

With the agility of a spider monkey, he scampered up the supports and over the balcony. It was a great trick, all right. So Geoffrey tried it. Then Sylvia and Jenny took a turn. Joan, a bit afraid, said she'd do it another day, and it was beneath David's dignity, but soon the Howards, neighbor children, were joining in the stream of balcony scalers.

When Joe came home, they put on their show for him. Joan, by this time, had been goaded into an attempt and found it was fun. Even David had given it a try or two. Joe wasn't impressed. He was all too familiar with the destructive power of children at play.

"Come on, you kids. Get off of there before you break something."

"But, Daddy," Jenny wailed. "We aren't hurting anything."

"Please, Daddy," Sylvia joined in. "It's strong enough."

Robbie went up once more to show Joe how safe it was, and they all let forth with another barrage of "Please, Daddy"s.

"Oh, hell." Joe waved them away. It had been a long day, and he was too tired to argue. "All right, all right. Just be careful."

Mother was a better audience. She gasped and moaned and ordered me to do something. She'd forgotten how my brother Geoff and I used to occupy ourselves on boring summer afternoons in Port Blakely when we were kids.

We'd crawl out the upstairs bedroom window, step on a board we'd nailed to the side of the house, and inch over to the dining room roof. Then we climbed to the upper roof. When we got to the top we yelled down the chimney and waited with ever-increasing excitement as we heard Mother calling, "Where are you?"

The finale—and it was always worth the wait—was when she realized where we were. She vaulted out of the house and stood in the middle of the lawn shaking her fist and demanding we get down "this instant." Robbie's balcony trick was mild compared to what we'd done, but grandmothers have a lower excitement tolerance than mothers, and the comparison didn't appease her much.

Sven, however, outdid even Mother in pessimism. She foresaw broken bones, torn cartilages, and fractured tibias. He took the next logical step. Logical to him.

The day he came over was the day Geoffrey had bought a stopwatch. He and Robbie and Wade Howard were trying to beat the one-minute climb. Joe was on the top of the ladder putting a vent in near the peak of the roof. I was handing him nails.

"Oh, God," Joe said as Sven drove up. "That's all I need."

"Be calm. Maybe he won't stay long."

Sven got out of his truck and watched as Robbie flipped over the railing and appeared three seconds later at the back door.

"Hey, Joe," he called. "Are you letting these kids do that?"

Joe grunted and Wade whooshed by.

"Boy, you're really asking for it. The way they're pulling on the railing, it isn't going to last out the week, and if the Howard kid breaks a leg, you're going to be in for one fine lawsuit."

Joe dropped his hammer. It landed in a can of nails and sent nails flying all over.

"Sven," I called out. "Could you look at the peonies once more? I think the earwigs are back."

11

You Don't Have to Eat
Your Macaroni

Writing is not an avocation to be entered into unadvisedly or lightly, especially if you're remodeling your house. Somehow there's always a hunk of lumber lying on your manuscript, and the minute you think of a new, fresh way to describe the rain someone yells, "Hey, come here, I need you to hold this board!" and the thought is lost forever.

At first my biggest problem was I couldn't find a place to write. It wasn't that I expected a studio with a massive desk and wall-to-wall bookcases. I didn't—at least not until we'd built a bedroom for David and I could take over his room next to the library. I was simply looking for a clear flat space, large enough for my typewriter and a pad of paper.

There weren't a lot to choose from. Most of our flat surfaces were occupied with hammers, crowbars, and cans of finishing nails. This limited my selection to either the dining room table, the counter next to the stove, or an unused breadboard, which I'd have to balance on my lap. I chose the table.

For a while we had it in the kitchen, so every morning after the children had left for school I cleared off the dishes, wiped up the crumbs and the rings of syrup, and sat down to write. For at least twenty minutes I was left undisturbed.

You don't have to eat macaroni in order to get rid of it, I wrote.

About this time the back door swung open and Hal came in. Then as I tried to think of a second sentence he and Joe spread the house plans out on the table, over my manuscript and discussed what they'd do today.

I moved my typewriter over to a corner.

You needn't eat all your macaroni in order to get rid of it, I wrote x-ing out what I'd written before.

Once they'd mapped out their next project, they moved on to another room, and I tried to remember what it was I wanted to say about macaroni. It didn't seem very clever now, so I poured myself another cup of coffee, rummaged around in my purse for a pen that worked, and then rolled a new sheet of paper into the typewriter. I stared at the blank page for a while and listened to the whine of the power saw as Hal and Joe cut through two-by-fours upstairs.

Who said you had to eat all your macaroni in order to get rid of it? I typed. *Not I.*

"Hey, Annie!" Joe's voice boomed down from above. "Can you run down to the hardware store and see if they have my saw blade sharpened yet? This one's getting dull."

So off I went, and by the time I got back I had to find another extension cord, and then the Phillips-head screwdriver, and there was lunch to fix and dishes to do and laundry to fold and hamburger to defrost, and as I sat down and wrote, *Cook that macaroni if you must, but don't feel you have to eat every bit,* the children rushed in, home from school.

I wasn't gracious about it at all. I complained a lot.

"How the hell am I supposed to get anything published if I have to sit in the kitchen and try to write in between running to the hardware store and answering the phone and looking for the screwdriver?"

"I don't know." Joe shrugged. Obviously he thought anyone who'd amassed the number of rejection slips I had and who lived in a house that needed as much work as ours did ought to turn her talents to carpentry instead of fooling around describing how her children have inundated her with macaroni jewelry.

But I persisted. When we framed in the dining room and moved the table there, I followed. I stared at sheets of plywood stacked up against the four little windows, and I wore Joe's wool socks because the wind under the chicken-house door was freezing my feet. I typed and retyped and sent a long harrowing tale of my attempt to climb Mount Fuji out to seven magazines. It came back each time, and Joe told me the spackle was drying up in the bucket and he had to have someone help him carry in the plasterboard.

Finally I got my own desk. In a fit of prosperity a real estate office on the Island was redecorating, and all the old furniture had to go. So for $25.00 I had a flat surface that was mine. It was big enough for my papers and books and clippings and notes and even an occasional hammer or chisel.

I looked around for a place to put it. The kitchen was out. There was no room left in the dining room, and the children practiced their piano lessons in the library. So I stuck it in a corner of our bedroom and gazed out the window at the dogwood tree while I typed, *We buy wading pools the way some people buy boats—a newer, bigger, better one every year.*

Then Joe and Hal, like bulldozers razing a forest for a condominium, moved me out into the hall. I objected, muttering under my breath about my right to create and have my own interests. Joe suggested perhaps I should show more interest in creating a couple of decent walls. So, with the martyred air of someone who's misunderstood and the frantic connivance of someone who's determined to avoid spackling, I joined a writer's workshop in Seattle.

My joy knew no bounds. It was like a vacation every week. On Thursdays I rose at dawn, showered, dressed, and combed the putty out of my hair.

"No, I can't pick up a new tape measure today," I declared. "And I won't be able to finish the bedroom wall till tomorrow. I have to go to class."

And Joe, like a tolerant parent who hopes his child will outgrow this phase in time, said, "Oh, yes, that's right. Today's your class day. Well, have a good time."

I did. I met Jan and Carole in the coffee shop on the 9:10 ferry, and we journeyed in together.

I was always there first. Joe's Air Force training and his compulsion for promptness had apparently rubbed off on me. So I was in the group straining at the barrier while the deckhands rattled chains and slid the gangplank over from the ramp to the boat.

Sometimes Carole was early too. I'd see her coming down the ramp—tall, cool, and statuesque—with a purse slung over her shoulder and a sheaf of papers clutched in her hand.

"Hi," she'd say, swerving to avoid a two-year-old who thought the ramp made a dandy airstrip. "Do you have anything to read in class today?"

"Just a first draft. I thought the idea was hilarious originally, but now I'm not so sure. How about you?"

"I reworked the fishing scene, so now it sounds more plausible. I'll read that."

And we surged forward with the rest of the crowd.

Jan never came till seconds before the boat pulled away from the dock.

"God, kid!" she'd roar, swinging into the coffee shop. "You wouldn't believe what I've had to go through this morning." Thus would unfold a tale, bombastically told, of a phone call at 6:00 A.M., of Maria forgetting her lunch at home and having to have it delivered, of the car that wouldn't start because the doohickey under the hood was stuck again, and of Martin who wouldn't be able to drive us up the hill to class because he had to be in court early with a case he was defending. "The last straw," she'd bellow, shaking her fist in the air, "came when I forgot to put money in the meter. I'll probably get a ticket, or they'll tow the damn thing away. Oh, well." She'd take a deep breath. "Who'll get me a cup of that rotten coffee? I can't face the line."

Once we got into town—unless we got a ride from some poor soul who hadn't planned to go anywhere near the YWCA —we had to walk the eight or ten blocks up and over. With rain usually lashing at us and the wind whipping up the streets off the waterfront, we ducked into any buildings we could and took escalators and elevators from one level to another. Finally, just after ten o'clock, we staggered wet and windblown into class.

A writer's workshop is not like an advanced class in Spanish. There aren't specific assignments or conjugations written out on the blackboard. It isn't like a course in cooking either. No one hands out recipes or tells you the basic rules.

A writer's workshop is more group therapy in longhand, with an accent on grammar and phrasing. Our class was loosely run by Jane Bryant, a nonconformist with a critical ear, an intuitive sense of what works, and an unusual and unpredictable approach to life. She refused to call herself the teacher. "I merely keep the mayhem to a minimum," she explained to anyone new.

And that's pretty much how it was. We all sat around a huge table in one of the upper rooms at the Y. Whoever had written something that week read it aloud, and then we criticized.

Jane said she felt a woman being raped by a Sasquatch was pretty far out, and she asked where Laura intended to send her story. Jan stated flatly that the repeated mentions of how he smelled made her sick. Someone asked why the heroine would take a bath in the middle of the yard if she knew the Sasquatch family was lurking in the bushes. Carole suggested she tone down the rape scene itself and pointed out that the husband, even if he were asleep in the cabin, would have heard her screams. I, who love to latch onto the picky details, told her she'd used the word "clutched" three times in one paragraph.

Laura took voluminous notes and said she'd do a rewrite and bring it back next week, and we were on to the next piece.

About ten or twelve of us formed the nucleus of the class. We took one eight-week session after another, writing, rewriting, sending things out, getting them back, and sending them out again. It went on all year, and most of us grumbled if Christmas or the Fourth of July fell on a Thursday.

We were a diverse group—not at all the sort you'd find giving luncheons or joining the tennis club.

There was Amanda, a woman in her seventies, gentle, quiet, and matter-of-fact. She was a lady in the best sense of the word, but she hadn't joined to write essays on how to pour tea or make antimacassars. She was working on a novel set on an Indian reservation in the 1920s.

"Next week's the final love scene," she'd say after her turn at reading. "And don't expect a happy ending," she'd add, her eyes sparkling.

Marilyn was our glamour girl with coordinated outfits, hairstyles that could only be referred to as coiffed, and eyelashes that defied gravity. Her stories were brisk and chic accounts of life in New York and Florence, but they always had a moral and they were always romantic rather than passionate, for Marilyn disapproved of explicit sex.

Not Bonnie, though. Bonnie was writing a book about incest and her own terrifying relationship with her father, and she never alluded or inferred. She said it right out.

"I felt his hand caress my buttocks," she'd read out loud and clear, as Marilyn gasped, snapped her notebook shut and blew her nose. The rest of us assumed an air of nonchalance. We were there to judge form, not content. Jan nodded. I made a note to suggest a better transitional sentence. Carole lit a cigarette and inhaled slowly. Right after Chapter Six, Marilyn dropped out of class.

Beth wrote introspective pieces, liberally laced with Freudian symbolism. Denise's characters belched and scratched and came at each other with pickaxes. Amy recounted her ten months as a surrogate mother to a baby gorilla.

Cassie was our intellect, our voice of ERA. Her thoughts marched out in logical order, made their statements, and exited. Teddy told of hooking rugs with scraps of wool cut from a pair of pilfered long johns and described buying an antique carousel horse and having to transport it home in the rain in an open jeep.

Mary was the feisty member of the class. "I don't care what anyone says," she often argued. "There's no proof Sasquatches exist, so who knows if one would get turned on by a nude woman in a redwood tub."

Some people came to only one or two sessions. And there was Valerie, who wrote one story, reread it every week for ten weeks with only minor changes, and was never seen again.

Martha, a tiny mouse of a woman, only joined because she wanted help telling a story about her parakeet. It took her six weeks to get up the nerve to read, and when she did and we suggested she cut it some, she took out all the articles.

"Walked in room." Her meek voice trembled. "Saw cage door open. Didn't know where Cheery had gone."

"Jesus Christ," muttered Bette, who wrote murder stories set in the vast expanses of the Yukon. "Who wants to read that kind of crap?"

Martha dropped out before we found out where Cheery had gone.

Jessica came sporadically. When she came, she came late, banging and clattering and shaking her umbrella out. "I missed the bus," she'd announce in the middle of someone's reading. "I thought I had time, but I guess my watch was slow." When her turn came she dragged out pages and pages torn from an old notebook. "These are stories I wrote in 1927," she'd announce. "See what you think." And then with the slow, deliberate cadence of someone in love with the sound of her own voice, she'd begin, "It was a cold, gloomy, slushy, snowy day."

I knew what I thought. I thought she'd taken a correspondence course in adjectives.

Jan wrote short humorous pieces about bust developers, inflatable exercise suits, and a zucchini plant that ran amok. She got discouraged when *Cosmopolitan* rejected her poem, "Lust's Labor Lost." "Hell," she complained. "You'd think they'd buy the title if nothing else."

Carole wove gossamer memories of Christmas and Halloween and painted word pictures describing how it feels to be ten and wake up to a summer day.

And I plugged away. One week it was a diatribe against Barbie dolls, the next a hymn to daylight saving time.

"Keep sending them in," Jane told me. "I don't care if they come back fifteen times. Keep at it."

So I did, and one day when I came home from class, there in the mail was a note from the *Tacoma News Tribune*. "We liked your piece on macaroni necklaces. It will be in next week's Sunday magazine section."

"Say, Annie!" Joe yelled out as I galloped into the house. "Can you bring up that can of wood putty?"

"Well, all right. I'll do it this time, but"—I waved my acceptance in his face—"I'll have you know I'm not just an errand girl anymore. I'm a writer."

12

Six Bedrooms in Early Wamsutta

The difference between replacing old walls in an old bedroom and putting up brand-new walls in a brand-new room is like the difference between having your old suits altered and buying a whole new wardrobe. The first is sensible and satisfying. The second is exciting.

In late June of 1971, we bought a whole new wardrobe. We moved the theater of operations to the attic and began to frame in the children's bedrooms and the second bathroom.

It was the moment I'd been waiting for—the long-promised generation gap. I wanted a gap of fourteen stairs and several walls between them and me. I'd lived next door to rock and roll, pillow fights, and "Mom, make him stop jumping on my bed" long enough.

So when Joe called the lumberyard and ordered a gross of two-by-fours, and he and Hal trundled upstairs with the saws and hammers and nails, I responded with a jubilant "Wahoo!" It took a while. They sawed and nailed and braced for weeks, hammering in top and bottom plates, lining up studs, and fitting in headers and cripples. Since it was dark up there, big and dark and empty, Joe confiscated the floor lamps from the living room and carried them upstairs to help light the work area, and Hal strung extension cords from beam to beam and suspended light sockets from large nails in the ceiling joists.

They measured off the two-by-fours, and as they cut them the sound of the power saw reverberated from one end of the attic to the other.

Occasionally, however, on a clear, warm day, the sunlight tiptoed inside the open balcony doors, and a cool breeze whiffled through, stirring up the scattered piles of sawdust and wafting the clean, fresh smell of pitch and fir into the musty corners.

This project—unlike some others—attracted helpers, and the assistants varied with each room. When Joe and Hal worked on the north side, over in the east corner where David would eventually settle in, he was only too willing to carry up two-by-fours or look for the extra hammer. As they worked along that side, first Robbie and then Joan volunteered to gather nails and fetch the coffee.

Jenny egged them on impatiently when they got to her little room on the west corner.

"How long's it going to take?" she asked. "Do you think you'll be finished by tomorrow? Can I move in when you're through?"

"We're working as fast as we can," Joe said. "Now, hand me that board over there."

Then they crossed the hall and framed in the new bathroom. Hal put in a tiny window looking out over the balcony and the driveway. It matched the one in Jenny's room, and I fantasized about taking baths, downstairs, alone.

Sylvia's room, between the bathroom and the stairway, turned out to be the largest. She gloated over this and reminded the others that when we put the dormers in she'd be able to look out over the bay and see the herons waiting for the tide to turn. Every evening when Hal and Joe put down their saws and called it quits, she swept up the sawdust and wood chips and arranged the furniture in her mind.

They came to Geoffrey last. Before they could do his room, they had to frame in a linen closet next to the stairs. But finally they were through and the attic looked like a storage room for giant playpens.

The afternoon they finished, Joe and I stood in the doorway of Geoffrey's room staring down the row of two-by-fours that made the hall.

"Not much longer," Joe said. "Soon everyone will have his own room."

"Hooray!" I answered. "And not a moment too soon."

The next logical step would have been to put up the plasterboard, spackle the seams, paint, and put in the trim. We are not a logical family. We went on to bigger and better projects, mainly because of the weather. We had about two and a half months of possible good weather left before the fall rains, the winter rains, and the spring rains socked us in. In those two and a half months we had to construct two dormers and reshingle the roof.

So we postponed the finishing touches, and when the children asked to move into their rooms as is, we agreed. Why not? They were used to camping out. The girls had lived upstairs before it was completely floored. They'd shuffled their belongings from one end of the attic to the other so as not to impede progress during the framing in. They'd even survived a couple of nights when both ends were open to the elements as the French doors to the balconies were being put in. So to them it was a luxury even knowing where the boundaries of their rooms were.

I must admit, though, I didn't foresee the decoration mania that was going to follow. I suppose it's from their upbringing in the Air Force. You settle in quickly and decorate immediately, since you may have to move at any time.

David, sedate and not as much of a pioneer, elected to remain downstairs till we furnished his room with a few more amenities—namely, walls, a ceiling, and some lights. The rest set up housekeeping before we could get all the sawdust swept up.

Sylvia took the lead. She always does. She's the innovator in the family—or is it the instigator? She tacked up mock canopies over her bed, using sheets, blankets, and occasional bolts of shantung I'd bought in Japan. I retrieved the shantung with only a few nail holes around the edges. On the two-by- fours she penned notes to posterity declaring that on this day in the year 1971, she, Sylvia Ann Combs, age eleven, daughter of Joseph R. and Ann G. Combs, sister of David, Jenny, Geoffrey, Robbie, and Joan Combs, had moved into this room. We were all included, with ages and brief descriptions, which I censored when she started asking around about our various weights.

For walls, she dug out a few more sheets. She insisted she needed privacy. It didn't do much good. When she had friends over to spend the night, Geoffrey and Robbie hid in the hall and peeked through the gaps. I imagine they were hoping to catch a glimpse of something close to a Playboy foldout. They were disappointed. An eleven-year-old girl in her underwear is not the kind of vision that encourages potential Peeping Toms. They were, however, delighted with the response they got— shrieks, threats, and bellowed demands.

"Daddy, will you kill Geoffrey and Robert?"

Jenny used sheets too. In fact, they all used so many sheets and blankets on the walls there weren't enough left for the beds. Jenny hooked hers up with nails that would easily pass for railroad spikes. Over them, and with more railroad spikes, she hung pictures: pictures of ballerinas, kittens, woods, meadows, and steamy tropical forests. Here and there around the room she put pots of ferns and lichens, terrariums, and old bottles filled with rocks and colored water. The whole room looked like a jungle—or at least a verdant pasture.

Joan's decor fluctuated with the mood of her older sisters. If Jenny got tired of the alpine scene she'd created in a long wooden box, she lifted up the sheet and shoved it through the studs into Joan's room. If Sylvia decided she wanted only four pillows on her bed instead of seven, she tossed the extras across the hall into Joan's room. She wasn't above taking them back either. The only constants in the scheme of Joan's room were Heloise, Abelard, and the plastic flowers.

Heloise and Abelard were figures on two old and fraying tapestries. Heloise was a maiden of medieval ilk, standing forlornly in the deep woods. From the ornateness of her costume, it was obvious she wasn't in the woods hunting mushrooms or because she'd been separated from a Sunday picnic. She was gussied up for Abelard, and he was late.

Abelard, on the other hand, stood leaning casually on a stile, possibly waiting for the proverbial cows to come home but more likely hoping to catch a glimpse of Beatrice or Cassandra, maidens living in the neighboring castle. You could tell he'd forgotten his date with Heloise.

Despite the whole melancholy situation, Joan adored both tapestries. And she adored her plastic flowers. Living, as we do, near a church where rummage sales are a way of life and where no rummage sale worth its salt doesn't have a bin or two of plastic flowers, Joan was able to feed her habit regularly. Bouquets of plastic geraniums and marigolds sat on her dresser. Little wicker baskets of plastic daisies were hammered into the two-by-fours, and a plastic pot with a plastic hyacinth in it sat next to her bed. She even had some plastic ivy she stuffed into an old violin-shaped holder I'd had as a child. Joan's room was forever in bloom. It still is.

The sheets ran out when we got to Robbie and Geoffrey. Robbie didn't care. He preferred being able to slip through the walls and climb up into the rafters.

He had no particular theme for his room, and no one object or set of objects dominated, for Robbie is a collector in search of a collection. Till the right one comes along, he's sampling everything: large cars, small cars, trucks, dinosaurs, tiny porcelain squirrels, large, live lizards in old peanut-butter jars. He has airplane models, ship models, rowboat models, bicycle tires, and rocks. He had a lot of rocks that year, not polished stones or agates. They were more what I guess you'd call driveway rocks or common garden rocks. He was ahead of his time. Four years later, the pet-rock craze would sweep through the country. By then he was into bent nails.

All these potential collections he displayed casually—on the closet floor, on the windowsill, in his bed, on top of his dresser, in his dresser drawers. His clothes he put on the floor.

Geoffrey's room was off by itself, next to David's when he should choose to occupy it. Because of his tragic flaw—neatness—he didn't adorn the walls excessively or pile up mounds of socks and underwear in the corners. He tacked a couple of posters on his studs, made his bed, and arranged his clothes in his drawers. The top of his dresser had neat stacks of Monopoly and Parcheesi games, a couple of books, and a model or two. This left his floor free, so he and David set up their jointly owned racetracks. They threaded them under the bed and through the two-by-fours into the storage and out again. The room was a giant speed trap, and when I tried to go in, cars whizzed by and nipped at my ankles.

Of course, the arrangement was temporary. All six were shuffled back and forth, upstairs and down, depending on what the construction project of the month was. Finally, however, each was established in his or her own room.

Decoration fever never abated. When Sylvia's room got plasterboard and paint, she put strips of foil on her ceiling and adorned one wall with gruesome pictures of Alice Cooper in the throes of what appeared to be something terminal. Jenny brought in more and more plants, including a couple of baby firs that threaten to go through the roof in a couple of years. Joan gave up Heloise and Abelard in favor of an Indian maiden and two Daughters of the Revolution—a wise choice, I think —and Robbie still searches for the perfect collection.

David moved up, when the walls moved in, and ensconced himself amid computer tapes, books for the mathematically inclined, tennis rackets and cans of tennis balls. And Geoffrey took to making fleets of ship models. They hang from his ceiling, and the other night when I went in to say good night I sank the Titanic all over again.

And in the linen closet between the stairs and Geoffrey's room are neat stacks of sheets and blankets, all with holes in all four corners.

13

Is It Five Pounds of Sixpenny Nails or Six Pounds of Fivepenny Nails?

Some people who are desperately in need of comfort and advice go to a psychiatrist or a counselor. Others turn to their doctor or to a priest. Not me. I have Vince at the lumberyard. He knows my failings—that I broke the chisel trying to open up a can of paint; my shortcomings—that I hate spackling; and my innermost secrets—that I dropped the tape measure down inside the stairwell wall. And he doesn't act superior or blame me or say, "Isn't that just like a woman?"

It wasn't always this way. Years ago, when Joe and I were first married, Joe knew almost as little about home repair as I did. It was, however, beneath his dignity to admit it. So he sent me to the lumberyard to ask dumb questions and make a fool of myself.

I remember the first time. It was a Saturday and I was headed out the door, on my way downtown in Wichita Falls, Texas. As I started to leave Joe, who was hanging up some pictures for me, called out, "Hey, Annie! While you're down there stop at the lumberyard and get me six nails."

I didn't want to. I hate going into strange places, but I was a new bride, eager to please, and I wanted the pictures on the wall, so I agreed.

When I got to the lumberyard, it was fairly crowded, full of Saturday carpenters buying two-by-fours and siding and having their crosscut saws sharpened. I hung back, waiting my turn by the plumbing display, and tried to figure out what closet spud washers and a beveled close-coupled gaskets were. Finally the salesman came up to me.

"Yes, ma'am, what can I do for you?"

"My husband wants me to get six nails, this long," I said innocently, producing a slip of paper Joe had given me. On it was an accurate picture of a nail.

The salesman took the paper, stared at it for a minute, then showed it to three men behind me who immediately broke into convulsive laughter. The salesman bit his lip, turned away, and coughed violently.

"Are you sure it was six nails he wanted, not six pounds?" he asked when he'd regained his composure.

"He said he needed six nails." I silently cursed the messenger who gets stuck with the message.

"OK." He shrugged his shoulders and went off to get them.

When he came back, he rummaged around for a bag and dropped the nails in one by one as if he were a magician about to do his disappearing nail act. Then he handed the bag to me.

"There you are, ma'am. Six nails."

"How much do I owe you?"

"Lady." He paused, checking to be sure the men behind me were catching every word. "For six nails, I'll let you have them for free."

His audience applauded. I thanked him, grabbed the bag, and fled.

In the two decades since then, I've been sent to lumberyards all over America. Things have improved only slightly.

"Hi there. We're redoing our kitchen floor. Can you tell me what we need?"

"Sure, do you have the dimensions of your kitchen?"

"Well, it's about half as big as this corner of your store."

"Lady, I'll need the dimensions."

"Couldn't you estimate?"

"I've got to have the dimensions so I can compute the total square footage of the room."

"All right, I'll get them. But first may I see what you have?"

"OK. Do you want linoleum or tiles?"

"I don't know. Tiles, I guess. Aren't they easier to install?"

"Depends. Do you want vinyl, cork, asphalt, or rubber? Do you want the nine-by-nine size or the twelve-by-twelve? We even have a few of the nine-by-eighteens left."

"I want one that doesn't show the dirt—in a light green."

"Lady, we gotta lotta green ones. I don't know if they show the dirt or not."

Somehow, till Vince, no one ever cared about the important information, such as will the tiles show the dirt? But he has all the answers.

"Don't pick that one," he tells me. "It even looks dirty when it's clean. And stay clear of those over there. They look great, but when you stand on them for a while you ache right here in the back of the leg."

But I didn't have Vince when we redid our first kitchen floor.

I made two trips back home to check the dimensions. I got something wrong the first time, and the man guffawed and slapped the counter at the thought of a kitchen thirty feet long and four feet wide. Finally I got it straight.

"All right," I said. "Now what?"

He mumbled, scribbled on the back of an order blank, then looked up. "Let's see, you can either get five hundred and thirty-four nine-by-nine tiles at twelve to fourteen dollars a box, or three hundred twelve-by-twelves at—"

"Wait a minute. I have to see the colors first, then I'll know which size tiles I want."

His pencil snapped in half, so he grabbed a new one and took me over to the display. There were hundreds of different colors. Two I liked especially, one predominantly green with gold and brown flecks, the other a pale yellow with orange and green flecks. I couldn't decide. Then I noticed the prices and chose a white with black flecks, or was it black with white flecks. I can't remember. I do know it showed the dirt and I ached in the back of the legs.

After I'd picked out the tiles, the salesman scratched out some more figures, computed the waste allowance, and stacked the boxes of tiles on the counter.

Then things got worse. He sneered at my ignorance when I said I had no idea what condition the underfloor was in. And he took personal offense when I shook my head and said we didn't have a propane torch for getting up the old tiles.

"Why do I need a propane torch? I just want to rip the little devils up, not bum the house down."

His second pencil snapped, and he tried to signal another salesman to come and take over, but that man was in the middle of a two-hundred-dollar sale and wasn't about to give it up to help some female who didn't have a propane torch. They're chauvinistic in most hardware stores and lumberyards.

Eventually I got all the materials. Then I took them home and tried to impart what I'd learned to Joe. It was like being cross-examined in court.

"What's this?"

"A trowel."

"What's it for?"

"Spreading out the mastic."

"Is this the right one? I've seen them with lots bigger teeth."

"I don't know. It's the one he gave me. Why don't you go down and ask him."

Joe looked at his watch. "I can't. I have to be at the base in twenty minutes for a mock alert." It was a lie. I knew it, and he knew it.

"Then go next Saturday."

"We can't wait till then. We have to get the floor down."

He was determined not to submit himself to a salesman's ridicule. I can't say as I blamed him. It's easy asking stupid questions when they expect it of you. They didn't expect it of Joe.

"Well, call them and ask. Mention my name. They'll remember me."

That was one thing about my trips to the lumberyards, hardware stores, carpet emporiums, and assorted do-it-yourself palaces: They always remembered me. When we first moved to the Island, I went to the lumberyard so often and asked so many questions that once, as I approached, I heard a voice in the back shout, "Oh, no, I'm not waiting on her again. It's your turn, Bill."

When Joe graduated from weekend tile setter to a full-fledged home remodeler and mastered the difference between a crosscut saw and a ripsaw, my trips to the lumberyard became more frequent and far more complicated. Luckily, this was about the time I met Vince.

It was when Hal and Joe were making the stairs. I was in the kitchen reading the paper, thrilled that there was yet another way to use leftover lobster. Joe and Hal were nailing in the last of the treads.

"Hey, Joe," I heard Hal say. "Hand me a couple of sixpenny nails."

There was a pause while Joe banged around. "We're out of them, Hal. Will these do?"

"No, we need sixpenny. Have Ann go up to Island Lumber and get about five pounds. We can always use them." Joe came into the kitchen. "Annie," he said, "run up and get five pounds of sixpenny nails. Hurry."

I folded up the paper. "OK." I replied, and put on my coat.

As I walked into the store, the salesmen fell over themselves rushing for the back. Then Vince came out.

"Hi. Can I help you?"

"Yes. I need six pounds of fivepenny nails."

Vince went over to the revolving bin, scooped out some nails and weighed them. "There you are, six pounds of five- penny nails."

I thanked him and headed home.

Joe and Hal were waiting.

"Here you are." I held out the bag. "Six pounds of five- penny nails."

Hal groaned and Joe clenched his teeth. "Annie," he said, "I told you, five pounds of sixpenny nails. We can't use these."

"Five pounds of sixpenny nails... five pounds of sixpenny nails," I chanted as I drove back to the lumberyard.

Vince was outside loading a wheelbarrow into a man's car when I drove up. "I made a mistake," I said. "They want five pounds of sixpenny nails."

He laughed. "It's an easy mistake to make," he said, and I adored him immediately. He exchanged the nails and I was back in the car.

This time as I came in the back door, Joe grabbed the bag and peered in. Then he swore. "Dammit, Annie, you got galvanized." The words marched out of his mouth like mechanical soldiers. "We need brite. Five pounds of sixpenny brite nails."

Off I went again. Vince was still calm. He even claimed responsibility. "I should have known they needed brite," he said.

This time Joe was satisfied. "Here they are, Hal," he called. There was another one of those awful pauses. I held my breath.

"Joe," Hal said, "we don't use box nails on treads. We need finishing nails, the ones without a head. You can't countersink a box nail."

Joe came back into the kitchen. I pretended to be copying down the lobster recipe. "One more time, Annie," he said. "Five pounds ... sixpenny ... brite ... finishing nails."

"Couldn't you go this time?" I pleaded. "I can't face them again."

"No, I've got to stay here and help Hal."

That had a familiar ring about it, and I choked back the urge to ask if he and Hal were having a mock alert.

Off I went. "Five pounds ... sixpenny ... brite ... finishing ... five pounds ... sixpenny ... brite ... finishing."

Vince was still there.

"Vince," I said. I knew his name by now. "I did it again, but this time it's not my fault. They didn't specify finishing nails."

He shook his head. "They ought to write down what they want in the first place. You could spend all day coming up here. Tell you what, why don't you call and make sure you have what they want."

I called.

Apparently Joe was on the top of the ladder when the phone rang. He had to come down, climb over the sawhorses, and squeeze through the two-by-fours. "Good God, do you know where I was?" he snapped. "How do you expect me to get any work done if I have to spend all day answering the phone? I told you before. Five pounds… sixpenny … brite … finishing." He slammed down the phone and I said goodbye to the dial tone.

The ritual has varied since that day. Sometimes Joe gives me a written list of the supplies he needs. Sometimes he calls the order in himself, and I only pick it up. Whenever I have to call back to make sure it's brite, not galvanized, I make Vince do it. He doesn't mind. But then Joe never swears at him.

No matter what, I always go to Vince. If I'm picking up a can of plastic wood to fill nail holes, he doesn't let me get out of the store without asking, "Are you staining or painting over this? This stuff is cheaper, but it doesn't take stain."

When we were stripping paint off the beams in the living room, he not only recommended the brand of paint remover but told me to lather on two coats of remover before scraping. This saved weeks of work.

All this aside, however, Vince would still have my unwavering loyalty if only for one reason. He never lectures me about tape measures.

We consume tape measures at our house, at least the children do. They have more uses for tape measures than Heloise does for nylon net.

Robbie uses one when he can't find a hammer. To Geoffrey they make handy paperweights, especially when his Monopoly money gets out of hand. David fiddles with one when he's nervous, and Joan and Jenny stretch one out to divide up couches, tables, and chairs. Once they've divided up something, they dare each other to venture over the boundary.

Of course, they also use tape measures for measuring. They measure their feet, their heads, their noses, my nose, and the dog's tail. They measure the distance from the refrigerator to the living room, how far apart they can stretch their fingers, and how much bigger than Sylvia's David's piece of pie is. When they tire of measuring, they time how long it takes for the tape to snap back from a distance of four feet, then six, then eight.

This is all very educational and would make a whole segment on "Sesame Street." But when their measuring is done and Hal and Joe are figuring out the width of a new windowsill and the tape sprongs or won't snap back or breaks at the three-inch mark, I'm sent, with a volley of accusations hammering at my back, up to Vince to get another refill. Hal lectures me about the proper care of tools. Joe says I've lost control of the children and that they have no respect for people's property and that "in his day... Vince doesn't complain or roll his eyes heavenward. Why should he? One day he may be able to retire on the profit from our tape measures alone.

Two years ago, about the time we were putting in the upstairs bathroom floor, Vince left town on vacation. It was like having your psychiatrist leave on one plane and your mother-in-law come in on the next. But I felt strong enough to make it alone. I made a list of equipment needed. I left nothing out. I had the room dimensions. I'd figured the waste allowance and even knew the linear measurement for the molding. There wasn't a hitch. I bought a trowel with the right number of teeth per inch and I bought the right floor cement. Then I brought it home and Geoffrey and I decided to surprise Joe and tile the floor in one afternoon.

I read the directions carefully. I'm a great reader of directions, probably the foremost authority on when to and when not to induce vomiting. Anyway, we began. It was tricky in places, in the corners and around the shower, but we took our time, working slowly and carefully.

As we put down each tile and pressed it into place, a bit of cement oozed up. I wiped off what I could and went on to the next.

"We'll clean it thoroughly when we're through," I told Geoffrey. But it was late when we finished, and I postponed the cleaning till the following day.

The next day I went to the local hardware store.

"Yes, ma'am, can I help you?"

"You certainly may. I installed a bathroom floor yesterday and I need something to clean up the cement that oozed up between the tiles."

There was a snicker behind me and memories of the six nails flitted in and out of my mind.

"You didn't clean it up before it dried?" the man asked. "No, I didn't have time."

"But you have to or it won't come up."

"It didn't say that on the directions. I read them twice. It said not to have the room too cold. It told me how to apply tiles to a wood surface and a concrete surface. It said not to induce vomiting, but there was nothing that said, 'Clean it up before it dries'."

The man bit his lip. "Lady," he said, slowly, patiently. "Everyone knows you clean it up right away. It doesn't have to go on the directions. Everyone already knows it."

"Well, I didn't," I said. And I left the store.

Two weeks later I was waiting at the door when the lumberyard opened.

"Vince," I called as I dashed in, "thank heaven you're back. I've done it again."

The bathroom is clean now, even in the corners.

14

Come on, Take Five on the Fourth

"**O**h, no, you don't." Joe's voice had the same tone he gets when I try to slip Red Flannel Hash into the dinner menu. "You're not going to get me to waste another complete day on one of your Island parades. I have work to do."

"But, Joe," I pleaded, "this isn't just another Island parade. This is the Fourth of July. It's special."

"That's what you said about the Scotch broom parade. 'But, Joe,' you told me," and his voice rose in a too-perfect imitation of me, " 'where else are you going to find a celebration with a chairman who leaves town the minute he's appointed? Where can you be in a parade simply by driving through town with some Scotch broom stuffed in your car or threaded through your bicycle spokes? Where will you find a queen who isn't young and nubile and half clothed?' " He paused and looked at me over his glasses. "I like to see queens who are young, nubile, and half clothed. But no. I give up the whole afternoon, when I could put a coat of sealer on the balconies, and what do they do? They roar into the liquor store and grab the cashier and make her the queen. And do you know how it felt to stand on the sidewalk and have people come up to me and say, 'Wasn't that Lady Godiva on the horse your wife?' "

"Oh, you're stuffy. Besides, I was fully clothed."

I was too. I'd dipped Joe's long underwear in coffee to make it look more the color of skin, and I'd let down my hair, which reached to my knees at the time, though I usually kept it piled in a dignified Episcopal knot on the top of my head. I'd even worn sunglasses and a garland of Scotch broom.

"Most people didn't even recognize me," I protested. "Anyway, it was fun. I was sick of staying home and working on the house. But we're getting off the subject. We were talking about the Fourth of July. It's different. You're probably thinking of the old Strawberry Festival they had when we were kids. This isn't the same at all. This is uptown time on Bainbridge. They have booths on both sides of the street, selling quilts and pottery and jewelry. You can buy a hot dog or have an ice cream cone, some strawberry shortcake—anything you want. There's a bingo game down in the Thriftway parking lot. You can buy a chance on a new car. You can listen to Dixieland jazz. There's even a dunking booth, and Jan tells me both Father Edwards and Father Barnstable are going to be on the collapsing springboard."

I took a deep breath and Joe broke in. "But I was counting on getting everything cleaned up upstairs so we'll be ready when it's time to work on the dormers."

"Oh, phooey. We have lots of time for that. Besides, you'll have to stop when everybody comes anyway."

"What do you mean, when everybody comes?"

"Didn't I tell you? We're having a picnic at our house, and when it gets dark we're going over to the beach in Eagledale. They say it's the best place for watching the fireworks."

Joe shrugged and shook his head. "No, you didn't tell me, but it doesn't look as if I can do anything about it now."

He was right, he couldn't. I'd planned it weeks before, and I'd had to be sneaky about it. Joe was so caught up in the momentum of remodeling he refused to take a break. He's like that. He has a singleness of purpose that makes a mule look flighty, and the only way to jar him loose is to be underhanded. Through the years I've become expert at it.

"Right," I went on. "I've asked Carole and Alex, Jan and Martin, and Greg and Kathy Harper."

I'd met Greg and Kathy a couple of months before, when they opened a bookstore in Winslow. Till they came the only thing faintly resembling a bookstore was a tiny shop on a side street that carried paperbacks. If you went in to order a copy of the Bible, the first question was, "Who wrote it?" and things went downhill from there. I used to search the outgoing tide to see if book orders were being sent out in old Coke bottles. And I still expect to hear from someone in Tierra del Fuego saying my request for *Wuthering Heights* has been received and will be taken care of as soon as the fog lifts.

When Greg and Kathy came, Shakespeare, Ross Macdonald and Norman Mailer came to Bainbridge too, and I spent hours thumbing through Chinese cookbooks, odd dictionaries and illustrated volumes that promised to teach me how to tap dance and how to play better tennis. They even let me rush in and check a quote or look up a market for short stories and then rush out again. In return, I overlooked the fact that they were both young and gorgeous.

"The party was Kathy's idea," I said. "And I offered to have it here because we're close to Winslow and we have so much space. They can come down here whenever they want after the parade. We'll put up the badminton set and make a table out of sawhorses and a sheet of plywood. You'll have a marvelous time. Everyone's going to bring something and it will all be very casual."

"But, Annie." I could tell he was beginning to weaken. "You don't have guests over when there's lumber in the living room and plasterboard stacked up against the walls."

"Of course you do. It's the perfect time. Then no one expects the place to be spotless. Who cares anyway?"

"Well, all right. But promise me one thing."

"What's that?"

"Promise me you're not riding in the parade."

"Of course I'm not. I can't. I couldn't find a gorilla suit."

Once Joe got used to the idea, his enthusiasm grew. He fashioned a barbecue grill out of an old wheelbarrow and a rack from the oven. He paced out the badminton court and marked the boundaries in chalk, and he mowed the entire lawn in one day, which if you're in top physical shape and have the wind at your back only takes seven and a half hours.

The Fourth that year dawned typically—cold and gray. The forecasters, lying through their predictions, had assured everyone that after a low morning fog the skies would clear. I looked out around seven o'clock. The fog was low, all right. It was lying on the ground, and above it clouds, thick and dark, lolled around on the treetops and showed no signs of moving on.

I began to wonder if I'd made a terrible mistake. Like fools we'd planned the whole affair on the assumption the sun would shine and we could be outside. We should have known better. Having the sun shine on the Fourth is comparable to having a white Christmas in Miami Beach. July here is a mild winter, and summer if it comes usually arrives in August on the weekend you're out of town. But I'm a great believer in the impossible dream and I relied on faith, my horoscope, and the message in a stale Chinese fortune cookie to bring good weather. Therefore, in the intervening weeks since the first idea for a picnic, I'd let the guest list grow considerably.

The additions included Mother and Daddy, who said they'd love to come, and would it be all right if they brought Doris from Vancouver? Jan mentioned they usually spent the Fourth with their friends, Mike and Peg, and their four children, and I told her to bring them along—the more the merrier. We couldn't leave out Martin's mother or her sister-in- law, Carrie, or Alex's parents, either, and as long as Carole's mother and dad were going to be on the Island anyway, they should be included. Her father even agreed to bring his sax in case we needed music. Naturally we invited Paul Stewart, our neighbor, friend, and resident architect. His plums and blackberries made some of the wine we were going to serve. Besides, he said he'd furnish an accordion if his guests from Seattle could come too. I didn't even ask for a signed statement that they would overlook it if the plumbing backed up or a child dropped through the living room ceiling.

Now, however, with rain an ever-increasing possibility, I wondered whether or not we'd have to seat people on the bed and if I'd have to haul out the laundry hamper to use as an extra table.

"Don't worry," Joe assured me, "it won't rain. Those clouds are going to burn off. I give you my word."

They hadn't by noon when we left for the parade. In fact I could almost hear replacements roaring in from the Pacific. I put on a warmer pair of slacks and grabbed an extra sweater, and we drove up and parked as close to the main street as possible. We got out of the car and the front-runners from the annual Fort Ward to Winslow race sprinted past, their feet slapping the pavement, their faces contorted with pain.

"I want to run that race," Geoffrey said as we moved aside to let someone pass.

"Why?"

"I don't know."

"Do you think you could make it all the way?"

"Sure, watch." He ran ahead. Sylvia and Robbie took out after him.

By the time we got into town the streets were already crowded and people milled back and forth, stopping to check the price of a handmade apron here or to buy an ice cream cone over there. Kids wove in and out through the sea of people, chasing each other, and fathers hoisted their two- and three- year-olds onto their shoulders for a better view. We looked for a place where all of us could sit and luckily found an empty table next to the dunking booth. Peter Edwards, in a wet bathing suit and a soggy Oxford sweat shirt, and Lance Barnstable, his beard still dripping, stood together on the sidewalk shivering and accepting congratulations.

"Good show, Father Peter," someone yelled. "We made more money trying to dunk you than all the others put together."

Peter smiled grimly through chattering teeth. "Everyone's out to get God," he mumbled. "But"—he turned to Lance—"I didn't think you'd be one of them."

The parade started right on time, with fire engines and the medic car and a couple of representatives from the Kitsap County Sheriff's office leading off. Next came the bank's float, a battered old truck decked out in streamers and bunting. The loan officer and several of the tellers, dressed in red, white, and blue, threw handfuls of candy to the children in the crowd. Joe caught a piece and gave it to Joan, who'd been outmaneuvered by an agile teenager. Next the sheriff's posse rode by, sitting straight and tall on their horses, and behind them their wives —a cleanup committee in bathrobes and slippers—shuffled along with shovels and brooms and an old wheelbarrow. Glenn, of Glenn's Gas Station, drove his wrecker dubbed "The Happy Hooker." There was a pipe band from Vancouver, B.C., the jazz band in straw hats and summer jackets, and the Eagledale Lawn Mower Marching and Drill Society. Obviously they'd practiced, for when they got halfway down the street they broke ranks and wheeled their Toro backbaggers around and executed figure eights and other precision maneuvers. Their finale came when they formed the word MULCH and moved on. Following them was a long procession of open convertibles with yacht club commodores and their wives and poodles. Then we saw a trail of official real estate cars, some old Fords and Pierce Arrows, and finally an interminable line of Corvettes, roaring their engines and weaving from side to side to show off their tail pipes.

"Let's go!" Joe yelled in my ear. "I can't take the noise!"

So we gathered up the children, who by now had made numerous side trips to the hot dog and ice cream cone booth, and headed back to the car.

"When do the clouds bum off?" I asked as we threaded through the crowd.

"Don't worry," Joe said. "I told you, it's not going to rain." We hadn't been home long when the picnickers began to assemble. Greg and Kathy came first, and while I helped Kathy assemble her salad, Greg and David took on Joe and Geoffrey in a game of badminton. After a bit, Alex's parents (who said they couldn't stay long) and Martin's mother (who'd made plans for later) came, and from then on a constant stream of cars rolled in and out of the driveway. Half of them I'd never seen before. They were friends of friends and cousins of cousins. Some people waited in line to play the badminton winners. Others sailed Frisbees back and forth across the lawn. Martin started a game of catch, and the unathletic sat in groups sipping wine and deploring the necessity for "that many Corvettes."

Meanwhile, bowls of potato salad and shrimp salad and three varieties of tossed salad, loaves of bread and packages of potato chips, pans of fried chicken, pots of beans, jugs of wine, hot dogs, buns, and every imaginable condiment came in the back door and went right out the front onto the makeshift table. The children, about fifteen in all, swarmed around the food, and except for Clarissa—who belonged to someone, I don't know who—they looked like contestants waiting for the starting gun in a pie-eating contest. Clarissa howled, "I don't like hot dogs. I want a burger from McDonald's." She was ignored and eventually she stopped and elbowed her way to the table.

Mother hovered in the kitchen and worried. "Do you think there'll be enough to eat? Did you say Jenny could open that bag of chips? Do you think we should eat outside? It looks as if it's going to rain."

"It's all right," I assured her. "Joe says it'll hold off for another couple of hours at least."

It didn't, though. It started to sprinkle just as we were about to give the signal to eat. By the time everyone had grabbed a bowl or a dish or the plates and rushed them inside, it was pouring. We plunked everything down on the table in the kitchen and the children, their salivary glands caught in midair, milled around whining, "I'm hungry. When are we going to eat?"

Then the lightning and thunder began, and Golly and Sheba—devout cowards, both of them—threw themselves in a panic at the back door. It sounded as if the Huns had arrived.

"Come and get it," I bellowed above the din. "You kids, help yourselves, then take your plates upstairs to eat. Watch where you go, though. Not all the flooring is in."

Immediately they formed a line, Clarissa in front. They filled their plates and trooped upstairs. They loved it up there. I could hear them walking through walls, shinnying up the two-by-fours, and swinging from the rafters.

Downstairs, Joe stacked the last of our alder logs in the fireplace. I broiled another batch of hot dogs, and the adults took a plate and a fork and helped themselves. It wasn't too crowded. At least I didn't have to bring out the laundry hamper, though we did use the piano bench, balanced a couple of boards on bricks, and Joe sat on the floor in a modified lotus position and put his plate on a suitcase.

But there was plenty of food—though the dishes ran out — and Mike, who'd lost his plate, had his second helping of baked beans in a silver bowl.

"That's class," I heard someone say.

"No, that's Bainbridge."

The wine flowed too, and when everyone was through and the paper plates had been thrown in the fire, Martin brought out his harmonica, Paul strapped on his accordion, and Carole ran out in the rain to the car to get her father's sax. Then the music soared. We sang every song we could think of. Kathy and Carole and I harmonized on "The Battle Hymn of the Republic" and "Give My Regards to Broadway." Mother requested "When You and I Were Young, Maggie." Joe stood for the Air Force Hymn, and he and Jan started a conga line and wove in and out around the living room while the musicians belted out "When the Saints Go Marching In." Every time there was a lull in the requests we went back to "God Bless America." Kate Smith should have been there.

Finally, like a mechanical soldier winding down, the music slowed. Martin and Paul played odd arrangements of songs without words. Carole's dad filled in with the bass notes, and Mike, off in a corner, strummed absently on a guitar that was missing a string. The conversation had slowed too, and the children, tired of acrobatics upstairs, worried and fretted at their parents' side. I looked for a clean cup and checked to see if any coffee was left.

Then all of a sudden Alex stood up. "Time for fireworks!" he announced, and the room came alive again.

"Has it stopped raining?"

"Honey, where'd you put my coat?"

"Does anyone want the last of these potato chips?"

"Come on, let's go."

Kids raced around trying to find their sweaters. Jan told me to keep the extra hot dogs, and everyone left with someone else's bowl or plate. Then we all crammed into our cars and took off for Eagledale.

Others had come before us, and by the time we got there the beach was lined with people. Still, it was quiet down at the water's edge. Waves from a motorboat going by slapped up against logs and rattled the stones as they swept back out again. Conversation rumbled like distant thunder. Every now and then a firecracker popped or someone lit a sparkler that sizzled, sputtered, and then went out.

We sat on the logs and dug at the sand with the heels of our shoes.

"When does it start, Mom?" Robbie asked, huddling up against me.

"Pretty soon. Why, are you tired?"

"No, no. " He sat up straight. "I just wondered."

"It won't be long now. Look, here comes the ferry." We watched as the boat, ablaze with lights, rounded the bend and eased into the dock. The rhythmic clank as the cars drove off onto the dock and headed up the highway echoed from across the bay. Then with its new load it pulled away again.

Finally the show began. From a barge across the bay in Winslow, rockets shot up into the sky and exploded in chrysanthemums, shooting stars, and umbrellas of red and green and blue.

"Oooooh." Robbie poked me. "Look at that!"

"There's another one," Joan squealed.

For twenty minutes we watched, comparing each burst of light with the one before. Finally, three went off simultaneously and it was over.

"Is that all, Dad?" Sylvia asked, her voice not wanting to let go. "Let's wait a minute. Maybe there's more."

But the Fourth of July was finished, and we called out, "Good night," "Good-bye," "I'll get your salad bowl to you tomorrow," then piled everyone back in the car and joined the long line heading up to the main road.

It was quiet in the car going home. By the time we got there three of the children were asleep.

"See, Joe," I said as I held open the back door while he lifted Jenny out. "Wasn't that fun?"

"It was." He gave me his 'I'm-charming' smile. "I don't know why you wanted to work on the house instead."

15

On a Clear Day You Don't Mind a Hole in Your Roof

For most of the month of July, the argument raged on. Should we raise the roof or build dormers? I wanted to raise the roof. I always want to raise the roof. In this instance I felt it would add class, be aesthetic, give the exterior pleasing lines.

Joe wanted dormers. Roof raising terrified him. He envisioned joints giving way, timbers splitting, giant winds whistling out of the south to blow the raised part to Victoria. He was sure the ceilings and walls would cave in, and the house like a dynamited apartment building would roar and groan, then settle down in a heap of rubble.

"But, Joe," I said, searching for a familiar analogy that would make the project appealing. "Paul says it's simple. It's like one of those cupcake desserts where you slice off the peak, lift it up, stuff in some whipped cream, then put it back on."

"Great. And who holds up the cupcake while I'm struggling with the whipped cream?"

"I don't know. Aren't there jacks or something for lifting up houses?"

"Sure. But where are we going to put them?"

"On the comers ... in the middle ... I don't know. Where does one usually put them?"

"They have to be over a major support beam."

"Don't we have some of those?"

"Sure. But they're in all the wrong places, and most of them—like those two skinny poles in the living room—won't hold the weight."

In the end I ran out of arguments and kitchen analogies. Besides, Hal agreed with Joe. Mother agreed with Joe. So did his mother, my Aunt Sylvia, his sister, the first mate on the ferry, three of the bag boys at the grocery store, and the substitute mailman. The only ones on my side were the children, whom I'd brainwashed, Paul, who was out of town, and Sven. When I found out Sven was on my side, I gave in completely.

Dormers it would be—one on the north for Joan's and Robbie's rooms and one on the south for Sylvia's room.

As the day for constructing the dormers approached, the tension built. Joe, having been relieved of the worry about lifting the roof, now put all his energies into worrying about the dormers.

"What if the roof collapses before the bracing's in? What if it rains? What if the chimney outside Robbie's room has to be extended? What if it rains? What if we make a false cut? What if it rains?"

He was right to worry about rain. Northwest weather is, at best, capricious. On good days trees shimmer, the mountains hang out their snow against the sky like Monday's wash, and the wind is soft and caressing. On bad days it's like sitting on a November beach in a wet bathing suit.

Therefore, when the day was set Joe became obsessed with the weather. He monitored local forecasts from dawn through the 11 :00 p.m. news. He tapped at the barometer each time he passed it, cheering as it rose, despairing as it dipped and slid. Twice he said we'd make it, but then a high-pressure ridge off the coast dissipated and foul weather ambled in and lounged over the countryside.

We postponed—a day, another day, then a week. Finally July sloshed to a close and August skipped in bright and clear.

A new day was chosen—August 9. I got up at six o'clock on the appointed morning. The barometer was high, the wind from the north, and the sun already high in the sky. Joe had been up for an hour. He was worrying anew.

"Where did I put that chisel?" he muttered to himself. "Did Hal take home his wrecking bar? Where's the saw? I've got to find the saw. Have you seen it?"

He stormed through the kitchen and pointed an accusing finger at Geoffrey, who sat with David finishing off breakfast. They looked up and shrugged.

"Sit down, Joe." I gave him a cup of coffee. "You took the saw upstairs a minute ago. Don't get so upset. Hal will be here, and for once we'll have help, gobs of it."

I wasn't exaggerating. Whereas groveling under the house dragging heating ducts through the chicken manure had brought no cries of "Hey, let me give you a hand," everyone wanted to help with the dormers. There's something about cutting a hole in a roof that awakens the pioneer spirit. Even the children—by now experts at being absent when walls needed bashing, nails needed pulling, and plasterboard needed hefting—were anxious to join in.

"I dibs to get on the roof."

"Can I help pull off the shingles, Dad?"

They could hardly wait.

My brother Geoff, out West on vacation with his four children, volunteered his skills too. It was a gift of love, not expertise. Geoff is not a carpenter. He's an intellectual, more at home explaining how gravity makes a plumb line work than he is at using one.

When we were children, he spent two weeks building a doghouse. He drew up the plans himself, agonized over the pitch of the roof, made sure the shingles matched those on our house, and used the world's most expensive paint. Unfortunately the dog never used the house. The door was Chihuahua size, the dog was a collie. I think he passed his skills on to Robbie.

Geoff hadn't honed his talents in the intervening years, but he was willing and we needed willing bodies.

We had enough workers, all right—three in the Skilsaw and crowbar category, three designated as apprentice shingle rippers, and two (Robbie and our Geoffrey) in training as hammer and nail retrievers.

I was to be on hand at all times for trips to the lumberyard. The girls, my three and Geoff's Laura and Louisa, had no specific function. I'd suggested exporting them, but they demanded to be part of the goings-on. They had camped out overnight in a tent on the lawn and came in and out like the tide: in for excitement and food, and out again when it looked as if they'd have to work.

Of the whole entourage only Joe and Hal had the faintest idea of what they were doing.

Around eight thirty the motley crew assembled. Geoff and his boys, Burry and Lile, arrived first. Minutes later Hal drove up. He was ready to work, but I think he had doubts about the rest of us. From the look on his face I could tell he felt like Toscanini given the task of coaxing Beethoven's Ninth out of the sixth-grade band.

At the sound of the cars, the girls ran into the house again.

"Breakfast time!" Laura shouted.

"I get to make the pancakes!" Sylvia, in baby-doll pajamas, raced ahead.

Jenny was close behind. "I get to turn them!"

The two factions, workers in the back door and cooks in the front, met like waves crashing against a rock, and the kitchen splashed and tumbled with babble and shrieks. Hal shook his head and waded through, up the stairs. Joe followed, and eventually so did Geoff and the boys. I sensed that leaving the kitchen was the better part of valor, so I joined them. The men were conferring.

"Right here's where we'll cut," Hal was saying. "I'll drive nails through to mark the comers. You and the boys get out on the roof and tear off the shingles. Then we'll open her up."

Burry, at the time an awkward teenager, stepped back to survey the scene. Too far. The floor didn't extend to the eaves. There was a crash, and his leg shot through the ceiling tiles into the living room below.

Everyone rushed to help him, but he dragged his leg up through the splinters and broken plaster, then lurched forward, going through again in a new place. Joe's face registered an exquisite combination of panic, horror, concern, and control. I waited to see which emotion would win. It was control. He reached over and gave Burry a hand out of his latest hole.

Burry was embarrassed and shifted back and forth, first on one foot, then the other.

"Gee, I'm sorry," he said, coming dangerously close to going through again. "I'm really sorry."

Joe pointed to a safer spot. "Just stand over there," he suggested. "But don't worry. We're going to replace the living room ceiling anyway."

Geoff chortled. "You may have to sooner than you'd planned."

Hal bit down on his pipe stem and the puffs of smoke shot up like an Indian Letter to the Editor.

This was too much for me. I retreated.

In the kitchen, the girls had breakfast in full swing. Bowls clanked, beaters whirred, eggshells arched through the air in the general direction of the garbage can.

"We're making blackberry pancakes." Joan held up a pail of blackberries, stems and all.

"And I'm going to turn them," said Jenny, as she stood by the skillet, spatula clutched in her hand.

The confusion here was worse than upstairs. "Fine," I said. "I'm going outside. Clean up the mess when you're through."

"We will." Jenny waved her spatula and the others nodded.

Outside all was quiet, a peaceful morning. On the far edge of the lawn a mother quail and her babies pecked at the grass. I walked toward them and they scattered, running in frenzied circles till they escaped into the underbrush. I glanced back at the house. Except for a bald spot on the north side of the roof, there was no visible sign of impending activity. I could hear hammering and now and then the whine of the saw.

I walked around the yard and listened to the popping sound as Scotch-broom seeds burst out of their pods in the summer heat. The apples on the tree were fat with a tinge of red on one side, and the branches, heavy with their weight, drooped almost to the ground. I picked one that looked ripe and took a bite. It was tart and crisp. They'll make good applesauce, I thought, if we don't eat them all first.

I stood there in the sun, waiting and watching the roof. Downstairs my bedroom window flung open.

"Mom, Sylvia says I have to eat my pancakes, but they're yucky. Can I make French toast?"

I heard angry protests, a gagging sound, and the window slammed shut again.

Up under the roof the saw was insistent now. They'd started to cut the hole. The saw stopped, then started again. Again it stopped. I could hear the hammer. *Whap!* A board pushed up. A few more strokes of the hammer and it came free. Joe's hand shot through the hole and waved.

"Hooray!" The cheers exploded into the still air.

Soon more boards popped up, and as I watched, Joe peered out.

"Hello, Annie!" he called, looking not unlike Sir Edmund Hillary at the summit of Everest. "We've begun!"

After that everyone took turns looking out—except Hal, of course. When you know what you're doing you don't have to congratulate yourself at each juncture.

Once the first step was taken, the work went fast. As soon as all the boards had been tossed off the roof and it was clear below, Lile was dispatched to the scattered pile on the lawn to remove the nails. David and Geoffrey, grumbling at their menial task, then stacked lumber. Robbie, always the free spirit, scrambled to the peak of the roof and was ordered inside. Reluctantly I came in too.

In the kitchen, breakfast was obviously over. Every counter, table, and flat space was littered. Half-eaten pancakes lay lazily soaking up syrup till they could soak no more. Butter puddled in a plate on the stove. The coffee no one had turned down perked in black, murky spurts. I hadn't seen disaster like this since I witnessed the bombing of Manila.

The girls lounged in the living room, inert bodies perusing copies of Modem Romance and True Love.

"Ye gods!" I said. "I thought you were going to clean up this mess."

"We will. Just a minute."

"Just a minute, my foot. You made the mess, you clean it up—now."

Sylvia sat up. "It's not my fault. Joan was the one who wanted French toast instead of pancakes."

"Yeah, but Sylvia spilled the powdered sugar on the floor."

"And you're the one who let the syrup boil over."

"I did not, Louisa did."

"Did too."

"Did not."

They swarmed into the kitchen pointing out each other's transgressions. In the midst of this the back door flew open and David charged in with a two-by-six for a battering ram. His face reflected disgust at having to work while his sisters fooled around. He negotiated the utility room, made it across the kitchen, then turned to go upstairs.

"Watch what you're doing, dummy." Jenny snatched a stack of dishes out of his way.

"Watch it yourself. I'd like to see you carry one of these." Taunts and accusations volleyed across the room like tennis balls at Wimbledon. I whistled. It's my only talent, other than being able to tap dance in one direction. I curl my lower lip around my teeth, arrange my tongue, and let forth with a shrill, vertigo-inducing whistle.

There was silence. Even the hammering upstairs stopped, and I heard Joe mumble something. He hates the whistle, having stood too close when I use it to summon the troops to dinner.

"All right," I said, "everyone out. Out of the house. I don't care where you go, but get out, right now."

Sylvia, Jenny, and Joan, seeing a chance to avoid work, headed out to their tent. Laura and Louisa, used to a more dignified life, looked at me, startled, then turned and followed.

I lifted a bowl partially filled with a lumpy, blue batter out of the sink and put in some hot, soapy water.

An hour and a half later, I stuffed the last of the pots into the cupboards, wiped up the counters, and plugged in the dishwasher. I poured myself some coffee, which by now tasted like burnt corn husks, and sat down.

Suddenly the back door flew open and Mother staggered in with two bags of groceries. She set them down on the counter and one tipped over, spilling out cans of tuna, packages of sliced ham, cantaloupes, grapes, bread, and cheese.

I stared at her. "What's this?"

"I brought lunch—at least I brought the ingredients. I'd stay to help you, but I have to get home and get something for your father to eat. See you later."

She whirled out again, and I looked at all the food waiting to have me do something with it. I was less than enthusiastic, but finally I heaved myself to my feet and with a sigh I declared the kitchen open for business once again.

Half an hour later, after I'd whistled down the workers and they'd migrated out to the front porch to eat, I went up to see if Joe was coming down. He tends to stay behind and admire the job. It's only because he can't believe what's been done.

He was standing looking out the dormer hole. All the shiplap had been ripped off. The rafters, like giant ribs of some prehistoric beast, were all that kept out the sky. It was quiet. From the kitchen I could hear the girls chattering, and the sound of laughter drifted up from the front yard. Joe grinned and put his arm around me.

"We did it, Annie," he said. "We cut through and the roof didn't cave in."

I thought of five years before in another house when I'd goaded him into building the first shelves. He put them together in the basement and then, because they were too big for the stairway, had to take them apart, carry them upstairs then reassemble them.

"We've come a long way," I said.

He nodded and gave the framing a gentle pat, and I turned to go.

"Come on down before the sandwiches are gone."

The afternoon was somewhat calmer. Mother stopped by once more, this time to admire the work. At the sight of the discarded lumber in the front yard, she gasped appropriately, unable to keep the lid on her little basket of horrors.

"Someone's going to step on those nails," she warned, almost willing it. "I know a boy whose leg—"

Lile, who'd spent the better part of three hours pulling out nails as fast as he could, glared at her and she stopped in mid-disaster.

When she left, Sven dropped by.

"See you didn't raise the roof," he called up to Joe who had the misfortune to be visible. " 'Fraid you'll be sorry. The dormer looks OK, but with that long span it's bound to sag." Hal ignored him. Geoff looked alarmed, and Joe accidentally let go of his hammer. It slid down the roof, bouncing merrily over the shingles, and narrowly missed Sven as it plummeted to the ground.

He didn't stay long. He'd only come by, he said, to let us know what the county was doing to screw up our shore rights. I assured him we had no rights as we had no shore, and he left, calling back over his shoulder when he was out of range, "Good luck. You'll need it."

At four thirty Hal called a halt.

"I'm tired and I'm going home," he said. He unplugged his saw, stacked his tools in the corner, picked up his thermos, and fought his way through the children and dogs out the door and to his car.

The hole was completely empty now. The ribs were gone, the framing and the bracing in, and the sky filled the room.

"Daddy, Daddy." Geoffrey tugged at Joe's sleeve. "Can we keep it the way it is?"

Joe looked up. The rays of the setting sun caught in the branches of the poplar tree and the leaves trembled in the breeze. "I wish we could," he said. "I wish we could."

He picked up the broom and began sweeping up the sawdust, and I ran downstairs to help Geoff, who was whipping up a batch of martinis. Then we all went outside and sat in the cool grass and drank and congratulated ourselves.

"You know," Geoff said, "I could learn to love carpentry if I had someone like Hal to show me what to do."

"He's amazing, all right," Joe agreed. "Say, why don't you quit your high-priced job back East? Come back out here and be a gentleman farmer, like me."

Geoff laughed, but he was caught in the spell too. The hard day's work, the hush of sunset, the peace—they felt good.

"Don't think I wouldn't like to," he said. Then his voice changed. "We better get going. Mother'll have a fit if we're late again. I guess as long as we're staying with her this trip, the least we can do is be on time for dinner."

He rounded up his children and got them into the car. "See you tomorrow," he yelled as he drove off.

The next morning we all got up early again.

"Guess what?" Jenny said at breakfast. "I pushed my bed over near the hole last night and I went to sleep watching the stars."

She watched them that night too, but then her luck ran out and the magic was gone. The roof went on and the walls went in. Just in time too. The third night it rained.

By the time we got to the south dormer, all our help had left town. Joe, Hal, and I were ready with hammers poised and wrecking bars at the ready, but we needed another strong back and none was available. David was in school, as were Robbie and Geoffrey. We asked Sven to help, but he declined with the excuse that he had to pickle his zucchini. Joe sounded out some of his co-commuters, but he'd been too explicit in telling them about the north dormer and to a man they all developed back problems. We were back to a dearth of volunteers.

Then we remembered Bob Sims, a history professor and a friend of my Aunt Sylvia. He and his wife had been over several times. He'd even helped bash out a wall. A perfect choice. The university's fall quarter hadn't started yet. Joe rushed to the phone and I got on the extension to help persuade.

Bob sounded less than enthusiastic.

"But we need you," Joe said.

"I don't know. I should be getting ready for fall quarter."

"It'll only take a couple of days. The exercise will do you good. Besides, you already have a stake in the future of this house."

"How's that?"

"Well, weren't you here when the water came in?"

"No."

"But surely you remember last Valentine's Day when you and I knocked out the wall into the living room?"

"Oh, yes." he paused. "That was when your daughter Joan came down with scarlet fever—"

"You don't have to worry this time," I interrupted. "They're all in school and in perfect health. Besides, now you've had the shots."

The conversation went on for another half hour. Finally he agreed to come.

Poor Bob. Once committed he was gallant about it all. He claimed he enjoyed getting up at dawn to catch the ferry from Seattle. I think he left his house at quarter to six. He assured us he hadn't worn good slacks, when they caught on the nail and ripped. And he only rested for a few minutes when Joe, turning quickly with a two-by-six, accidentally hit him on the side of the head.

But on the last day, Bob plucked his last straw. Joe borrowed his hammer. It had been Bob's father's and his father's before him. Joe didn't intentionally break it. The handle split. Luckily the window was open or the hammerhead would have gone right through the glass. Luckily, too, Bob jumped back as it sailed by.

As I remember he had to catch the next ferry. We haven't seen much of him since then. Come to think of it, Geoff hasn't been back since that summer. Surely we weren't the reason he moved to Africa.

16

I Get Tense in Tents

"**M**om!"
Jenny's voice from the back of the car whined at me above the din.

"Mom!" she howled again. "Tell Robbie to get his feet out of my hair."

I sighed. It was August—camping time again. Joe, who'd fought taking a break on the Fourth of July, who'd vetoed a weekend for two in Canada, and who'd decided against a trip to the ocean, had suddenly declared time out while we all packed up the sleeping bags and the camp stove and traveled up to the Dungeness spit on the Olympic Peninsula to camp out for the weekend.

"But Joe," I asked when the idea was first sprung, "shouldn't we be starting on the north side of the roof? It's going to take a while, and you know how it usually rains the first two weeks in September."

"Look," he said, "you've been after me for weeks to take a trip, and now with Hal in California visiting his mother it seemed like a good time to go camping."

"But Joe," I said again, "when I said a trip, I meant you and me off together to swim in the sun, dance till dawn, and have breakfast in bed."

"Good God." He shook his head. "We can't afford that sort of thing. Did you see the lumber bill we got the other day? We'll be lucky if we can pay it off without taking out a loan. Besides, the kids are all excited, and you'll have a good time once you get there."

I thought about it for a while. I had nagged about getting away. The constant whine of the saw and whap of the hammer were beginning to get to me, and I knew if we let the summer go by it would be another year before I had even this small chance. Maybe it would be fun. Dungeness, famous for its huge crabs, was supposed to be a perfect place to camp. Carole and Alex had gone there one year, and they said the beach was sandy and good for swimming. The spit itself, Alex explained, was a hook of land with a lighthouse on the end.

"It juts right out into the Strait of Juan de Fuca," he said, "and on a clear day you can see Victoria across the water in British Columbia."

"And it's usually clear," Carole added. "That whole area is in the rain shadow of the Olympics."

Oh, why not? I thought, whipping half a pint of fervor into a minor froth. I suppose we'll have a good time. At least it's a change of scene.

But now, as we hummed along the highway, my enthusiasm was dwindling rapidly. It wasn't because I, pampered by years of rest, recreation, and room service, was being forced for the first time out in the woods to mingle with Mother Nature, but because I was being forced to mingle with her for the tenth year in a row. I had, as they say, gone to the well once too often.

It seems inconceivable that anyone not born to the canvas would submit willingly to ten summers of sleeping with a sharp stick under the kidney. It amazes even me. But the explanation was simple—and financial.

A family with six children does not vacation in the Bahamas or spend two weeks in Tahiti, even on the economy plan. It was either camp or stay home and clean out the basement. So we camped—here, there, and everywhere.

Every time we moved to a new base Joe had insisted we famil-
iarize ourselves with the terrain by sleeping on it. David and
Sylvia had gone as toddlers. Jenny and the twins went as babies.
Geoffrey even went prenatally.

I'd snuggled in the sand on a beach east of Tokyo and wakened
at dawn to see the entire population of a fishing village nude so
their good clothes wouldn't get wet running down to the sea to
launch their ships. I'd slept on a shelf in a stone hut halfway up
Mount Fuji and listened as other climbers shuffled past in the
night on their way to sunrise at the summit.

I'd spent days in South Carolina, trapped in a leaking tent
with six bored children, a claustrophobic husband, and a large
bag of rancid diapers. And I'd wakened in the Colorado mountains to find snow piling up against the door.

Virginia to me is a clear lake in the Blue Ridge Mountains.
It's a roll of chicken wire strung around the trunks of several
trees, making a giant playpen for Robbie and Joan, who were
likely to wander off into the bushes never to be seen again.

Pennsylvania is a sudden thunderstorm and soggy sleeping
bags. Ohio is a raccoon stealing a pan of leftover spaghetti, a field
of fireflies at dark. Indiana is listening to Beethoven's Third on
the radio and watching the moon rise over a hill. Missouri is Joan,
just two, falling off a slide and being carried home by Sylvia.

Kansas is two campgrounds, one with mosquitoes large enough
to be registered with the FAA. On the other side of the state, it's
another campground, a picture-postcard, travel- folder site with
trees, grassy meadows, and wild flowers. We could have stayed
there for days, but a tornado blew through the first night, so we
packed up all the gear that wasn't in Oklahoma and moved on.

During our three-year tour in Colorado, our tent was rarely
folded, the soot seldom scraped off our coffeepot. We'd camped in
every kind of weather. We'd camped at altitudes unfit for human
habitation and set up our tents in a grove of quaking aspen.

We'd camped by mountain streams, by dams, and at the
edges of gorges. Once, inadvertently, we camped by a railroad

track. It was hidden in the tall grasses. At two in the morning the milk train screeched by and collapsed our tent in the back draft.

I'd baked birthday cakes on a camp stove, bathed in a toddler's wading pool, changed my clothes by Braille in the privacy of my own sleeping bag, and frequented every Laundromat from Washington State to Washington, D.C.

Somewhere along the way my zest for the great outdoors began to wane. Perhaps it was the third time we made a midnight run for home with a nauseated camper in the back of the car spewing into his sleeping bag. Or maybe when a stray Frisbee knocked the coffeepot off the stove and scalded my leg. It could have been the time I found a black widow spider in my shoe.

Whatever the reason, I knew now as we headed out toward the campground that I was not looking forward to the weekend. I looked at Joe, lover of frosty mornings in clammy clothing, and searched his face for a sign telling me he could be persuaded to turn the car around and head for a motel with a swimming pool, a dimly lit restaurant, and hot showers.

It wasn't there. He pulled into site number thirty-six and turned off the motor. The children untangled themselves and sat up.

"Daddy, can we move to another place, one nearer the bathroom?"

"No, Dad, I like this one. All she does is go to the bathroom."

"At least I go somewhere. You sit and read comics all day."

"I do not."

"Do too "

"Says who?"

"Says me."

I took a deep breath. A large fly lit on my arm, and I could feel its teeth sinking into my flesh. I swatted at it and got out of the car. Joe, supervising the unloading, handed me our sleeping bag.

"Here. Stick this somewhere."

I looked for a spot. The only space left was over by an old log. There was a definite slant to the ground. There always is. I think "camping" is an Old English word that means sleeping on a slant. The only choice one gets is deciding which way to lie.

With my head up I always slide to the bottom of the bag like so much dirty laundry. Head down and my clothes creep up in the night and gather around my neck like a noose. Sideways means I spend the night with muscles taut and clutching so I won't roll into the campfire or under the picnic table.

I threw the bag down. Visions of a vacation in Hawaii swam before my eyes. I could see bodysurfing, endless beaches, and breakfasts on a lanai with fresh papaya and just a squeeze of lime, muffins nestling under the folds of a linen napkin, and hot coffee in china cups.

Joe tapped me on the shoulder. "You want a cracker and a sardine before the kids eat them all? This one fell in the dirt, but I brushed most of it off."

I shook my head. "No, thanks."

"OK." He popped it in his mouth and turned to set up the stove.

I watched him dejectedly. Gritty crackers suit him fine, I thought. He loves the dirt and grime and smelly socks. Every nerve in his body is relaxed and singing. The children love it too—the games of hide and seek, leaping over fallen logs and crouching behind rocks. Wet towels dragged through the sand don't bother any of them. They think it's an adventure to stumble through the dark in the dead of night searching for the pit toilet. Why else would Geoffrey get a faraway look in his eyes at the mere mention of our two-week trek across the country when he was five? Why would he sidle up to Joe and say, "Dad, don't you think that trip was the best time we ever had in our whole lives?" Why would Joe agree?

I shuddered and saw myself, an old woman of ninety, being wheeled out to site thirty-six for "one more camping trip."

"Sit there," I heard Joe's shaky voice tell me, "and once I get the tent up, we can toss the Frisbee for a while."

Suddenly something in me snapped. I grabbed a stick and banged on the coffeepot to get everyone's attention.

"Hey," I said. "I want to make an announcement."

The children stopped scuffling for a moment and looked up.

"I simply want to say that this is my farewell camping trip."

There was a silence. Even Joe stared at me as if I'd just spit on the flag.

"I mean it," I continued. "I've had it. After this weekend my body will crawl into no more sleeping bags. I will make no more vats of camper's stew, and I will patronize no more pay showers."

No one spoke for a minute. Then Geoffrey turned to me. "But, Mom," he said, "we always go camping. It's fun."

"Right, it's fun, but enough's enough, and after ten years this is it for me." I swatted at the fly that was still hovering. It dropped to the ground. "Now, I tell you what we'll do," I said, trying to break up the silence. "We'll make this the best trip we've ever had. Tomorrow we'll walk out to the lighthouse. Then we'll go swimming and after dinner we'll have a big fire and pop corn and tell ghost stories and..." my voice trailed off. I was overcompensating for the guilt I felt at not being the good sport mothers are supposed to be.

Joe came to my rescue. "Come on, kids, don't look so upset," he said. "I'll still go camping with you." He put the last box of groceries down on the picnic table. "Now, as soon as I find my sunglasses we'll all go down and see what the beach is like."

The storm was over. The chatter resumed, and the children trooped off down the trail. Joe waited for me.

"Thanks," I said as I caught up.

"It's all right." He took my hand. "I understand how you feel."

The next morning was bright and clear. After breakfast we washed up the dishes, had a final cup of coffee, and headed off for our walk to the lighthouse. We didn't pack a lunch since I figured it would only take a couple of hours to get out and back.

I was wrong, of course. The lighthouse that appeared to be but a short stroll down the beach was one of those wonderful mirages that shimmers and dances and moves farther away with each step. Our steps covered five miles each way.

Sylvia, Geoffrey, and the twins started off first. Half an hour later Joe, Jenny, and I followed. David stayed at camp. He wanted to finish the book he was reading.

"I'll be down later," he said when we invited him to come with us.

"All right." I bent down to tie my shoes tighter. "See you later." And we headed off for the trail that would take us down to the beach.

When we got there the tide was out. The breeze on the strait was crisp and invigorating, the smell of kelp strong and pungent. We looked for the children, but they were out of sight. I watched a flock of sandpipers skittering along the sand at the water's edge. A wave came in, and they raced up the shore just out of its reach.

"This is fun," I said.

"Yeah." Joe nodded and bent to pick up what looked like an agate. "I wonder where the others disappeared to?"

I looked down the beach. An older couple strolled toward us and a group of children played Follow the Leader, teetering along the old bleached logs that ran down the center of the spit like a spinal cord. Nowhere could I see our scouting party.

"They're probably already there," I said. "The shore bends just enough so everything is around the corner and we wouldn't be able to see them anyway. Let's keep going. They'll be coming soon."

Jenny by this time had deserted us in favor of lying down to get a tan. And as we trudged on, making brief footprints in the hard, wet sand, I wondered if maybe I hadn't been hasty signing off from the world of camping. Here we were. The sun was warm, the wind cool, everyone happy and occupied. What more could I ask? Then the place in my back that had spent the night on an old tree root twinged, and my resolve rushed back.

"Hey, look at this," Joe called out. He pointed to a message scrawled in the sand.

HELLO, MOM AND DAD, it said, and underneath were signatures: GEOFFREY, ROBERT, JOAN, SYLVIA.

"Well, at least we know they've come this far."

"Yes. I was beginning to think they'd turned back and passed us on the other side of the logs."

Twenty minutes later we found the second message. HOW ARE YOU? it said, and the signatures were the same, except that Sylvia's was missing.

"What happened to Sylvia?"

"I don't know. Maybe she got bored or tired and decided to get a tan like Jenny."

From then on we followed the messages like Hansel and Gretel, working our way from one to the other along the beach. The tide had turned, however, and was coming in, and only half of the last message was intact. Shortly after noon we spied them, three bright shirts bounding up and down the beach near the lighthouse.

"There they are," Joe yelled back at me. I was lagging by now, slowing down as through my mind drummed a soft chant: *Who walks out must also walk back.*

"I'm going to rest," I called. "You go on."

But he waited, so I plugged on, and by the time I caught up he was raring to go again. Finally the children saw us and ran back.

"Isn't this neat?" Robbie chattered. "We even went up to the lighthouse."

"Here, Mom." Joan showed me a handful of black and white and orange stones. "Can you hold these for me? I don't have a pocket."

I stuffed them in my shirt. "Where's Sylvia?"

"Oh, she got tired a long time ago and she went back. You want to come look at the lighthouse?"

"No, that's all right. I'm going to sit down for a while. Then we better start back."

"OK." They pulled and tugged at Joe, and he went on with them the last hundred yards or so.

The return trip took twice as long. The tide was way up by now, and whereas we'd strolled out on hard sand, now we had to pick our way through the driftwood and over the logs. What sand we found was soft and dry, and our feet sank in to our ankles. I felt the heat radiating off my legs and the backs of my knees, and the wind which seemed cold now made me wonder. What were the first signs of hypothermia?

Finally off in the distance we sighted the cliff, then the path up to the campground. Even the children were silent now, marching on like robots on automatic pilot, and with our last ounce of strength we climbed the hill and collapsed at our camp.

"You back already?" David asked.

"Yes." I lay there on my sleeping bag, wondering when anything had felt this good. "Where are the girls?"

"Oh, they went to the bathroom. Where else?"

That night I threw thrift to the winds and treated myself to a twenty-cent shower—six full minutes of hot water, guaranteed to run out before you finish rinsing. My leg muscles by then were twitching and convulsing involuntarily. The backs of my knees burned and throbbed. My hair, whipped and gritty, lay on my head like a thatched roof. As I stumbled in the general direction of the bathroom, I met a woman with towel and toothbrush in hand.

"Isn't this a lovely place?" she gushed. "I just adore camping."

I'd seen her earlier. She belonged to a trailer roughly the size of a four-bedroom house.

I nodded.

"It's so healthy, so invigorating," she went on. "Why, we've camped every year since our son was a little boy. Now he's married and he and his wife go."

We'd reached the bathroom, and I opened the door and held it for her. "In fact," she said, and paused so I'd appreciate the thrill of what was coming next, "last month they came here. They had the very site you and your family have now." She smiled. "It was his special treat for her. She'd been through six hours of surgery the week before, and he wanted to give her a rest from housework."

My mouth dropped open, and while I imagined ambulances stretchers and stitches popping like buttons on a tight shirt, she stood there with a smug grin on her face.

"My, that boy does love camping," she continued, ignoring the horror in my eyes. "He says the camping trips he's taken are the best times of his whole life."

I ran all the way back to the campsite. Joe was asleep. So was everyone else. I poked him.

"Joe," I whispered. "Joe, wake up."

"Huh? What's the matter?"

"Listen to me. First thing in the morning, we've got to get out of here. Before breakfast, even. We can eat somewhere on the road."

He looked at me, his eyes glazed. "What's the rush?" "We have to." I glanced at the children sleeping peacefully around the dying fire. Geoffrey turned over and snuggled down deeper into his bag. "We have to leave before they enjoy it any more."

17

Has Anyone Fallen
Off the Roof Yet?

In the world of plasterboard, two-by-fours, and power saws, you know you've arrived when you're given your own carpenter's apron. I got mine on the roof.

I already had a hammer of my own. It was a birthday present. And Joe gave me my own set of screwdrivers for one of those unexpected gifts that says, I love you. But when I qualified as a roofer, mastering shingle hammers, basic flashing, and the art of walking at a slant, he decided I'd earned my own apron.

Actually, my unbridled enthusiasm for life among the shingles came about not so much because I craved an apron of my own but because I wanted to be alone.

We were back in the harness. The north dormer was an accomplished fact with soffits and bargeboards in place, windows on their tracks, and two clerestories fitted into their triangular holes. Except for the weekend at Dungeness, Joe had hammered, sawed, braced, and framed most of his vacation away. Therefore, exercising one of his inalienable rights, he took a day off for a game of golf. This left me at home with the children.

Now, August and children don't mix as well as Norman Rockwell would have you believe.

In June, like taut rubber bands, they are full of pent-up energy. They cut off their jeans, throw on a tie-dyed undershirt, and plunge into summer. They stuff their days full of swimming lessons, bicycle trips to unexplored parts of the Island, and picnics in the woods. At night they strip off their bedding and sleep four abreast in a two-man tent in the middle of the lawn.

By July they're in full swing, building a tree house down near the bay, filching leftover lumber for a raft, floating in the sound on air mattresses, or rowing the dogs across the bay.

But by the time August saunters over the horizon, the tent smells like dirty socks, the bicycle tires are flat, the rafts have either sunk or been dismantled, the tree houses have been abandoned, the air mattresses leak, and the boat's lost its oarlock.

In mid-August it's too late to earn a fortune in the strawberry fields and too early to pick blackberries or make applesauce. It's too late to plant sunflowers and too early to go school shopping. They're bored, so they lie around the house all day complaining.

"There's nothing to do."

"Why can't we have a pool in the back yard?"

"I can't find my shorts."

Spending a mid-August day co-mingling with six summer-weary children is not my idea of fun. Therefore, the morning Joe bounced out of bed, laced up his golf shoes, dug out his clubs, and went out the door, I too leaped into action. I gathered up the shingle hammer, a bundle of shingles, Joe's apron, and some nails and sped to the roof.

They'll never find me here, I thought. Up here the sighs, groans, mutterings, whines, and accusations will be just so much muffled noise.

I looked around. The view was glorious. To the north I could see the high school water tower, the graffiti on its side a jumbled blur. Across the bay a tow truck hauled a mangled convertible into Glenn's Gas Station. To the east, the bay wandered in and out of coves, not really caring if it made the final turn into the busy part of Eagle Harbor. A flock of crows in the willow down by the water

squawked and complained, and I watched a sea gull circle higher
and higher and then dive into the water with a splash.

Obviously my escape to the rooftops was a good idea. The
sun was warm, the air was fresh, and I was alone. I thought of
leaving the shingles where they were. Why not juggle the sensa-
tions of August and morning and solitude a while longer? Then
my puritan ethic, coupled with rumblings from below, snapped
me to attention. No work, no solitude. I picked up a hammer and
filled my pockets with nails.

As I laid out the shingles, I tried to remember all Hal had told
us the night before.

"This is your baby," he'd said. "You don't need my help for this
project, and I've shingled enough roofs in my time to last forever.
Now remember, the first row upside down. Second row directly
over it right side up, then right side up from there to the ridge."

I hammered as quietly as I could, hoping to remain undiscov-
ered. It was futile. I was still on the first row when the children,
like missiles searching out a target, located me and exploded their
complaints in my face.

"Mom, David won't put his cereal bowl in the sink."

"Mom, it's Joan's turn to change the Kitty Litter."

"Mom, why do I have to …

"Mom, make Geoffrey …

"Mom …

I refused the job of arbiter. "That's too bad…. Did he really? …
I find that hard to believe … Now, hand me some nails. Reach
the hammer over there. Bring up some more shingles. Who'll get
me some coffee?"

The scent of work dispersed them, and I continued alone.
When Joe returned from the links, I'd finished the dormer roof.
He was pleased with my work. Of course he was. Joe is pleased
with any work, the more the better.

"Great." He patted the shingles. "Did you have any trouble?"

"No."

"Are you going to cut off this overhang?"

"No, Hal says it slows you down. I'll let you do it later." I emptied the extra nails out of his apron pocket into the can.

"I see you used my apron."

"Yes, not having to carry around a can of nails makes the work go faster."

"Tell you what," he said.

I flinched. He's never learned, despite all my nagging, when to say, "Good job. Take a rest." No, it's always, "Come on, one more hour, one more wall, one more row." I felt my morning's efforts had earned me an afternoon of reading under a tree.

"Tell you what," he said again. "After lunch I'll get you an apron of your own."

"Why?"

"Why what?"

"Why are you getting me my own apron?"

"What do you mean?" His face was innocent and cherubic, his eyes sparkled.

"What do I have to do in exchange for it?"

"Nothing." He sounded hurt. "I merely thought you'd want one when we start the main roof tomorrow."

I was sorry I'd snapped at him. "Of course I would. Thank you." I rubbed my right hip.

"What's the matter?"

"Nothing. My hip's a little sore from scooching along the shingles. Being left-handed, it's the only way I can sit."

"Well, don't worry. You won't have to scooch this afternoon."

I was right. The apron was a bribe for more work.

"Why not?"

"'Cause this afternoon we're going to rip off the old shingles." He jumped in the dormer window, landed with a thud on the floor of Joan's room, and went off downstairs, chuckling.

I didn't need the apron that afternoon, but I wore it anyway. We worked for hours. We tore up the old shingles, then hurled them out behind us like so many jagged Frisbees. The dogs ran back and forth barking and chasing each one as it sailed down the lawn.

By dinnertime, a good section of the roof lay bare.

"There," said Joe, "that's it for today."

He picked up a last hunk of shingle and tossed it. It caught the wind, sailed for a while, and landed in the top of the hawthorn tree. The dogs ignored it. So did I.

The next morning, as dawn was groping its way across the yard, something woke me up—a noise like leaves rustling in the wind, or mice scampering, or rain. Rain. I sat up in bed. That was it—rain. I poked Joe.

"Joe," I said. "Get up. It's raining."

Joe's a selective sleeper. It's a trait left over from the days when we both played dead during the 2:00 a.m. feedings. I can poke him and tell him three burglars are loading the living room into a truck and he doesn't budge, but the news of rain brought him bolt upright.

"Let's go," he said, rummaging around in a daze. "It's time to start roofing."

"But Joe, can't we just roll out the tarp or cover it with plastic or something?"

"No, we don't have enough. Now hurry up before it starts dripping inside."

By the time we got all the tools up there and had gulped down a hasty cup of coffee, it had stopped. I voted for going back to bed, but Joe said no.

"I'll go get a couple of bundles of shingles," he said. "You get out on the roof and start."

I love to shingle. It's a clean, neat, precise job and could be fun if it didn't start at the edge of the roof. It's not that I'm an acrophobiac. I'm not—never have been. I stride to the edges of gorges and peer down at the rocks below. I stand in the front in glass elevators and watch the buildings and cars fall away below me. I had no qualms about straddling the peak of the roof, but when I squatted down at the edge, an unseen force sat down behind me and whispered in my ear. *Watch it there. Oooops, don't swing that hammer so hard, you 'll go over.*

When I put down the hammer, the force gave it a kick, then laughed, saying, *Go ahead, lunge for it, and you '11 end up spread-eagled on the bicycle down there.*

So I let it slide over the edge. Then I climbed up the roof, in the window, down the stairs, through the house, out the door, and picked it up. The force stayed on the roof and cackled. I made the trip seven times in the first hour.

Unfortunately it didn't scare the children. One by one, as they got up, they bounded out on the roof and galloped up, down, over, and right to the edge. Robbie skittered back and forth, challenging Geoffrey to chase him. Sylvia sat on her haunches on the dormer roof and peppered Jenny with bits of wood and old shingles. Joan scooted along beside me like a shadow, handing me nails one at a time.

By noon every muscle in my body quivered from the strain of hanging on, and my voice was hoarse from yelling. "Watch out!... Get away from there! ... Stop that!... Don't run!" It was then that David, who'd slept late, appeared at the dormer window. "Not bad," he said, surveying our work. "Has anyone fallen off the roof yet?"

"David!" I screamed, and my hammer bumped down the roof and over the edge again. "Don't say such a thing."

He shrugged. "I just wondered."

The fear subsided in the afternoon. The farther away I got from the edge, the bolder I became. I lunged at my escaping hammer, ran up the roof to refill my pockets from the can of nails on the dormer roof, and stretched out to get additional shingles. Geoffrey's job was to keep Joe and me supplied, and he put them just out of reach, saying we'd be working up to them. We never did.

By two in the afternoon, we'd finished three rows. They were a little crooked, wobbling here and there like the path of a drunk on his way home, but we thought they looked marvelous.

"Hal wouldn't approve," Joe said, pointing to a large dip. Hal's blessing was like a papal benediction, and we often trembled till he gave it.

"No, but we're getting better, and when we're through he won't notice these first rows."

Hal must have heard me. Not twenty minutes later I looked up to see his car coming down the driveway.

"Thought I'd stop by and see how you're doing."

The next thing I knew he was out on the roof.

"Your lines aren't straight," he said.

Joe moved his leg to hide two shingles that dipped an inch out of line. "We're improving."

Hal grabbed some nails and whipped out his shingle hammer. "Here, let me show you."

He stayed all afternoon, and together we worked furiously —hammering, nailing, straightening out the rows. By five we'd made it across the roof six times, not an amazing amount but, with a roof the size of ours, an accomplishment.

I stood up when Joe called a halt. My right hip felt as if I'd skidded down a hill on it.

"Looks good," Joe said. Hal nodded. "Now if it doesn't rain—" He scanned the sky, and a couple of innocent clouds strolled by and headed north. "If it doesn't rain," he said again, "we should have it made."

"Oh, it won't rain." I headed inside to start dinner.

I heard the first clap of thunder as we got up from the table. Then the rain began. Not a drizzle, as it had been in the morning. It was pouring like an overturned bucket.

Joe jumped up. "Oh, God!" he yelled as we heard the first muffled splat coming from the direction of our bedroom. "Check for leaks ... then get something to put under them." Leaks weren't hard to find. It was as if the ceiling were made of gauze. The children, who thrive on disasters, loved it. It was like a treasure hunt. They shrieked with delight each time they found a new drip.

"Here's another one."

"There's two right together!"

"I found more than you did."

Water poured down the inside of the windows, filled the light fixtures, and ran down the walls. Joe pushed furniture out of the way and tried to stack our books in a safe spot. I balanced on the end of the bed, holding bowls and buckets aloft under a steady stream of water. Sylvia and Jenny emptied the full containers. David and Geoffrey brought in replacements, and the twins scouted for new leaks. In twenty minutes we'd emptied the cupboards of everything that would hold water— thermos bottles, vases, ashtrays, teapots, coffeepots, egg coddlers, crystal bowls. Joan even lined champagne glasses on top of the piano to catch some of the slower leaks. And still the water came. It cascaded off the windowsills like misbegotten waterfalls, and I got out the bath towels to mop it up.

Finally I went back to check our bedroom. A wall of water divided the room, pouring through the ceiling tiles. But at the foot of the bed it stopped, and the rest, like a quilted raft, remained dry.

"It's an omen," I told Joe, "a sign saying we might as well give up."

With that I put on my nightgown and crawled in under the covers.

The next morning dawned bright and clear, and the rains held off for a month till we had the south side bare.

The north side, like the north dormer, had been the community side. Geoff helped some. The children pitched in. Hal even came back for a second session. He never really trusted us to do it alone. But when we got to the south side, school had begun, Joe was back at work, and Hal was busy at home with his own projects. So except on weekends the roof was mine—all mine— and I loved it.

In the morning as the last child trudged off up the hill to catch the bus, I made myself a cup of coffee, grabbed my cigarettes and the radio, put them all on the dormer roof, and began my work.

It was a perfect autumn that year, and with no one to prod me I delayed and dawdled as long as I could. I sat on the roof sipping coffee and watching the day shake itself awake.

The jays, back from their summer vacation, screeched at me and darted in and out of the hazelnut trees, picking the nuts I'd planned to harvest.

"You know, you birds aren't too swift," I called out. "You drop more than you pick."

The jays looked at me and flew on.

Eventually I put my coffee down, turned up the radio, and reached for the hammer.

"Take a shingle. Line it up. Nail it. Take another."

I scooted along, talking to myself and singing along with the radio at the top of my lungs. "To dream the impossible dream,/ To fight the unbeatable foe...

My voice rang out over the bay, and the sea gulls and herons squawked back at me. This certainly was more fun than housework.

Utopia lasted for a few days. Then Joe decided I wasn't fast enough, so he hired Larry to help me. Larry was young, about twenty, strong, efficient, and, most of all, quick. He didn't waste time shouting at the jays. He didn't stride to the peak of the roof and stand there, arms flung wide, pretending he was Robert Goulet. Larry didn't even stop for coffee.

He hefted bundles of shingles out on the roof and snatched up his hammer. *Flap*. Down went a shingle. *Bang- bang*. It was nailed in. *Flap*. Another shingle. *Flap, bang-bang, flap, bang-bang*, he sped across the roof.

Joe was ecstatic with the progress. The roof was pulling up its covers faster than he'd dared hope, and by the eighteenth of September we pounded in the last nail.

There was a ceremony, naturally. We're great on ceremonies. We all scampered over the roof, admiring this row, that bit of flashing, and the work around the chimney. Everyone, even the twins, pointed out where he or she had put in a row.

Jenny climbed up to where Joe was. "Daddy, can we put up the pheasant now?"

The pheasant is our weather vane. He's a stately, hand-painted, wrought-iron beast, and he'd sat in a box waiting for the wind long enough.

Joe thought a minute. "Tell you what," he said. "As soon as you get all the shingles picked up off the ground and put out by the driveway, we'll put up the pheasant."

Jenny, allergic to any sort of work, headed for the window.

"Come back here." He stopped her in mid-flight.

"But, Daddy, I have a headache. I've had it all day."

"And I have homework." Sylvia inched her way to the edge of the roof, presumably to make her escape by jumping onto the balcony.

Joe hadn't spent twenty years in the Air Force for nothing. "Halt."

Everyone froze, even me, and I'd almost made it in the dormer window.

"Vince is lending us the lumberyard truck tomorrow, so we can take the stuff to the dump. We'll have to load fast, so everything must be in one pile."

Robbie and Joan crept over the top of the roof and headed down the other side.

"That means you too." Joe's voice yanked them back.

Once the mutiny was quelled, we worked till dark. We loaded shingles into the wheelbarrow, bumped them around the side of the house, and dumped them. I was granted a temporary leave of absence during the dinner hour, but Joe saw to it I took no deserters with me. After dinner we gathered up the last few piles. Then the pheasant ascended to his roost. I held the compass. Jenny held the flashlight. David held the pheasant. Joe nailed him in. He looked glorious, proud of his new home. Joe gave him a gentle spin, and he whirled noiselessly, caught the wind, and pointed north.

Once the roof was complete, the shingles disposed of, and the nails raked into a pile and thrown out, Joe was at loose ends. Like someone finishing a book without another waiting to be read, he prowled around the house looking for things to do.

I recognized the symptoms, but I was on my toes. The day I saw the words "new project" forming in his eyes, I jumped in.

"Tell you what," I said. "I'll do three weeks of laundry, swab the kitchen floor, clean out the refrigerator, and try to find the furniture under the dust dunes, if you'll go up on the roof and cut off the ends of the shingles. You know what I mean. The ones Hal said would hold us up if we cut them as we nailed them."

It worked. Fall went and winter came, and Joe perched on the roof, gnawing, chewing, cutting, snipping, and biting at the shingles.

"The hell with Hal," he said. "If we ever do this job again we're going to cut as we go along."

And I? I washed my apron and hung it on a nail in the tool room for the duration.

18

The Breeze From the Chicken House Is Freezing My Chow Mein

The phoenix rose out of its ashes. The cathedral at Coventry rose out of the rubble of World War II. And our dining room rose out of half a bedroom and the back hall to the chicken house.

As far as I was concerned, it could have risen out of a mud hole in the back yard, as long as it rose. I'd had my fill of dining ells and breakfast nooks and was determined to endure them no longer.

Dining ells are fine if the hostess can leave the table with her guests after a formal dinner, retire to the living room, and ignore the grease congealing on the plates she left behind. I can't. While the guest of honor is regaling all with his trip to Monterey, I stare at his vacated place wondering why he didn't touch his salad. Either that or my eyes are riveted to the wine stain still spreading slowly over the tablecloth.

Of course, I could clear the table, and I have, but then I miss all the fun. Some hostesses I know can clear the table, wash the dishes, launder the tablecloth, vacuum the carpet, and still keep track of the conversation. Not I. I can either listen to Myrna and Fred explain their strange and wonderful relationship or I can traipse back and forth from table to kitchen concentrating on nothing but which bowl to use for the leftover broccoli. Therefore, since broccoli is eternal and Myrna and Fred aren't, I elect to stay in the living room staring at the table. The only other solution I can think of is to throw a bed sheet over the table.

Kitchen breakfast nooks aren't any more appealing. They're fine for breakfast, and acceptable for lunch, but revolting for dinner. A kitchen does to dinner what pornography does to romance, and, as they say, I'll take romance.

Obviously the former owners of this house weren't riddled with my prejudices—or if they were, they ate out a lot—for nowhere could I find a room that said, "Hi, I'm your dining room."

Consequently, when Paul was drawing up the remodeling plans I was adamant.

"We must have a dining room," I told him.

We were in the kitchen at the time. He looked around at the sink, up to its gunwales in vegetable peelings, at the stove where a pan of gravy scummed quietly, and at the refrigerator, festooned in stickers declaring war on plaque, tooth decay, and pyorrhea.

"I agree," he said.

He cleared a place at the table and made some quick sketches. "If you take out this wall between the back hall and the bedroom and put in a new wall here, you'll have a good- sized dining room. Then, with a regular-sized window on the east and a large plate-glass window on the south, you'll have plenty of light, the morning sun, and a view of the bay too. Of course, you'll have to tear down the chicken house."

Nothing could have pleased me more. The chicken house was not a cozy structure, nor did it have rustic charm. It was simply an awkward building, an afterthought, that clung desperately to the side of the house trying to be accepted. Its walls were bare studs with a little shiplap and tar paper over them to keep out the elements. It was covered with a token roof, designed, I think, to sift impurities out of the rain. Its floor, covered with ragged islands of linoleum, had suffered a fatal attack by carpenter ants.

The children wanted to keep it. Of course they did. They wanted to keep the chickens too. In fact they would have liked a horse, two cows, a goat, three pigs, and a zebra.

"No chickens," I said.

"But we'd have free eggs."

"No."

"But they'd wake us up. We wouldn't need a clock." Jenny's eyes shone. She thinks I'll fall for any idea that saves money.

"No chickens."

"How about fried chicken? We could raise them, sell them, and make lots of money." She doesn't discourage easily.

"No. And that's that."

My trouble is I'm not a compulsive animal lover, and I felt I'd made enough of a concession with two dogs, two cats, and two birds.

The dogs are simpleminded but affable. Sheba, an odd mixture of several breeds, faintly resembles a sheep dog and always looks as if she's still in her bathrobe and curlers. Golly, her brother, received a different set of genes. He's sleek and handsome and dumb. Walk up behind him when he's sleeping and he'll leap to his feet and bark ferociously. When he realizes you're friend, not foe, he gets embarrassed and charges off into the woods, pretending he only barked because he heard a vicious beast off in the brush somewhere.

The cats keep out the mice—at least Tib does. Well, that's not quite accurate. She keeps out the live mice. Dead ones she brings in, depositing them indiscriminately on beds and floors. The other cat, Grey, has a condition. He doesn't do much of anything except glare at me from the mantel and wheeze.

The parakeets, Rex and Charlie, are no longer with us. After a short, happy life of kicking seeds and feathers out of the cage, they escaped out an open window and joined the great parakeet migration to Nicaragua. Before them we'd had Peter, a canary, who sang when the dishwasher was on. He lost a foot in a desperate escape from one of the cats. So we had to widen his perches. He was my favorite, but one week the dishwasher was out of commission and he died. We buried him in our pet cemetery, and Joan placed a bunch of her plastic geraniums on his grave.

With all these beasts to care for, I was not about to have any more animals, least of all chickens. This left us for a year or so with a vacant chicken house. Its demolition was scheduled farther on down the remodeling road.

We should have knocked it down immediately. But as it was we'd swept out the last of the straw, swabbed the linoleum as best we could, and filled it with a couple of old trunks, some rakes, and other garden tools.

Joe, in his first official act as a new owner, had put up a door in the opening between it and the back hall. It was an irregular opening, and the door, cut from one we found under the house, turned out to be more irregular than the opening by about half an inch on all sides. So we'd stuffed old bath mats up against the bottom and improvised some weather-stripping around the edges. This kept out most of the wind.

The back hall itself had become our storage area. First we'd put lawn furniture, packing boxes, and other paraphernalia there. Then, as carpentry began, we'd stacked plasterboard on one wall, two-by-fours on the other, and had filled the space in between with tools, sawhorses, and odd pieces of wood.

By October of 1971 we'd been at the remodeling for a year. The heat was in, the rain was out, and the stairs were up. We were, you might say, between jobs, so Joe got out the blueprints and studied them. It was a toss-up between starting the dining room and putting in more plasterboard upstairs.

"We might as well do the dining room," he said. "Tearing down the chicken house and putting in the windows will have to wait till summer, but we can do enough so we can move the table out of the kitchen."

My joy knew no bounds. The decals about plaque and pyorrhea were getting to me, and the thought of another Thanksgiving surrounded by pots and pans was more than I could bear.

The morning we began I could hardly contain my enthusiasm. The first order of business was to bash out the wall between the back hall and what had been the girls' bedroom. I'd had a taste of bashing when I hammered the heating ducts together, and I wallowed in it. It was the equivalent of a month of psychotherapy.

You see, I come from a long line of semi-controlled china throwers. When life pecks away at our thin skins for too long, we wind up and fling a set of dishes to the floor or sail a mustard jar through the air at some escaping tormentor. But this was better and less maiming.

Shortly after the children left for school, Joe gave the signal and I grabbed my hammer and a crowbar and advanced on one of the three barren closets that huddled like condemned school-bus stops on the bedroom wall.

I wound up and swung. The wood cracked and splintered, and Grey, peering down at me from a hole in the ceiling, wheezed and disappeared. I swung again. The wall fought back.

"Hot damn," I mumbled to myself.

I wrenched a nail out of the brittle wood. It squealed. The old house didn't want to let go, and the nail burned my hand with the heat of leaving.

"This is the life," I said. "Who says scrubbing floors is where it's at?"

Joe stuck his head around the corner. "Did you say something?"

"No." I pried a board loose with the crowbar, and it pulled away. "I was just talking to myself."

"Oh." He returned to his closet, and I heard him rip out another board.

I looked to see how he was doing. The floor was littered with nails, splintered boards, and torn bits of wallboard.

"Fun, isn't it?" I said.

A weird gleam came into his eyes. "Yeah." He wound up and hit a crosspiece.

I retreated. He had the look of a man aiming his own mustard jar.

All morning we wrenched, ripped, and tore down. By the middle of the afternoon, the back hall was waist deep in boards and bent nails. I didn't have any aggression left. I'd hammered away my hatred of laxative commercials, miracle diets, and name tags that say HELLO, I'M_____. I'd dealt with my feelings about scrubbing toilets, picking up towels, cleaning refrigerators, and looking for socks, shoes, pencils, library books, commuter tickets, lunch money, paper clips, and scissors. One whole section of the wall had been dedicated to laying to rest my frustration with mechanical devices: the car radio that plays only if you push the cigarette lighter, closet doors that come off the track, ballpoint pens that won't write, and the portable dishwasher with one locked wheel that must be carried to the sink and back again.

Suddenly I remembered the refrigerator repairman I'd waited for all day Monday. There was one board left dangling from the ceiling like a loose tooth. I swung at it, and it flipped across the room and bounced against the wall.

"That's what I think of you, fella," I said.

With the bashing done, Joe and I took a coffee break, and when the children came home he organized a lumber brigade to move the rubble from the back hall out to the lawn. Sylvia, over in a corner, handed boards to David. He tossed them to Geoffrey, and Geoffrey threw them out the door. Jenny and the twins did the same thing. It didn't take long, and soon it looked like a wood tide around the back steps. It was messy, but we didn't care. Lumber in the yard had become a family tradition—our own personal insignia.

"Have you met the Combses?"

"Oh, yes, aren't you the ones who live behind the pile of broken boards?"

We sawed it, stacked it, burned it, whittled it, and chopped it, and still the piles grew. Even now I come across splinters in the forsythia.

By dinnertime it was all clear. Ruts in the floor told us where the walls had been, and the breeze blew in under the chicken house door and sent little swirls of sawdust dancing around the room.

"Can we move the table in?" Sylvia and Jenny were already hauling in the chairs.

"No. Wait." Joe blocked the entrance. "Not yet."

"Why not?"

"Because."

"Because why?"

"We have to wait till Hal and I put the new wall up."

"We don't need a wall. I like it this way."

"We're putting in a wall, and Hal and I need room to work in, so back with the chairs."

They grumbled but put them back, and once more we wedged ourselves around the table in the kitchen.

"Don't worry," I said. "It won't be long, and when they're through we'll have a party."

And we did, on the eleventh of November, shortly after Hal and Joe finished putting in the studs. It was a twofold celebration, commemorating not only the grand move out of the kitchen but also the fiftieth anniversary of my father's ordination as a priest.

Daddy had, up to now, participated in our numerous remodeling projects from afar. He relied on Mother's often horrendous accounts of our progress to keep him abreast of the general situation, and when he was forced by circumstance to view a dormer or comment on the excellence of a taping job, he harumphed and puffed on his pipe and made up an outlandish story about the time when George Washington asked him to build a barracks at Valley Forge. Naturally no one believed him, not even Joan, who doted on his every word. The whole idea, aside from being historically impossible, was incongruous, for Daddy is the epitome of the British vicar, a gentleman and a scholar, at home with Chaucer and Melville and "the efficacy of prayer" but totally confounded by joists and claw hammers and the use of a power saw.

However, it doesn't take an appreciation of carpentry to enjoy a dinner party, so in his honor, as having survived the Ladies' Auxiliary and the Bishop's Committee for fifty years, and in honor of not having to sit in the kitchen any more, we invited him and Mother and all our friends and held a banquet.

The new dining room performed beautifully and was as dignified as its bare studs would allow. To play down the fact that there was no plasterboard on the new wall, Sylvia made a banner and strung it up on the two-by-fours. HAPPY FIFTIETH,

GRANDADDY! it proclaimed. To play down the fact that the floor was painted two different colors and had three symmetrical holes in it that looked as if they'd been used for ice fishing, we nailed the tops of cat-food cans over the holes and spread out an old rug. To play down the sheets of plasterboard stacked up against the windows I covered them with streamers, and to play down the bare light bulb I bought candles. Then I got out the linen tablecloth, the china, the silver, and the crystal, and I roasted a leg of lamb.

It was a dream fulfilled. The conversation bubbled and sparkled out of sight of the potato peelings. When we were through we retired to the living room, and the broccoli stayed behind.

After the first dinner party, progress on the dining room slowed—what with Thanksgiving and Christmas and all. Then in a burst of January energy, David and I slapped up a few sheets of plasterboard. We worked well together. We usually do. He made accurate measurements, and I remembered to mark the location of the studs so we had something to nail to. Aside from that, the rest of the improvements had to wait for warmer weather.

By June we were ready to begin again—with the demolition of the chicken house. We let Robbie help with this. He was in seventh heaven, and he should have been. Tearing things apart comes naturally to him. In July we rebuilt the east wall and installed a window there. It was one salvaged from another part of the house, and to my delight it swung out.

August was declared picture-window month. The four portholes on the south wall—the ones Joe had nailed shut a year and a half before—were going to be replaced with an enormous picture window. Joe trembled at the thought of it. Glass in any size intimidates him, but huge, shatter-prone sheets of it fill him with terror.

As usual he began to prepare weeks ahead. One day toward the end of July he called home for the noon briefing. It's a daily ritual and a remnant of his Air Force days. The calls are brief and consist of three questions and a directive: "What came in the mail? What are the children and/or you doing? What's for dinner?" and," Here's what I want you and/or the children to do today."

My report was succinct. The mail hadn't come. The children were messing around. Dinner was undecided. He wanted me to do what?

"Rip out the south wall of the dining room. Have David help you." (David hates the noon briefings and takes them with little or no grace. I'm not much better.)

"But Joe, we were going swimming. Does it have to be ripped out now? It's two weeks till you and Hal will be able to work on it."

"I want to be ready."

"What if it rains?"

"Good Lord, Annie, it's not going to rain. It's July."

"But Joe—"

"I've got to go," he interrupted. "There's a customer here."

Sometimes I think he keeps a backlog of customers handy just so he can terminate conversations with me.

Still, David and I ripped out the wall, and twenty minutes after the last board was tom off, clouds rolled in from China and the Kamchatka Peninsula and for ten days the rain fell, the wind blew, and the temperature sat at 50 degrees.

"I can't understand this weather," people told me. "We've never had a summer like this."

I could have told them who brought it on. Joe did, with his "Good Lord, Annie, it's not going to rain." I could have told who brought floods to north Texas the year we moved there. I could have told who crippled Washington, D.C., with a blizzard and dragged a typhoon into Tokyo. But I didn't.

By the time the bad weather lost interest in us and the warm days returned, Hal and Joe were ready to make the window frame. They took a while, selecting the perfect wood, then measuring, cutting, and measuring again, and finally, like surgical residents who step aside at the critical moment, they called up the glass company. This was a job for professionals, and Joe, happy to be relieved of the responsibility, arranged to have the window installed.

On the day the glass was to go in, he got up early. He was worried as usual. What if something happened? What if they tripped and fell? Right after breakfast he went outside and planned the route they would take carrying the glass from the truck. Then he went over it. He picked up rocks and threw Golly's bone under the house and cut the trailing branches off the rosebush. By midmorning we had our instructions: "When they come, don't make any loud noises. Don't ask any questions. Keep out of the way."

Noon found him haunted by the specter of a sudden wind whipping up from the south to send the glass sailing out over the lawn. He checked with the weather bureau.

"Five miles an hour out of the northeast."

By two in the afternoon, when the truck was spotted lurching down our pockmarked driveway, his nerves were like a hand grenade with the pin half out.

"Annie!" he screamed. "Get the children out of the way!" The children were nowhere in sight, and I went in search of someone to keep out of the way. I needn't have bothered. The dogs had decided to be watchdogs. Before the truck was halfway up the driveway, they hurled themselves at it, barking, foaming at the mouth, baring their teeth.

"The dogs!" Joe yelled. "Get the dogs!"

"Here Golly! Here Sheebie!" I whistled and slapped at my knees. The dogs ignored me and tried to bite the tires off the wheels. I advanced on them, and they split up. One circled in front of the truck. The other dashed behind. Joe went one way. I went the other. The men sat in the truck cackling as they watched beast outwit man.

Finally Jenny, the only one who can control them, appeared, and together we caught them and hauled them away to the front lawn. Then we sat on them while the men, still snickering, unloaded the glass and carried it around to the back.

I could hear Joe's voice exploding like a string of firecrackers.

"Geoffrey, move the garbage cans. David, get the lawn chair out of the way. Watch it. Careful! Don't stand there, Sylvia, move the rock."

Jenny and I sat on the dogs, thankful to have a reason for being out of the way.

All of a sudden Joe stopped yelling, and there was a hush. I poked Jenny. "They must be putting the window in now," I said.

She nodded. The dogs were asleep, but we sat on, ever vigilant. Not till we heard the truck doors slam and the engine start up did we rise.

"Go get 'em, Golly," I said, but he was bored by now. There was no challenge left. He stared at me and yawned, and Jenny and I ran around back to see how the window looked. Joe was there, sitting on the scaffolding, smoking a cigarette.

"How do you like it?" he asked.

"It's magnificent. And see, they didn't have any trouble, did they?"

"None at all." He chuckled. "I don't see why you were so worried this morning."

I threw my sweater at him. "Some day," I threatened, "some day I'm going to get you."

It's hard to remember now how the dining room looked when it was half a bedroom and a back hall to the chicken house. Now winter sunrises tap at the east window. In the spring we sit at the table and see the plum tree toss blossoms into the air like confetti. Summer lavishes our dinnertime with various shades of green, and in the fall the copper beech, from where I sit, burns and crackles like a bonfire.

"See?" I say to Joe as we linger over coffee. "Doesn't this beat watching potato peelings turn black?"

19

I Used to Be Six Feet Tall

I'm certain I used to be taller, maybe not six feet, but tall enough to reach the top of the refrigerator without a stool.

Then Joe and I started putting in plasterboard.

We were finishing the stairwell—walling it in, so to speak. Joe, under Hal's direction, had rigged up a scaffolding of sorts with boards strung through ladder rungs and balanced on open beams. It looked like a training camp for trapeze artists, but since I had no aspirations to join the big top and was being forced to work without a net, I inched along the planks with every nerve end in my body screaming, Down, get me down!

A couple of times, because we were using some warped two-by- twelves we'd found in the attic, I got halfway across the chasm when the board tilted and lurched. Fearing certain death, I screamed, flung hammer and nails into the air, and lunged for safety. Joe didn't take to this kindly. Aside from the fact that he was in constant danger from flying debris, he was convinced I was hamming it up to get out of work. If I was, I failed.

"Get back there before you lose your nerve," he'd shout, and I'd blink once or twice to erase the vision of him with a whip and a chair and edge back out.

But Joe didn't start me out at the heights. The first section we attempted was the slanted part of the ceiling, easily reached, with a bit of stretching, by standing on the stairs.

"This should be a cinch," I said when he mapped out the first day's work. "When do we start?"

"Not yet. I have to get some nails, some new knife blades, and of course the plasterboard."

Ah, the plasterboard. I didn't realize it at the time, but in the next year or so thousands of sheets of plasterboard were going to be hauled in the house, stacked up against every available wall, then cut and hammered into place. I would soon grow to hate even the sight of it.

The first day, however, I was blissfully unaware of what was to come. When Joe drove up with the bus loaded down, I helped him haul it in, and we put it in the living room.

"Now what do we do?" I asked.

"First we measure. Get me the tape."

"Is it still hidden in your underwear drawer?"

"Lord, yes. I left my other one out last week and Robbie took it down to the boat. Now it's rusted solid."

I got the tape, and we measured—exactly, right down to the last sixteenth of an inch. Then we laid the plasterboard out on the rug, marked it, and snapped a chalk line. Then Joe cut it and we flipped it over, gave it a whack, breaking it in a straight line, and he cut again. With the second cut a fine line of plaster settled into the shag. I got to my feet.

"I'll get the vacuum and get this up."

Joe looked at me over the top of his glasses. "We don't have time for that. We'll get it when we're finished."

"But it'll grind in."

"Not in a couple of hours."

So I gave in, and by the time I was free to vacuum, the living room looked as if we'd mapped out a badminton court. It still does. In fact, to this day I have the urge to play hopscotch in a section in front of the library doors.

When the first sheet was cut, we carried it through the kitchen into the stairwell. We almost swept the breakfast dishes off the counter as we maneuvered around the comer, but I sidestepped in time, and only a plastic glass bounced off onto the floor.

At the bottom of the stairs, Joe paused, trying to figure out how to get around the newel post, which isn't really a newel post but a support to the ceiling.

"Let's do it this way," he said. "We'll carry it up the stairs. Then you hold it while I come down again and get up on the ladder."

I stared at him, incredulous. One sheet of plasterboard weighs fifty-five pounds and is about as easy to control as a hang glider in a hurricane.

"I can't hold it by myself."

"Sure you can. Grab it right in the middle."

"That won't work. I can't reach across."

"Well, rest it on the banister then."

"But it'll slide."

"No, it won't. Here." He helped me put it down again. "Now, just hang on." He ran down the stairs and up the ladder and snatched it as my fingers were letting go.

"OK. We're going to lift it up now and fit it in right in the corner there."

We lifted it up over our heads against the ceiling. It didn't fit. It was too big.

Joe swore. "Let it down—easy there! Can you hold it while I get the knife to cut some off?"

"No."

He swore again. "Then hold it till I get down from here, and we'll take it back to the living room."

I didn't dare complain again, so I held on till he got down, and back we went. We repeated the process twice, and on the third try it was still a hair too big.

"Hit it in the corner with the flat of your hand," Joe said. "Maybe that will force it in."

I hit. Nothing happened, except it wedged in tighter.

"Hit it again."

I did. Still nothing.

"Give it a good whack. It's almost in."

I gave it a good whack. The corner crumbled, and plaster dust sifted down into my eyes.

Joe didn't say anything. He simply stared. Finally he spoke.

"Let's take it down. We'll cut another piece."

It took us ten minutes to get it unwedged and ten more to cut out a new piece. This time our measurements were not so exact. This time it fit.

"Now, hold it there," said Joe, considerably cheered. "I'm going to get the hammer."

I leaned forward and stretched my arms out, praying it wouldn't fall, and Joe climbed down the ladder. Before he had reached the kitchen I could feel my muscles quivering. Then a dull ache crept into my shoulders, and I knew how the Statue of Liberty must feel having held the torch aloft all these years. I could hear Joe rummaging around in the living room, muttering. "Now where the hell did I put that thing?"

I shifted my weight. His rummaging sounds moved into our bedroom. I stepped backward up one stair and leaned forward, the top of my head against the plasterboard. This enabled me to lower one arm. I could almost hear the blood rushing back into my fingers. Joe was muttering again, this time from the direction of Robbie's room. Carefully I lowered the other arm. Nothing fell, and I stayed that way like a flying buttress. My head flattened slightly.

"Annie!" Joe called from what sounded like Robbie's closet. "Did you let those kids use my hammer again?"

"No," I shouted back. "Hurry up."

"I'm coming as fast as I can. Are you sure you didn't let them take my tools?"

My head inched down into my shoulders, and my knees headed for the tops of my shoes. "I didn't let anyone play with anything. Please hurry."

"I'm coming. I'm coming."

There were a few more unintelligible mumblings, a couple of damns, and finally, " I found it."

He wasn't a moment too soon. I felt like a telescope, retracted, with no place to go.

Under orders, I remained as I was while he hammered in enough nails to hold. Then I sat down on the stairs and rubbed my head.

"See?" Joe said when all the nails were in. "That wasn't so bad, was it?"

We worked this way with all the ceiling pieces, and I grew shorter and shorter. Then one day Hal dropped by to see how we were doing. I was on the plank, suspended over the hallway with my head wedged against the ceiling when I heard the back door open.

"Anyone home?" Hal called.

"In here, Hal." Joe started to get down.

I grabbed his arm. "Keep nailing," I muttered.

"OK, OK."

Hal came to the bottom of the stairs and stood for a moment, taking it all in.

"How do you like it?" Joe asked, inching his way around me.

"Not bad. Not bad at all. But what's that you've got Ann doing?"

"Holding it in place till I nail it. Her arms got tired," he added as an afterthought.

Hal took off his hat and scratched his head, "Dammit, Joe," he said, "you always do things the hard way. Why aren't you using a T bar?"

"What's a T bar?"

"Just what it sounds like—a brace shaped like a T. Prop it up with the crosspiece against the ceiling and you can practically do the job by yourself."

"Where were you three ceilings ago?" I said as I edged my way back to safety, but Hal didn't hear me he was already picking through the stack of lumber, looking for a couple of pieces to make a T bar.

My working conditions improved after that, but that's not to say it was easy.

For one thing, the plasterboard still had to be hauled in and put somewhere. It was a two-man job, and no matter who was number one, it seemed I was always number two. I could be on my hands and knees scrubbing behind the toilet, and I'd hear the old familiar cry.

"Annie! Can you come here? It'll only take a minute."

And there would be Joe with another load of plasterboard.

"Take the other end," he'd say. "We'll be through in no time."

After a few months of this, something began to dawn on me. It seemed no matter which end I took, I always ended up being the one to go backward. I'd stagger from the car, up the porch stairs, and in the back door, stepping on cats and kicking over wastebaskets as I went. Then up the stairs I'd go, bent over like a croquet wicket, and without fail when I got to the top I'd realize I'd been had.

"You did it again," I'd say.

Then Joe would smile innocently. "But, honey, you do it so well."

I carried plasterboard in with Joe, with David, with three of the children on the other end. I even helped the delivery men. This was the worst, and it was my own fault. If I'd had any sense, I would have offered nothing more than to hold the door open or keep the dogs out of the way. But no, I had to offer to help.

At first we carried one sheet at a time. Then the man suggested we take two to make the work go faster. Because I'm never one to admit I can't do something, I'd go along with his silly idea. I'd clutch one end, my fingers would turn white and I could feel all my internal organs dropping, and together we'd stumble into the house to some far corner Joe had designated as that day's storage place.

We stored it everywhere—in the back hall, in the dining room, in our bedroom, upstairs in the children's rooms, in the library, in my study. There was a time or two when the house was so full of plasterboard we had to leave some outside covered with plastic. The more we brought in, the faster we used it. We measured, marked, cut, slapped the sheets up, and hammered them in.

After the stairwell, a closet, and a few rooms, I got fairly adept at it. So one day—why, I don't know—I decided to try it without Joe. I think it was one of those let's-surprise-Daddy projects.

I couldn't do it completely alone, so I drafted David again as my assistant. It was a logical choice. Aside from the fact that he's strong, he also can subtract one and a half inches from three and a third inches without having an emotional breakdown. I am not so blessed, and as a result the holes I cut for wall sockets and light switches end up near the ceiling or in the middle of the wall.

David was lukewarm about becoming an apprentice plasterboarder. Actually he was cold. He was against it, but then he's an intellectual and doesn't take well to physical labor. "Why do I have to do it?"

"Because I can't manage alone."

"What about Geoffrey or Sylvia or...

The list went on and on, and I countered each suggestion with a logical reason. "Because."

Finally, seeing no way out, he gave up and we began.

One thing I'll say about David: he resists work, but when at last he agrees, he's a joy to work with. So it was in the dining room that day.

"All right, Mom. It's four and five eighths inches up from the floor and three inches in from the left side. Got it?"

"Got it."

"Let me check it once more."

"Was it right?"

"Pretty good. Now we allow an eighth of an inch for the width of the saw blade and it should fit perfectly."

It usually did, and we nailed in whole sections as fast as we could cut them.

When Joe came home he was ecstatic. "How'd you do it?"

"David helped me."

"David? Fantastic." He walked around the room patting the walls. It's a tribal ritual with him. He always pats his walls. "You even got a nice tight fit around the switch."

"That's because David did the measuring."

All evening Joe raved. We basked in his praise. We shouldn't have. We were being set up. I realized this the next morning when I drove him to the ferry.

"Say," he said as he got out of the car, "since you and David are so good at putting up walls, how about finishing off the den today?"

He slammed the door and was off before I could protest.

David balked when I broke the news. "That's not fair. Every time I do something and do it well Dad makes it my permanent job."

"Oh, that's not true," I lied.

"It is too. Remember when I had to paint all the trim on the house, and when I had to carry all the shingles up to the roof just because I brought up one bundle for you?"

"But David, it has to be done."

"But why do I have to be the only one to do it? Besides, I can't today. I have to go into Seattle to get my tennis racket restrung."

Unfortunately, the rest of the children had unlimited excuses too, that day and most days thereafter. Oh, once or twice they agreed to lend a hand, and they were more than willing if we were working on their rooms, but most of the time it was:

"I can't. I'm inventing invisible ink."

"I can't. I have to fix my bike."

"I can't. I have to wash my hair and steam my pores open."

Sylvia washed her hair and steamed her pores so much the bathroom broke out in moss. Geoffrey took his bike apart and put it back together three separate times. Jenny wrote all her Christmas thank-you letters in invisible ink. At least she said she did. Once the words disappeared there was no getting them back.

So most of the time Joe and I worked together, or I pleaded with David and he and I worked together, or he and Joe worked together. This was the best combination. It let me out altogether. As I told Joe, "If you and David can get along without me, I'd appreciate it. I have to do the laundry, scrub the floor, vacuum the hall, hem up the draperies, clean out the fireplace, prune the forsythia, comb the dogs, wash my hair, fix my bike, and invent some invisible ink."

20

Hide! Here Comes the Garbage Man

Everyone has natural enemies. I know. I've had plenty. There was the insurance man who turned up at my wedding and, in between sips of champagne, quoted actuary tables. He wanted me to know he could make me rich should Joe not survive the honeymoon. And there was David's second-grade homeroom mother. She had a cookie fetish. This—coupled with a desire to celebrate every holiday, even Mecklenburg Day and National Pussycat Week—left me chained to my oven for nine months.

When we bought this house and the remodeling began, a new enemy turned up—the garbage man.

Now garbage day on Bainbridge Island is not a haul-your-stuff-to-the-street-and-forget-it-affair. Our garbage men are an independent lot. It's something you come to accept. Some of them are more accommodating than a politician in an election year. Others make you wonder if Hitler has any living relatives on the Island. But all are either appreciated or tolerated— unless, of course, you want to stow your garbage under the house or throw it in the back seat of the station wagon and take it to the dump.

When we first moved here, garbage day was a delight. Not only did our garbage man take away mountains of packing cartons and dish crates, but he also told us where to get the TV repaired, how to fix the kitchen faucet, how to contact Harry Barker, the well driller, and how to fit a week's garbage into two cans and a paper sack.

"The secret," he said, picking a couple of apple-juice cans out of the garbage, "is to flatten these."

I tried it. He was right. Unfortunately, the children tried it too. Whap! They spun both ends off a couple of tomato sauce cans. Wham! They threw them on the floor and jumped up and down on them. It smoothed them out, all right, but tomato sauce shot onto the cabinet doors, onto their shoes, and onto the cat.

The kitchen looked like the aftermath of the Saint Valentine's Day Massacre. So I gave up and went back to the old way. The garbage man noticed, but he accepted my excuse with good grace.

Then he moved away, and after a couple of interim garbage men, the Wild Man appeared in our lives.

I don't remember when he first came on the scene. Perhaps we didn't hear him above the whine of the saw and the crash of collapsing walls, but soon I noticed things had changed. There were alien cereal boxes and milk cartons along the driveway. The broken parts of an old tricycle remained stacked up next to the garbage cans for weeks, while wastebaskets disappeared by the hundreds.

As time went on and our weekly refuse included such items as empty paint cans, boxes of bent rusty nails, and unburnable sections of wallboard, we realized he was not happy with us. Most of the time he ignored anything not in the garbage cans proper. Fine. We filled the paint cans with cantaloupe rinds, broke up the wallboard and stuffed it in where we could, and sprinkled rusty nails over the top like a dusting of paprika. This apparently enraged him, and he vented his spleen on the cans. It was as if he emptied them and then threw them against the house.

"I'd hate to come across this guy in a dark alley," Joe remarked one day.

"So would I, and I haven't even seen him yet."

"I'm not sure I want to."

I wasn't either, and all winter for one reason or another I missed his visit. Not because he came at dawn, as they do in the city, or because he came at odd times. I simply wasn't there, or else I was occupied in another part of the house and didn't hear him.

But he came, regularly. Every Tuesday he made his rounds. Every Tuesday old bread wrappers and pot-pie cartons blossomed along the Island roads like dandelions and Queen Anne's lace, and every Tuesday our cans lay in a crumpled heap at the edge of the driveway.

Then spring came, and one Tuesday morning I was outside clipping some lilacs when I heard a distant rumbling. I looked up. A giant white garbage truck was lurching up the driveway. I ducked behind the bush. I didn't want to be seen. I thought I might have to run for my life.

The truck pulled up and I peered through the branches, curious to see what manner of beast would leap out. The door opened and a form swung out, gave the dog a kick, and alighted on the grass.

I couldn't believe my eyes. He wasn't nine feet tall. His arms didn't dangle around his kneecaps, and there were no signs of fur on the back of his paws. He was merely a plain, ordinary-looking young man. He wore an enormous pair of sunglasses—the kind that reflect the world but hide the wearer, so you never know if anyone's home. Other than that he seemed harmless. As he strode up to the cans, I decided to brave it and try to make friends. I came around the edge of the house.

"Hello there."

He looked up but said nothing.

"Isn't this a glorious day?"

Still nothing.

"My, with all the rain we've been having, it's a treat to have a day like this. Not that I don't like rain. Why, when we lived in…" My voice trailed off, and I gave one of those high, empty giggles I do when I'm playing conversational tennis and suddenly notice my opponent has left the court.

He was staring at the garbage. Then he aimed his sunglasses at me.

"Are you ever going to finish this damn remodeling?"

"Lord, I hope so. It seems as if that's all we've been doing, but it's coming along nicely, and soon—"

He turned away, and again I was left with an unfinished sentence and nowhere to put it. As quickly as he came, he went —with one final kick at the dog.

After that I made a point of being out of sight on Tuesdays.

Joe laughed at my cowardice. "He can't be as bad as all that."

"OK, you go out and chat with him."

"I will. The next time I'm home."

He was home the following Tuesday.

"Watch this," he said as we heard the truck approaching. He strolled out the back door and came face to face with the sunglasses.

"Good morning. Nice day, isn't it?"

The Wild Man picked up the can and headed for the truck. "Not if you have to work around this shitty garbage all day."

"You're right," Joe told me later. "Stay out of his way."

I did, and for almost a year things went along uneventfully. Tuesday mornings we dragged the garbage cans out. Tuesday afternoons we carried the mutilated remains back to safety.

Then the following January we had a long period of freezing weather followed by a sudden thaw. The driveway became a spongy morass, and for a few days we parked up at the church and walked in. Not so the Wild Man. He plowed through the mud and muck and sank to his hubcaps a few times. Giant ruts developed. Then they merged and formed craters. When the rains returned, they filled up, and our car pitched and rolled up the driveway like an ocean liner tossed about in a tropical storm.

"How does the Wild Man like our road?" Joe said one morning.

"Don't ask. I'm afraid he'll tell me."

As so often happens, the thought was the mother of the deed, and the next Tuesday, as I was making up the beds, I heard what sounded like a battering ram coming through the back door. I ran to open it.

"Yes?"

The sunglasses glared at me.

"You're going to have to do something about that road."

"I wish we could, but we'd need a grader and a couple of loads of dirt and gravel. We can't afford it. If you hadn't brought your truck in that day—"

He turned, stalked off, and I retreated hastily.

From then on there was no pleasing him. One week he told me I'd have to move the car if I expected him to turn around without hitting it. The next week he had Robbie's bicycle in his hand.

"Tell your kid to keep his bike out of the way."

Then one day the twins found a bedspring on Lovers' Lane, down the county road from our house. They brought it up to the lawn and used it for a trampoline all week. Monday night Joe hauled it over and put it with the rest of the garbage. The next morning the attack on the back door threatened to bend the hinges. I opened it.

"Give me your name and address."

I was too startled to ask why, and I gave it to him, spelling out each word.

"Why does he want our name and address?" I asked Joe that night.

He shrugged. "I don't know. Probably to charge us for the extra stuff."

But when the bill came it was the same as always. Whatever his reason, it must have slipped his mind between Tuesdays, for every week he was at the back door wanting our name and address again.

That was when I started hiding, ignoring his attacks.

I don't hear a thing, I'd tell myself, as I groveled on the closet floor supposedly looking for a lost shoe. Not a thing.

As soon as the banging stopped, I'd run to the window and watch as he went down the driveway. He always paused next to the mailbox. Then he jumped out, wrote something down, presumably our elusive name and address, and went off in a cloud of chicken bones and coffee grounds.

I got away with hiding as long as the children were in school, but one week Joan was home when he came.

"Mom," she called as I cowered in the bathroom.

"Mom, the garbage man's knocking."

I signaled her to be quiet. "Tell him I'm in the shower," I whispered. Then, because it's not nice to lie and mothers have to be an example, I stripped down and leaped in.

Tuesdays became a nightmare. I worried about them all Monday and most of Monday night. Around two in the morning I'd wake up in terror.

"Joe. Joe, do you have the car parked out of the Wild Man's way?"

"Huh?"

"Did you move the VW?"

"Yes. Go to sleep."

Finally I'd had enough, and I decided to try a new tack. Spurred on by a spate of "How to win friends, intimidate enemies, and deal effectively with the general public" books, I made up my mind to win him over with gentle humor.

The perfect time came. We were in the middle of a big push to finish the upstairs. Refuse abounded, and the garbage cans were almost hidden under the mountain of junk.

"This should send him into a furor," Joe said, as he balanced a putty bucket on top of the pile. "You'll have to hide under the bed this week."

"Don't worry." I searched my pockets for a pen. "I'm going to leave this note to cheer him up."

I took an old paper bag, wrote *Sony, Luv* on it, and secured it under the lid.

I could hardly wait for morning to come. About eight thirty I heard the truck. I rushed to the window and peered out from behind the curtains. He leaped out as usual, kicked at the dog as usual, and strode over to the cans. Then he stopped.

"He's found it," I said out loud, and I chuckled at the thought of my cleverness. I watched him read. His face remained stony.

Then he reached in his pocket for a pencil, wrote something on the bottom of my note, ignored the pile of junk, and left.

I ran outside. Under my message was written *Sorry, Luv, it's too much and too heavy*.

Joe sneered at me when he came home. "I told you it wouldn't do any good. I'm going to call the company. We pay the maximum rate. He's supposed to take it all."

"No, wait. Have patience. These things take time."

The next week I had another message waiting for him. *But Luv, it won't bum, won't compost, and the Goodwill won't take it*.

This time he didn't even answer my note.

Joe was furious. "That does it. I'm going to call."

He did, that week and every week for a month. Each time they assured him all would be taken care of. Each time I penned another amusing plea. Each week the garbage remained. Finally, after threats of suit and mayhem, the garbage was taken away.

"See," I said, "he's come around. I think I'll leave him a thank-you note."

Joe snorted, but I was used to his derision by now. I made a large sign: *Thanks, Luv, it certainly looks neat now*.

That Tuesday, after the truck had careened off down the road, I went outside. Sure enough, he'd answered. Under my note was *You're welcome, Luv, and it's going to cost you a neat $3.00 extra too*.

I'm back to hiding, and as long as I'm in the shower on Tuesdays, I wash my hair.

21

Stay in Line Please, We'll Be Viewing the Laundry Chute any Minute

Had Joe been Michelangelo painting the ceiling of the Sistine Chapel, historians would have noted he spent an inordinate amount of time on the streets of Rome saying to passersby, "Say, I've just finished God's index finger. Come look. I'll give you a tour and show you how it turned out."

Joe loves to give tours. It's something about him we've come to accept. Let anyone get within a mile of our house and he persuades them to come take a look. Some go willingly. Some ask to go. Others have no choice. At his insistence newsboys have peered into our closets, marching mothers have inspected our drain field, and the UPS man was subjected to a short course on miter joints.

Joe's rebuilt the stairs in song and story so often the treads are worn. He's resurrected the torn-down chicken house till it seems to lurk out there beyond the dining room like a ghost limb after an amputation, and to this day I think there are only fourteen people on Bainbridge who haven't heard him describe the fiberglass itch. They're bedridden.

This tour business isn't anything new. He's been at it since the first day we moved in. Early showings were conducted with blueprints in hand. Some aged relatives we hadn't seen in six years would stop by to see us, and no sooner had they stepped out of their car than Joe had them trailing after him like ducks crossing the road. He had a regular agenda.

"This is the utility room. See the trapdoor in the ceiling? That's the way to the attic. If you'll hop up on this table I'll get you a flashlight and you can see how big it is up there. Well, if you'd rather not, I'll take you up the ladder later.

"To the left is the bathroom."

The bathroom door was minus a lock at the time, and after a few surprise visitations, I took to singing in the shower as a matter of course.

After the bathroom, the tour went into the kitchen, then to the back hall for a brief lecture on dining rooms—past and future. Then, skipping to keep up, the visitors were led through the rest of the main floor, the living room, the library, the bedrooms. It didn't matter if there were clothes all over the floor, if the beds were unmade, or even if I was still in bed. Joe would throw the door open and say, "This is our bedroom. We're going to knock down this wall, move that window, and put a closet in here. Oh... hello there. You remember my wife, Ann, don't you?"

For a finale he took them back to the kitchen and unrolled the blueprints on the table.

"See, this is where I showed you we'll be putting in the new wall."

Those who hadn't paid attention were taken back to the site to refresh their memory. Then, regardless of race, creed, or the state of one's arthritic knees, he herded them outside and up the ladder into the attic. Visitors in wheelchairs were exempt, but other than that Joe brooked no exceptions.

Once we began the actual work and found we could cut a hole in the ceiling without the roof caving in, Joe was like Archimedes and his bathwater. He couldn't believe what he'd done. Rather than run naked through the streets of Winslow, however, he dragged people into the house to marvel with him over the miracle of carpentry.

Deliverymen from the lumberyard were some he preyed on a lot. They trudged in, stacked plywood against the far wall, and when they were through, Joe sprang into the doorway blocking their retreat. "Have you noticed what we've done since you were here last Thursday?" His innocent smile belied his purpose. "You remember the soleplates and the top plates? Well, now we've finished the studding and have framed in the window." He gave the window a pat. "How do you like the looks of that header? Why, two weeks ago I didn't know what a header was."

His enthusiasm was contagious, and they all agreed: That was one fine header.

Strangers who happened in the driveway were another object of Joe's tourism fetish. He let a few get away at first. He was over-anxious and scared them off with his, "Hi! Wanna see a house?" Then he modified his approach.

"The Howards? No, this isn't their house. They live down the other road. Turn right at the fork. You can't miss it. It doesn't have a balcony like ours."

He paused slightly, giving them time to glance at our balcony. Then he chuckled.

"Of course, we didn't have a balcony last week. In fact I put in the last of the uprights only yesterday."

At this point someone always said, "You mean you made it yourself?" and Joe was home free.

Relatives and repeaters, who'd had the grand tour, were subjected to mini-tours—updates, so to speak.

"Come see the west wall. We finished it yesterday." Or, "Ann's finishing the grout. Bring your coffee in the bathroom and see how well she's doing."

If Mother hadn't blocked it from her memory, she'd be able to recall having seen each nail, each coat of paint, each pane of glass, and each piece of flashing we've put in. Jan and Carole have been forced on so many tours they won't get out of their car unless Joe promises he won't ask them to crawl under the house to look at the heating ducts.

This doesn't deter Joe. There are plenty who are willing to tour—or, better yet, who are willing to watch him work. He doesn't give them much choice. It's either watch or play Monopoly with Robbie and Joan.

Some people arrive, however, with no intention of moving out of the living room. They've come with pictures of their Hawaiian vacation or news about their new boat. They're not interested in clerestory windows or Formica cement. Joe outfoxes them every time.

"Before you sit down," he says, "let me show you what I'm doing upstairs. Annie, bring up a couple of chairs. We can talk while I finish. I have a couple of boards left to nail in."

These visits are usually short. You can't shout above the roar of a power saw and still describe a moonlit luau successfully.

Other people are simply not tour material. They have missions of their own—petitions to be signed, donations to be solicited, encyclopedias to be sold, religious conversions to be accomplished. Joe greets them effusively, then edges to the door.

"If you folks will excuse me," he says, "I have some work to do upstairs."

And he's gone, leaving me trapped. Periodically he wanders back in.

"I'm sorry. I didn't mean to interrupt. I'm looking for my hammer. Would you mind lifting your feet? I think it's under your chair."

Several of these trips usually send them rushing for their cars, encyclopedias and petitions clasped to their bosoms.

But for the hardier ones who remain, Joe uses other tactics. One lady, bent on revealing God's plan for our family, was one of his victims. She arrived at our door early one morning, starched and prim, full of missionary zeal. After blanching at the suggestion of a tour of our plumbing facilities, she perched on the edge of the couch, knees and ankles locked together in true Protestant fashion. Immediately she whipped out three pamphlets which, she claimed, would change our lives.

Joe got up and left. "I'm going upstairs to paint the bathroom cabinet," he said.

She glared at him, turned to me and flipped open a pamphlet.

"You'll notice on three here, Mrs. Combs, there's an article entitled 'God Has His Eyes on You.' "

"Annie!" Joe's voice bounced down the stairs. "Have you seen the screwdriver? I can't get this damn paint lid off."

I leaped up and rushed to the bottom of the stairs. "I think it's in Robbie's room. Look on his dresser."

As there was no reply, I went back to the living room. "I'm sorry. Now, what were you saying?"

She sighed and started her speech over again. "You'll notice here on page three, Mrs. Combs—"

Another bellow from above. "It's not there. How the hell can I paint if I can't get the can open?"

Again I excused myself, and again we went back to the beginning. I must say she persevered. She kept her finger glued to page three while Joe demanded turpentine and rags, called down twice for Band-Aids, and accused me of watering down his latex. She didn't bolt and run till Joe dropped the paint and let forth with a volley of obscenities that rolled her eyes back in her head. Her last words as she ran out the door, tripping over the dog's dish, were, "Page three, Mrs. Combs, page three. Don't forget, God has his eyes on you."

I glanced at heaven, then closed the door.

After that, I raced Joe to the exit whenever a lone crusader appeared on our doorstep.

At the height of the tourist season, somewhere between the construction of the balcony and the reroofing, one fact became abundantly clear. Tourism was great for Joe, but when he vaulted off the scaffolding to give yet another demonstration of shingle snipping, I was left with my hammer in my hand to carry on. So in self-defense I joined him, and together we became quite a team.

Joe astounded his audiences with facts and details. "This project, finished on the twenty-third of February, took three and one half months to complete and used up seventy-six sheets of plasterboard, one hundred and twenty-seven two-by- fours, and approximately forty pounds of nails."

I furnished the background material. I described blisters, the pain of stepping on a nail, and how it feels to stagger out of bed at three in the morning, go out in the rain with my nightgown flapping around my ankles, climb to the attic, and put coffee cans under the new leaks in the roof.

Then, lest I not get credit for my efforts, I mentioned my part in each accomplishment. "I dug the furnace hole myself... This wall David and I put up... You can't see any nail holes, can you? That's because I countersunk them and filled them with putty."

The children, when they were along, supplied their own brand of color.

"Three days after we put the rug down, our dog threw up on it. That's why it's a different color over here."

"When we tore down the bathroom wall there were dead rats in the wall."

"Do you want to know what Mom wrote on the inside of the wall when she was mad at Daddy?"

Hal didn't give tours at first. In fact, his jaws tightened and he bit down on his pipe stem every time Joe dropped his hammer and hurried to take another party through. But one by one as the projects were finished and the house became as much a monu-ment to his skills as to our efforts, he started giving after-hours tours. They differed from Joe's. Joe's were usually conducted mid-project, so upheaval was excusable. Hal came when supposedly I had restored order. I never had. The first time was the worst.

It was around nine in the morning. The breakfast dishes were heaped on the counter. Piles of laundry lay on the bathroom floor hoping for a turn at the washing machine. I was doing what I always do when the projects pile up and I don't know where to start. I was reading the paper, up to and including the want ads and the Marriage Dissolutions Granted.

I'd poured my third cup of coffee and was halfway through the crossword puzzle when I heard a car pull up. I ran to the window. It was Hal and a young couple who looked as if they were charter members of the White Glove League. Hal pointed to the balcony and with gestures rebuilt it. They nodded appreciatively. I snatched a pile of towels off the bathroom floor and stuffed them in the washer. Then I bounded into the kitchen, filled the sink with hot sudsy water, and slid the dishes in under the bubbles. The voices were circling the house, apparently heading for the well. I dashed into the bedroom, pulled the covers up into some semblance of neatness, grabbed magazines and papers off the floor, and shut the closet door. I was whirling through the living room when they came in.

Hal looked sheepish at being caught giving a tour, but he had a ready excuse. "These folks want me to help them with some kitchen cabinets. I thought I'd show them yours."

"Fine," I said. "Fine. These are marvelous cabinets. See, the shelves slide out." I pulled one out to demonstrate and the catfood box tipped over and showered Friskies all over the floor. I scooped them up with my hands. Everyone looked the other way.

"Is it all right if I show them the rest of the house?" Hal asked. "They've heard me tell about it so often."

Mr. and Mrs. White Glove nodded like puppets, and I trilled a panicky, "Of course, of course."

Then my mind snapped awake. Oh, Lord, they were going upstairs. I pushed past them and dashed ahead to flush toilets, hide Sylvia's *True Romances*, gather up David's underwear, and kick a path through Robbie's room. Then I pulled up my girdle, pulled down my sweatshirt, and joined the group.

"Excuse the beds," I said. "Today's sheet-changing day, and I see Joan has all her laundry ready for me here by the door."

"My, it's lucky Jenny took her curtains down. I'd almost forgotten I was going to wash them for her this afternoon." I could tell Mrs. White Glove was impressed with all the laundry I was going to do. So was I. I'd be at it for two weeks at least.

Hal didn't seem to notice the mess, which proves people can be conditioned to predictable situations. His friends, however, didn't place their feet down with abandon, and in Robbie's room the navigable path was so narrow they held on to each other lest they topple.

"Oh, one thing I forgot to show you," Hal said as we completed the upstairs viewing. "I want you to see the drawers in the kitchen." He led the way down and opened up the silverware drawer. "I divided the drawers so Ann could keep her silverware separate."

I reached in quickly and retrieved a dirty sock from the spoon section. "Strange where children will put things when they're helping Mommy clean up, isn't it?" I said, inviting them to join in on the hilarity of it all. They declined, and Hal sped them to the next exhibit.

Nothing was missed that day. The closet under the stairs that resembled a Goodwill drop box. The bathtub with a ring that looked like a high-tide mark. The dining room where a bouquet of spent forsythia shed silently like dandruff. And the den, a mine field of lumber, carpet remnants, and coffee cans filled with nails.

By the time the tour ended my laugh was wispy and vapid, my pockets were bulging with debris I'd picked up off the floor, and my resolve was strong. This wouldn't happen again.

The rest of the day was spent vacuuming, washing, mopping, and dusting.

"Who's coming?" Jenny asked as I led her to the closet and handed her a hanger for her coat.

"No one," I snapped.

I was right. No one was coming, and no one did—till I relaxed my hold on the broom and the dustcloth and the house disintegrated again.

Most of our tourists were properly impressed with our work. They oohed and aahed and fed our egos with appropriate gasps of surprise and amazement.

"Do you mean with six children you still find time to shingle the roof?" (There's a certain mystique about having six children and still managing to make it out of bed in the morning. I don't understand it, but I capitalize on it.)

"Oh, it's not too bad. I try to organize my time."

Other people, women mostly, got so caught up in the mood of it all that they poured forth suggestions for changes.

"Why don't you make the upstairs into two big dormitories, one for the girls and one for the boys? I bet they'd like that better."

They didn't know our children. Their experiences together have brought new depth to the old adage "Familiarity breeds contempt."

A few gloom mongers, like Sven, claimed we'd done everything wrong, but we ignored them.

For five years our tour schedule kept a steady pace. Even the children tramped through with friends, friends of friends, dogs, and dogs of dogs.

Then one day the assessor drove up. Had I known who it was I'd have hidden in the shower as I do for the Wild Man. As it was, I rushed out to greet him.

"How do you do," he said, handing me his card. "I'm from the county assessor's office."

I slumped. I'd been dreading this day, and my whole remodeling life passed before my eyes.

"Let's see." He flipped through a sheaf of papers. "It looks as if you've done some remodeling here. Isn't that balcony new?"

I glanced up at our beautiful balcony. "Oh, that thing, it's not much, really."

He nodded suspiciously. "It states here that the upstairs is an empty attic. It doesn't look empty to me. Do you mind if I see it?"

What could I say? "Not on your life, buddy," or, "Are you kidding, over my dead body"? All I could think of was where was Joe now that the big tour had arrived.

"Of course, please come in." I went ahead. "I'll open the door. You know how shaky these old doors are."

I heaved it open, hoping it would fall off its hinges. It didn't and we went in. For the first time in months the kitchen was neat. Hal had been down with a group the day before. I cursed myself for having cleaned it.

"Nice," he said.

I pried loose a piece of Formica on the counter, and kicked at the cabinet door that doesn't close properly. It sprang open again.

"Nice if you don't mind counters that are falling apart and doors that won't shut." My disloyalty astounded me, but I kept going. "Nice if you can live with wind coming in the cracks and through the wall plug."

I grabbed his hand to let him feel the breeze. He shook me off. Apparently he's used to desperate women.

"And look here." I spun the dishwasher into the center of the room. "See where the tiles have come up? This spot used to look like Texas backward, but with the leaks from the kitchen sink more and more tiles have disintegrated. Now it looks like Alaska. See, here are the Aleutians."

I poked at it with my foot and Attu came loose and slid across the floor. But he was unimpressed. He was looking through into the dining room.

"Isn't this new?"

The sun was shining in the window and the mottled green carpet gave off a glow that transformed the room into a summer hideaway in the forest.

"Oh, that. We had to have somewhere to eat. The floor is so full of holes we nailed lids from cat-food cans over them and glued down the rug." I pulled at the rug, but he stopped me.

"That's all right, I believe you."

Next we went upstairs.

"Watch the banister. The cats use it for a scratching post. It's got slivers. No, no, don't lean on it. It'll give way."

We went into Geoffrey's room. His eyes lit up.

"Another balcony, I see."

"Totally useless," I broke in. Unless, I added to myself, you like to stand out there and look at the moonlight through the branches of the fir tree.

The tour continued. I pointed out the water marks on David's wall where the roof had leaked. I explained that the double sink was a gift. "If we'd had to buy one we'd be using a bucket instead."

I repeated all the local propaganda about skylights when he showed interest in ours. And still he took copious notes and mumbled, "Large rooms," "carpeting," "second bath," "built- ins."

He was impressed, I could tell. I was depressed, he could tell. Finally the tour ended.

"Thank you, Mrs. Combs," he said. "Now, if I may, I'll take a look around the property."

I shrugged. I was drained. "Go ahead, but watch out for the rat carcasses. The dogs strew them all over."

I shut the door and leaned on it as they do in the movies when there's no hope of saving the farm. As if on cue, the phone rang. Joe's ESP is, at times, unsettling.

"Hi," he said. "What's going on?"

"Nothing much, Michelangelo. I've just given my last tour. That's all."

"Huh?"

"Well, Joe, let me put it this way. The county assessor came, saw, and loved God's index finger."

22

Tile and Grout and Things That Collapse in the Night

We bought this house for various reasons. For one thing, it's comfortable, like a grandmother's lap. For another, it's all by itself, nestled in among the trees and overlooking the bay. But one of the major reasons for slapping down our earnest money right away was that it has an enormous bathroom. Now, we didn't crave sunken tubs or saunas or infrared heating units in the ceiling. Space was what we wanted, and as it turned out, space was all we got.

The previous owner had redecorated the bathroom with paint and paper and gilt accent pieces, but like an old whore in a new dress, the embellishments failed to hide the imperfections.

The tub, seven feet long and deep enough for submarine maneuvers, was encased in a warped plywood box, and it nestled in a niche of the same warped plywood, giving the bather a feeling he and his tub were plowing through the high seas in a typhoon. The toilet extended the nautical theme by rocking gently back and forth on its base, and the cabinets, made out of rough shiplap with a coat of paint to hold down the splinters, completed the picture. It even seemed fitting that the cabinet doors had been installed with their hinges upside down, and once or twice a week the pins fell out and the doors clattered to the floor.

Unquestionably, it was not modern, but we could live with that. What we couldn't live with was the absence of a shower. A shower is a necessity in a family where a school morning finds seven half-clad people in line outside the bathroom door while the eighth lounges in suds and perfume and contemplates shaving her legs. "Line 'em up, run 'em through, dry 'em off"—that's our motto. And it's only possible with a shower, a whip, and a stopwatch.

We knew when we moved in that the bathroom was due for an overhaul eventually, but in the meantime Joe and I were determined to tile around the tub and rig up a shower of sorts. This was in our pre-Hal days when our expertise was picked up off the streets and when we had more confidence than caution. Therefore, ignoring any possibility of failure, we gathered trowels, tiles, grout, and mastic and set to work.

Joe doesn't take well to piece work. He says his hands are too wide, his fingers too stubby. Not me. The more intricate something is the better I like it, so I got the installation job. I loved it. Of course I did. I love anything that takes me away from housework. I felt like a brain surgeon with assistants waiting on my every whim.

"Hand me the trowel... now the rag. Cut another tile. Make this one two and a quarter inches wide... Easy does it... Is this row plumb?"

Joe and the children were at my beck and call. They brought me coffee, sent lunch in on a tray, took phone messages, cleaned up the kitchen, and cooked dinner. I stood in the tub, slapping on row after row of tile. Joe scored and cut the tiles and handed them to me. Every now and then I hopped out, stood back, squinted one eye, and admired my work. Then I hopped back in and began another row.

One place gave us trouble—the space between the edge of the tub and the wall. It was shaped like the remnants of cookie dough after the cookies have been cut, and, as one plumber we consulted pointed out, it was too small for regular tiles. After soliciting and discarding random suggestions, we decided to break up some of the tiles we had, place them strategically like broken walnuts on top of a cake, then fill in the spaces with grout.

The plan worked perfectly, with one slight exception. Cookbooks don't require one to level a cake, and it didn't occur to me to level the tile bed either. Days later, after the grout had dried and the shower was in commission, Joe noticed water gathering in scummy little pools in the corner.

"I don't like the looks of it," Joe said. "Standing water means trouble."

"Oh, that." I sucked up the water with a sponge. "That's easily fixed. If everyone wipes up after their showers, it'll be fine."

I didn't really believe they would any more than I counted on towels being hung up or the toothpaste cap being put back on. And I was right. Still, the water never stood long.

"Where do you think it goes?" Joe asked one day.

"It evaporates. The Christmas cactus sucks up the moisture. That's why plants thrive in bathrooms."

I like this theory, and I stuck to it till the floor started to buckle. Even then I was loath to give it up.

"Come now, Joe, this can't all be due to seepage, especially since the toilet overflows every twenty minutes."

He had to agree there. Eight of us were living with a twenty-year-old septic system designed, I think, for two old spinsters, one of whom was never home. Though we tried to ignore it, it was obvious to even the most casual observer that a new septic tank was needed. We weren't casual, however— not about the cost. So we muddled along, mopping, bailing, swabbing, and blaming the undulating floor on the seepage around the tub.

Then Sylvia and I broke the toilet bowl. We had the best of intentions. I'd bought a new seat to replace the cracked one, and we were in a hurry to install it. In our haste we tapped one of the bolts too energetically with the hammer, and a hunk of porcelain fell off in our hands.

I rushed off to the lumberyard and cornered Vince just as he was getting ready to close up.

"You've got to help me," I panted, and with modified gestures and laundered terminology I explained what had happened.

"Don't panic," he said. "This ought to hold it for a while." And he handed me some porcelain glue.

It was one of those glues they advertise as being strong enough to lift an elephant. Heaven help the elephant, for it didn't hold the porcelain for long, and every time the piece fell off we were awash again.

Finally, Joe could stand it no longer.

"The toilet has to be replaced, and something has to be done about this floor before it rots out."

Luckily, by this time we knew Hal, and Hal knew plumbing. We outlined our plan to him.

"Is it feasible?" Joe asked.

"Sure, nothing to it. Rip everything out and we'll start from scratch. Then you better consider a new septic tank."

"Yeah, yeah." Joe waved away the idea as one waves away a mosquito.

Hal went on. "Take out all the tiling, then call me," he said, and like a doctor who's prescribed two aspirin and bed rest he went home, leaving us to pry tiles off the walls.

It took us several days and several nights. The tiles didn't come off as easily as they'd gone on. Some chipped. Some split in half. The mastic stuck on the walls and looked like skin peeling after a sunburn. We stacked the whole tiles in one box, and the larger of the broken ones in another. When we were through, Joe called Hal. As luck would have it, he said he could come the next day.

Joe told me the news, then added, "By this time tomorrow the tub and the toilet will be gone. Are you ready?"

I wasn't and never would be. I consider plumbing indispensable, like hot coffee, a refrigerator, and a dishwasher. I'm not one to yearn for the simplicity of the good old outhouse days, and the prospect of nocturnal sprints into the woods awakened none of my romantic instincts.

As a concession to propriety and the capriciousness of Pacific Northwest weather, Mother had presented us with a contraption called a Porta-toi. Its presence gave me little consolation. It wasn't one of those sleek chemical affairs you find in four-room tents at the ocean. This monster was designed on the order of a folding chair, with the same propensity for collapsing at inconvenient moments. With it came a decade's supply of plastic bags. I glanced at the directions, then put them away. I didn't want or need to know that much about camping with toddlers or surviving long motor trips with the newly trained.

"No, Joe," I said. "I'm not ready."

But ready or not, the next day—Sunday—came. So did Hal, and by noon tub and toilet had been wrenched free from their moorings and set outside on the lawn. Robbie immediately leaped into the tub and set sail to find the pirates who patrol the tall grasses just off our property.

We bid him bon voyage, then Joe was all business again.

"OK, Annie," he said. "Hal and I are going under the house to hook the pipes back up. I want you to stay in the bathroom so you can hear me when we need the water back on. David, stay here in the yard. Your mother will let you know when we're ready. Geoffrey, your post is in the pump house. David will signal you."

Geoffrey grumbled, "Why me?" David asked for time to get his tennis ball and racket so he could volley against the side of the house while waiting. The rest of the children, sensing they might be called upon to volunteer, scuttled away like crabs escaping from an upturned rock.

I trudged inside, sat down on a little stool in the bathroom, and peered into the hole in the floor. I couldn't see much except dirt, cobwebs, and what I suspected were the remnants of a long-dead rodent. The suffocating smell of damp, musky darkness enveloped me, and I pushed the stool back a ways and turned my attention to the shapes in the wallpaper design.

After a while, I got up. "How's it coming?" I called.

There was no answer, only mumblings and an occasional burst of laughter. I waited, staring at the wallpaper. I found if I squinted I could see the face of a dragon and a ballerina.

David broke my reverie. He had a message from Geoffrey. He was tired. He had a stomachache. He wanted to go down to Toby's and work on their fort. Could he get out?

"No."

Again I waited. The cat came to investigate, sniffed around, and disappeared down the hole.

So this is how Paul Revere felt as he waited for one light or two, I thought. It's a wonder he didn't say to hell with the British and go home to bed.

Finally Joe yelled up, "Turn on the water!"

I went to the window and called to David. "Turn on the water."

He loped over to the pump house. "Turn on the water."

There was a pause.

"It's on," he called.

I went back. "It's on."

I listened. I could hear the gurgling and spluttering as the water churned through the pipes. Then there was a gush that sounded as if a fire hydrant had been knocked over.

Joe bellowed, "Turn it off! Turn it off!"

I raced back to the window. "Turn it off!"

David looked quizzical for a moment, then relayed the message. "Turn it off."

I went back to see what happened, and the cat, a wet mass of fur, shot past me and bounded upstairs.

"What happened?" I called.

"I don't know. Don't bother me now." Even Joe's voice sounded wet.

After another half hour at our battle stations, the cry came again. "Turn it on!"

The cry echoed from me to David to Geoffrey, and I held my breath. Again there was a gurgling, but this time no eruption. I turned on the faucet in the sink and water spurted out, then settled down to a steady stream.

"It's OK up here," I called.

When Joe and Hal crawled out from under the house they looked like Welsh coal miners coming off the last shift.

"What happened?" I asked.

Hal shook his head and walked away.

Joe glared at me. "Don't ask," he said.

I never did find out.

The next few days—or was it months?—were living proof of Einstein's theory of relativity. Time expanded like leftovers. On Monday morning, bare moments after Joe had promised me plumbing by dusk, he and Hal decided to postpone the installation in favor of framing in the upstairs bathroom. I wasn't in on the decision, and I saw Joe's guilty backward glance as they headed out the driveway on their way to the lumberyard.

All day they hammered, sawed, laughed, and chatted. Every now and then I crept upstairs and hissed to get Joe's attention.

"When does the toilet go in?" I whispered.

"Soon... soon. We're getting there."

He lied. By evening the bathroom was in, but we were still roughing it. The children, cowed by the eccentric nature of the Porta-toi, took to the underbrush. It was the better part of valor, and finally I too headed for the Scotch broom. Not knowing who might bound down the driveway or be peering at me from the upstairs windows, I feigned an air of casualness, as if I were on an expedition to gather firewood.

The next day was no more productive. Soil pipes were extended and elbow joints joined, but the American Standard remained in its crate.

On Wednesday—though my memory insists it was at least a year later—Joe went back to work.

When I drove him to the ferry, I grabbed his arm as he struggled to get out of the car. "Is Hal coming today? Please tell me he's coming and he's going to put in the new toilet."

"He's coming, he's coming." He pried my fingers loose. "Let go of my coat. You're making a spectacle of yourself. I have to go. I'm late."

With that he slammed the door and sprinted off to a boat that was still out in the bay.

By the time Hal arrived, I'd given up all hope and was considering taking to drink, except that my problems would be compounded.

Hal was in a jovial mood. "Joe tells me you're getting desperate." He laughed as I turned a deep scarlet.

"Heavens no. It's inconvenient, that's all," I said. "Can I help you carry in your toolbox?"

"No, no. I can get it." He went out to the car, and I trailed after him and loaded myself down with pipes, wrenches —anything so he could start immediately.

"Not that," he said. "It's the tire iron." He took it out of my hand and put it back. "You're lucky, you know. Lucky we're doing this while the weather's warm. I remember one Thanksgiving. I think it was ten years ago—no, maybe it was eight. Let's see—"

"Excuse me," I said. "Do you want this taken in too?"

He nodded and went on. "Anyway, it was really cold that year, and Thanksgiving morning about seven o'clock I got a call from some folks who lived way out in the country. I'd done some work for them before."

Like a sheep dog, I nudged him back in the direction of the house.

"They were having a family reunion, the first in ten years, and Grandpa'd had too much wine. Well—" He stopped halfway to the door and chuckled. "It seems the wine made him sick, and when he threw up, he threw his teeth up too."

"Good Lord. You mean his teeth had gone down the drain?" I opened the back door and went in. Hal followed.

"Right. So I got dressed, grabbed a box of cornmeal, and drove out there."

I went into the bathroom, put the wrenches down, then took Hal's toolbox and put it down too. "What was the cornmeal for?" I located a screwdriver and started prying the staples off the carton housing the toilet.

"I'm getting to that. First I bailed out the toilet."

"Was it like this one?" I asked, hoping he'd remember why he'd come.

"Exactly. Anyway, once I got it bailed out I poured in the cornmeal. The teeth were still in the commode, and it surrounded them so they wouldn't break when I took off the fixture."

"Speaking of fixtures ..." I had ours almost out of the box.

"Then I took it off, carried it outside, and ran a hose through, and the teeth floated out."

"Were they all right?"

"Sure. Grandma sterilized them and Grandpa had them back in his mouth before the turkey came out of the oven." Hal shook his head, remembering. Then, as if waking up, he shook his head and whipped off his coat. "Say, I can't stand around talking to you all day. I've got to get to work."

The actual installation didn't take long, and soon afterward the water was hooked up again.

"There you go," Hal said. "It's all ready."

I went into the bathroom, and he pressed down the handle so I could see how it worked. I watched. The water rose slowly, menacingly, up to the rim. It hovered at the top, threatening to spill over, then ever so slowly it receded.

"What's wrong?" I said.

"Oh, I don't know. Probably something in the line that has to clear out."

The water disappeared and he gave it another flush. Again it crept up to the edge and went down.

"Is it going to work?" I tried to keep the panic from spilling over in me.

"Sure." Hal was gathering up his tools. "Give it a flush every now and then. It'll be fine."

With that he put on his coat and left.

All afternoon I flushed and watched, mesmerized like an Indian cobra. Whatever was clogging the line was in no hurry to come out. Once or twice the toilet overflowed, and I attacked it with one of our large assortment of plungers.

Joe was exhausted when I picked him up at the boat. It was his first day back at work in ten days, and things had not gone well. He'd had to unload a truck by himself, then load it up again. The bottle washer had broken down, an order for champagne corks had been mistakenly sent to Boise, Idaho, and, finally, the bus was late and he'd had to run three blocks to make the ferry. Therefore his silence in reply to my "Hi, honey, how much bad news can you stand?" was understandable. I said no more and prayed instead that we'd get through dinner before he discovered the toilet didn't work.

It was not to be. The first sight as we came up the driveway was a cascade of water pouring down the back steps.

"Daddy, Daddy, come look!" The children, ecstatic at another disaster, splashed down the steps to greet him.

"What in the hell happened?"

"It's the toilet," I said. "For some reason it keeps backing up."

"But didn't Hal just put it in?"

"Yeah. He said it was probably something in the line that would clear up."

The children danced around him, escorting him inside. "Mr. Jorgenson was here," they babbled. "He says to tell you, you need a new septic tank."

Joe might have been able to cope had they not mentioned Sven, but that was too much. He pushed the children aside, marched over the field of soggy towels into the kitchen, poured himself a stiff drink, and went to bed.

"Daddy's discouraged," I told the revelers. "Help me put these towels in the washer. Then go eat your dinner. It's all ready. I'll set up the siphon."

I went outside, dug up the trap on the septic tank, hooked up the siphon, then threaded the plumber's snake into the pipe. There was something stuck about twenty feet from the opening, and though I pushed and poked, nothing happened. Finally darkness fell, and I gave up and went in to my own stiff drink and my own bed.

The next day the flushing was somewhat improved, but it still wasn't right. Joe, however, was rested, and he thought he had a solution.

"I'll bet the pea trap's clogged," he said as he sprang out of bed around six. "Get me my boots. I'm going to check."

"Like that?" He was in his underwear.

"I haven't time to fool around. I have to make the seven- fifty boat."

I shrugged, handed him his boots, and he disappeared under the house. I could hear him mumbling down there, and once or twice he yelled up for me to flush or run the water in the sink. Finally he straggled up. Cobwebs draped over his hair like a snood. Dirt was caked on his elbows and knees.

"I don't know what it is," he said. "Work on it today."

I worked on it—that day and the next and the next. Finally I decided I'd clear the line if I had to lie out in the yard poking and pushing till midnight. As soon as everyone left, I grabbed the snake and flung myself on the ground beside the open trap. I threaded the snake in the line. The clog was a bit closer. I poked at it. Nothing happened.

"Stupid pipe," I muttered. "Do you think I enjoy lying out here all day?" I gave it another jab.

"Looks like you're having trouble." A voice leaped out of the morning air. I jumped and dropped my end of the snake into the sewage. Sven was standing behind me.

"Where'd you come from?"

"I walked down the road. You were so busy talking to your septic tank, you didn't hear me. I see you still haven't fixed it." He grinned. "You might as well give up and put in another tank."

"It's not the tank," I snapped. "There's a clog." I hauled the handle out of the sewage and rinsed it off with a hose. "I've worked on it for days, but it won't come loose."

"Maybe there's a root growing through the line."

"No, we checked that."

"Then it must be in the pipe."

I nodded and started poking again. Sven watched.

"My God," he said, "no wonder. You're doing it wrong."

I glared up at him from my prone position. "What do you mean wrong? I didn't know there was an art to reaming."

He ignored my sarcasm. "Of course there's an art. You're poking. You should be turning. Why do you think the handle's bent, and they have a hook on the end of the line?"

I shrugged. I hadn't analyzed the snake. When one's prostrate, enveloped in sewer fumes, one tends to disregard the hows and whys.

"Thread the snake again," Sven ordered. "Now twist."

I threaded and twisted. Something caught. "I've got it!" I yelled. "I've got it. Now what?"

"Now pull slowly ... slowly." It sounded as if I were a novice fisherman reeling in her first marlin.

I pulled slowly. Something began to give way and water trickled out of the pipe. I kept pulling. The water was faster now. Then with a burst of excitement I gave one final jerk. There was a great rush and I hauled in my catch—a rag the size of half a bed sheet.

"What's a sheet doing in the pipes?" I said, and as the words came out I knew. Joe and Hal had stuffed rags in the soil pipe when they took out the toilet. It was to keep down the fumes. Apparently Hal forgot to take them out.

I looked up at Sven. He knew too, I could tell. And he watched me to see if we were going to admit it. We weren't. I got up and dusted myself off.

"See, I told you. We won't need a new septic tank."

I was wrong. The toilet continued to overflow—when the washer drained, when the dishwasher drained, when we emptied the sink, when we brushed our teeth. After the new tub was installed, it was even worse. Then the water backed into the tub too. A shower upstairs meant a bath and a flood downstairs. Everyone I talked to had a suggestion for solving our problem. Put yeast in the drain. Put vinegar in the drain. Reroute the drain field. We tried most of them. Nothing worked.

Finally, one morning by accident I started a load of wash not knowing Joe was in the tub. It was rags and old towels and filthy sneakers, so I added extra soap. All was fine for a while. The washer churned and sloshed. Then it began to drain.

I heard the bellow first, then a crash that sounded as if a giant wrecking ball had been hurled against the bathroom door. Apparently Joe, snoozing in the tub, had been invaded by the foaming discharge from the washer. In his haste to escape, he'd jumped out of the tub, slid across the floor, and smashed into the wall.

When I got there, the door flew open in my face, and Joe, clad only in sudsy slippers, stomped past me to the phone.

"Mr. Zimmer," I heard him say, "this is Joe Combs. How soon can you put in a new septic tank for me?"

23

Vesuvius West

Hearing Joe order a new septic tank was like being face down in a muddy battlefield with bullets whizzing overhead and hearing someone yell, "Cease fire!" The struggle with our explosive plumbing system had been going on for three years, and I was more than willing to surrender my plunger and snake. I was drained, even if the pipes weren't.

It hadn't been conventional warfare. The old, decrepit septic tank used hit-and-run tactics, striking when we were the most vulnerable—at dawn, during family picnics, even in the middle of the night.

At first, when we were still new to country living, we fought back with drain cleaners and septic nutrients. They were useless, so we switched to rubber plungers. When these too failed, I suggested dynamite. Joe vetoed that and came up with a less drastic solution.

"You have to lower the water level in the tank," he told me one day on the phone. He'd gotten this information from his fellow commuters on the morning trip to town. It seems, though we didn't know it at the time, that Bainbridge has more septic tanks than residents, and the theories on their care and training are as numerous as meat-loaf recipes. "You can't unclog the lines till the water level's down."

I didn't care for his choice of pronouns, but gave him the benefit of the doubt, assuming he meant the editorial you. He didn't. He meant me. At the time septic tanks were still a mystery to me.

"How do I lower the water level?" I could see myself bailing or digging channels to the sea.

"Simple. Find the trap. Dig it up. Then put in a siphon."

"Wait a minute. How do I find the trap? I haven't the faintest idea where it is."

"Sure you do. It's right next to the septic tank."

"Where's the septic tank?"

"Near the back door."

"Near the back door where? I'm not going to spend the whole day digging up the lawn looking for the trap. Can't you tell me exactly where?"

My enthusiasm for finding the trap was rivaled only by my enthusiasm for not finding it.

Joe sensed this. We have a finely tuned relationship. I try, by feigned ignorance and wide-eyed naivete, to avoid the grubby chores that in the good old days used to be called men's work. He pretends to agree with me, though I can hear an undercurrent of impatience and annoyance. Then he paints a gruesome picture of the working conditions I'm forcing on him and, with a curt good-bye, leaves me with my conscience.

"Never mind," he said. "Leave it. I'll take care of it when I get home. It'll be dark then, but I should be able to see, if I can get the lantern working. You go on with what you were doing." And he hung up.

I was tempted to call his bluff, but guilt—the force that motivates us all—sent me outside.

The search wasn't as hard as I'd expected. The soil pipe was clearly visible where it emerged from under the house. All I had to do was follow it. I went inside looking for something to poke into the ground, and settled on a shish-kebab skewer. It worked beautifully. I stabbed along the pipe till I felt concrete rather than metal. Then I dug. There it was. I lifted the lid and staggered back a step or two as the fumes billowed out. Then I peered in. Sure enough, the mouth of the pipe was below the water level. Now all I had to do was siphon.

It sounded simple, but I wasn't going to start the siphon the way we do when we bottle the blackberry wine. I picked up the garden hose and put one end down in the trap.

"Now," I said to the dogs, who'd come to see what I was doing, "I need suction of some sort to draw the water up."

The dogs wagged their tails.

"How'm I going to do that?"

They looked at me. They didn't know, but Sheba licked my hand to tell me I had her unwavering support. Then I remembered a repairman who'd drained the washer by putting a hose full of water in it. As the water in the hose emptied, it had sucked up the wash water. I turned on the spigot and left it running till I was sure the hose was full. Then I undid it, held the hose high above my head, and bounded to the edge of the lawn. I put it down next to a couple of spindly lilacs and waited.

It worked, and after the water level was down, I was able to unclog the line.

After that success, I siphoned once or twice a week. In the winter during the rainy season, it became every other day, usually after dark. At the first cry of "It's flooding again, Mom," I grabbed my flashlight, the shovel, and the snake and marched out into the wet, frozen blackness.

Somehow I managed to kneel in the mud, hold the flashlight between my knees, and thread the snake at the same time.

By spring my fingers had lost all feeling, there were calluses on my knees, people were standing upwind when they talked to me, and the spindly lilacs flourishing on nutrients were snarling and pushing trees out of their way in an attempt to reach the sky. Joe's call to Mr. Zimmer came bare moments before they uprooted an old walnut.

I wasn't in on the planning session. Joe and Mr. Zimmer paced off the drain field and staked out the location of the new tank the evening I went to the Spring Program and Square Dance

Exhibition at school. It was fine with me, for when it comes to Joe and me and workmen, any knowledge on my part is a dangerous thing. If I know the drain field is supposed to make a right-angle turn at the maple tree, I become responsible for its doing so. This is because Joe is never home when the so-called experts come to work. It's not that he's not interested. No one could be more concerned. He simply is never home. It's an old military tradition—run the war from the blockhouse. No matter who is scheduled to come—be it tree surgeon or ditch digger—Joe flees to the office and calls home the minute he gets there.

"Has he come yet?"

"No."

"Have you checked to see if he's on his way?"

"Yes."

"Is he?"

"Yes."

"Call me when he comes." Only supreme willpower prevents him from adding, "Over and out."

Once the repairman arrives, the calls become more complicated.

"Have you told him we have near-surface hardpan?"

"No. Should I?"

"Of course. And don't let him talk you into leaching pools. We don't want leaching pools."

Eventually I hand over the phone and let Joe give his own orders. This seems to work. They chat for a while and the man then goes about his tasks as if divinely inspired. Only when Joe comes home and screams at me, "My God! I thought I told you not to let him talk you into leaching pools," do I realize I'm in trouble.

"Is that what those are?"

"Of course. Don't you know a leaching pool when you see it?"

"Not really. Besides, I thought you and he settled it."

"We did. I told him you knew what I wanted. What did he say when he was digging up this mess?"

"He said the Communists are behind the women's lib movement." Repairmen like to educate me politically.

"Good Lord! Can't you supervise a simple process like ditch digging?"

And on and on it goes, ending with a couple of choruses of "And another thing" and a crescendo of slammed doors.

But this time it would be different. I would greet the workers, admit that this was the Combs residence, then let them get on with it. Joe had given them their orders. I would not be consulted. I would relay no messages. I would carry on as if the back yard were not being burrowed through or tunneled under— or so I thought.

At seven thirty, Louie of Louie's Sump and Septic Service arrived to drain the old tank. He hadn't been in on the planning session, so Joe, who felt I couldn't possibly louse up a simple pumping operation, told me to go out when Louie came and show him where the trap was. "I wouldn't even ask you to do this," he explained when I sighed, "but they charge you a searching fee if they have to find the trap themselves."

I went outside as Louie was backing his truck around.

"Hi," he said, unhooking the hose and dragging it over. "Hear you've been having trouble."

"Trouble is putting it mildly."

"That's odd. How big is this tank?"

"Seven hundred and fifty gallons, I think. Whatever it is, it's too small for eight people."

"It shouldn't be." He started up the motor and the pumping began.

"What do you mean?"

"It shouldn't be too small. Our neighbors in Suquamish have one that size and they don't have any trouble."

"Then they must vacuum their dishes and bathe at the stream."

"No. In fact she does several loads of diapers every day. I bet something else is wrong with yours."

"Well, whatever it is, it won't be for long, 'cause we're having another one put in today."

"Oh, I wouldn't do that."

A feeling of panic swept over me. I could almost hear the rumble of machinery as the workmen approached, and this man was advising me not to get a new tank.

I must look helpless or dumb or both, for people are continually advising me about one thing or another. Salesladies exploding out of their knit suits caution me to hold in my stomach. Mothers of one child—a three-year-old docile to the point of being comatose—lecture me on sibling rivalry between teenagers. And my own children, whose rooms could be plowed under periodically, tell me I have to get organized. The worst thing about all this advice is that I take it, or at least I try to.

"What do you mean you wouldn't have a new tank put in?"

"Just that. This one should work. There must be something else that's making it back up. Let me take a look."

He turned off the motor and together we stood staring into the sewage. The dogs, ever interested, peered down too. I half expected a message to float up from the bottom telling us what was wrong. Louie got down on his knees.

"There it is," he said.

"Where?"

"Look here." He took a stick and pointed. "Your baffle's gone. That's what's wrong. All you really need is a new baffle."

"But the men are due any minute."

"You can send them back."

Me send them back? The tank wasn't the only thing that was baffled. I knew I couldn't make the decision by myself. I looked at my watch. Joe was still on the ferry, not due to land for another five minutes.

"I'll have to call my husband," I said, "and he's still on the boat."

"That's all right. I have to finish pumping this out."

I hurried inside. If I time it perfectly, I thought, I can have Joe paged at the ferry terminal. That'll catch him before they come.

I dialed the number.

"Good morning, Washington State Ferries, may I help you?"

"Yes," I said, "I have to get hold of my husband, could you page him?"

"Is this an emergency?"

"Well, sort of. We're having a septic tank put in today and the man who pumped out the old one says we don't need a new one, that it's only the baffle, and the others are coming and I have to ask my husband what to do." I stopped.

There was a pause, and the lady on the other end of the line sighed. "Is he on the Winslow or the Bremerton boat?"

"Winslow."

"What is your husband's name, ma'am?"

"Joseph Combs."

"Joseph Holmes?"

"No, Combs. Combs, as in brush and combs."

"How do you spell that name?" She raised her voice as the background noise swelled. I visualized the commuters, Joe among them, surging past and out into the street while I spelled.

"Combs, C-O-M-B-S, Combs."

"Thank you." I heard her put the phone down, and then a faraway voice announced what sounded like, "Hold the phones, hold the phones. It's messy at the Information Counter."

I waited, hoping to hear Joe's voice. Finally the lady came back on the line. "I'm sorry. He doesn't answer our page."

I hung up. How long before he'd be near another phone? Let's see. He had to walk up to Third Avenue. That should take five minutes. Then there was the wait for the bus. I gave up and went outside.

"It'll be a while," I said. "My husband isn't at work yet. Could you wait and explain it all to him?"

"Sure, no problem."

Silently I cursed Joe for going to work, cursed Louie for mentioning the baffle, and cursed myself for being in the middle again.

Half an hour later I reached Joe.

"Thank God I got you in time," I panted. "The man who came to pump the septic tank, Louie's his name, well, he says we don't need a new one, that we simply have to replace the baffle. He explained to me how it works and says we won't have to spend the money and Mr. Zimmer's men are due any minute and I tried to page you at the dock but you didn't answer and I've been trying—"

"What are you talking about?"

I repeated the whole dismal story.

"Let me talk to him."

I summoned Louie and went out to stand guard in case I had to hold back the trucks. I didn't. After a few minutes Louie walked out shaking his head.

"He says he's going ahead as planned. Too bad. You could have saved a lot of money."

He shrugged and I felt sorry for him.

"Oh, by the way," he added, "your husband wants to talk to you again."

Now I felt sorry for me. Joe was brief and to the point. He'd be home at noon I was to remain calm till he arrived. I promised I'd try.

The actual installation of the septic tank was uneventful. The men were professionals. Trucks came, trucks went. The front loader scooped out a pit, then it reversed itself and the backhoe wove in and out among the rhododendrons and the japonica digging a trench for the drain field. Minutes after one phase was completed and its machinery sent on its way, another lumbered up to take its place. Nothing deterred them from their appointed tasks. Not Joe, who when he came chased after the backhoe, leaping in and out of trenches, shouting questions above the roar of the motor. Not Sylvia and Jenny, who took one look at the young bare-chested men and immediately changed into shorts and halters and stretched out on the lawn for a sunbath. Not Joan, conservationist and protector of natural beauty, who stood guard in front of trees and bushes lest the backhoe get them. Even Robbie and Geoffrey, waited to leap into the trenches and reenact World War I. I didn't interrupt their steady forward pace.

By late afternoon most of the major work was over. The new tank was hooked up to the old, and both fed into the old drain field. The men parked their machinery out of the way and got ready to leave.

I came inside and stood for a while, staring at the toilet. Like an aging starlet on her eighth marriage, I prayed it would work this time, but I half expected another disaster. I heard a door slam outside and a truck start up. Then the noise moved off. Still I stared at the toilet. Finally I pumped up my courage.

I reached for the handle and pressed it down. There was a surge as the water rushed into the bowl. I held my breath, mop at the ready. The water rose, stopped, then swirled and disappeared.

"It works!" I screamed, running out to find Joe. "It works!" Joe was nowhere to be seen, and the rest of the family had vanished too. "It works," I said once more, and the dogs who were sniffing around the trenches wagged their tails. Of course it worked. They knew it would.

24

Two Steps Forward, One Step Back

Professional carpenters are an assured and jovial lot. They aren't plagued with nervous tics, fingernails gnawed to the cuticle, or unexplained rashes. Why should they be? They know what they're doing. I've watched them. They slap up a wall, tape it deftly, and obliterate all seams and nail holes with the swish of a putty knife.

Joe and I piece together a wall out of remnants we've collected from the workroom or else we measure a huge sheet of plasterboard six or eight times till it fits. Then we wedge it in and realize too late we forgot to mark off the studs. So we spend half an hour aimlessly nailing into nothing till, by chance, we find wood. By now the wall looks like a dart board in an English pub, but we stand back in awe anyway and congratulate ourselves on our dexterity. Then Hal comes in and asks why we covered up the wall socket.

Carpenters and contractors sweep through a house, hammering, sawing, nailing in a beam here, framing a door there. They don't nudge each other and whisper, "Hey, Charlie, you think that's going to hold?" They're confident.

Joe and I hammer in a nail and are stunned when it doesn't bend in half. We take ceremonial coffee breaks to celebrate a successfully mitered corner, and sometimes Joe stalks the house at midnight, like Vachel Lindsay's Lincoln, checking the walls to assure himself they're still standing.

I once read that Frank Lloyd Wright, on being advised by phone that his Imperial Hotel had survived the Tokyo earthquake of 1923, sniffed, replied, "Of course it did," and hung up. I marvel at his equanimity. Had Joe and I received such a call, we would have been thunderstruck and blathered, "You're kidding. Did it really?" For in our entire affair with carpentry and plumbing, nothing has ever been certain, and more often than not, two steps forward have meant at least one step back.

When we struggled to fit a ceiling piece in the bathroom, we pried loose a couple of tiles around the tub, swept three pictures off the wall, and bent the towel rack.

The day Joe and Hal finished the west balcony, the library window beneath it blew open, banged against one of the supports, and shattered in an explosion of glass.

Six months after we installed a new and barely affordable plastic tub, Robbie, bathing amid a fleet of homemade battleships, punctured a hole in the side.

We've bought more panes of glass than one would need to keep up a stable of greenhouses.

We've had more water crises than Noah.

And so many bodies fell through the ceiling the first winter that I began to suspect our living room was the target area for a parachute drop.

Most of our furniture will never be the same. Beds have collapsed under the strain of three adults holding up a ceiling, our tables have suffered more distresses than a warehouse full of simulated antiques, and we've put unbroken chairs on the Endangered Species list.

Long ago we lost count of the number of nails stepped on, the number of trips to get tetanus shots, the number of thumbs mashed into blue-blackness, and the number of splinters pried out of reluctant palms. But in fairness to ourselves, not all our mishaps have been due to our amateur status.

Fate has intervened several times. We did nothing to dry up the well. It wasn't our fault the septic tank was too small and, Lord knows, I don't see how we could have prevented the crack in the picture window.

The window was old to begin with. It was the one we'd installed with all the care one would take to transport nerve gas across the Rockies. Originally it belonged to the MacDonalds, friends who'd had it in their garage for several years. In their own throes of remodeling, they had replaced it with a door or a wall, but in the old Island tradition, they'd kept it till someone else could use it.

Half the houses on Bainbridge are patchwork quilts of other houses. We have two doors from a home in Arlington, a double sink from Suquamish, and a banister rescued from the ship President Grant. Conversely, four of our windows now look out on Everett, and somewhere a horse is quenching his thirst out of our old bathtub.

But a picture window was a real bonanza. A new one was financially out of the question, and the alternative was an assortment of smaller windows set in the wall like a display of medical degrees.

Besides being old, it was fragile. There were places where it looked as if cobwebs were embedded in the glass, but we were delighted with it and with the lush August view it afforded us. Then winter came, and the combination of bitter-cold nights and the direct morning sun were too much for it.

One day I noticed a tiny crack along the bottom edge. I kept the news to myself, pulling the draperies before dinner and keeping pots of flowers on the sill in front of it during the day. Joe was at the point where he discouraged easily. It wasn't his fault. When you choke on one salmon bone you shrug and go on eating. But after ten or twelve the tendency is to throw the whole thing out. So I decided I'd wait till the right moment—the day when things were going so well he wouldn't yell at the closest person, me, and say, "I give up. That's it. I spend all my waking hours trying to fix this place up, then when I turn my back everything disintegrates."

The day never came, and the crack, like a river searching for the sea, inched its way up the glass and branched off into tributaries. My flower arrangements got taller and wider. To no avail, however. Joe discovered it the day he caught me dragging a rubber tree into the dining room.

He stared at it for a long time, ran his fingers over it to be sure it wasn't a horrible mirage, then shook his head.

"I give up," he said with a catch in his voice, "that's it. I spend all my waking hours trying to fix this place up, then when I turn my back everything disintegrates."

I nodded silently and centered the rubber tree.

We lived with the crack for several months, charting its daily progress to the ceiling. Sven advised us to drill holes at the end of each branch. We declined to follow his advice. When, at last, the whole pane threatened to crumble we had it replaced.

The window wasn't the first instance of Fate's meddling in our affairs. When Robbie hurled his boomerang into the air, it wasn't skill that sent it circling around into Hal's windshield. When Joe catapulted off the scaffolding, none of us had loosened the nails at the other end. And only Fate could have derived so much pleasure out of tinkering with our water system.

I remember the snowy January when the pipes froze. I tried to get a simple electrical tape to wrap around them and defrost them, but Fate was playful that day. It flattened a tire, shrank the spare, stretched the chains, mucked up the wiring, and blew three fuses.

Then when Fate failed to humble us, Divine Intervention took its turn. One Easter night, out of a clear black sky, a small cloud drifted over our house and threw a lightning bolt down our well and burned up the pump.

We weren't aware of the damage at first. There was a flash of white light and an explosion of thunder. That was all. No windows blew out. No television sets caught fire. No trees were rent asunder. Geoffrey streaked downstairs, wild-eyed at the thought of how close the flash had been. David was right behind him describing how his bed shook, and the other children burst into our room in a frenzy of "What was that?" and "What happened, Dad?" But eventually they all calmed down and went back to bed.

In the morning when I got up, I discovered the damage. The water was off again. Oh, Lord, I thought, now what do I do? It was a silly question. I knew what I had to do. I had to break the news to Joe, and he doesn't take broken news well. For a fleeting moment I toyed with the idea of creeping back into bed and pretending I'd died in the night, but before I could implement my plan, Joe staggered into the bathroom where I was. aimlessly turning faucets on and off.

"The water's off," I said, edging to the door.

"What do you mean the water's off?"

"It's off. Look." I flicked the faucet on again. "See?"

"What happened?"

"I don't know. I think the lightning did it."

"I doubt it." He checked the faucets himself. "It's probably the pressure tank. Remember, before, it got waterlogged and we had to repressurize it?"

"I still think it was the lightning."

"Well, I don't, and I'll prove it." He strode out of the bathroom, picked up his flashlight, and marched outside in his traditional dawn repair costume—underwear and boots.

In a few minutes he was back. "Something's weird in the pump house. The light goes off when it should go on and vice versa, and the pressure switch is a mass of metal."

"See, it was the lightning."

"Maybe." Joe's not effusive when I'm right. "Anyway, call the electrician around nine o'clock and have him come down."

"Can I tell him about the lightning?"

"Lord, no. Those guys think of enough strange explanations for what's wrong without you supplying new ones." He rummaged around in his drawer for some clean socks.

"But he should know."

"Then let him find out. Last time something went wrong the guy said it was because the dogs walked on the well cover. If you mention lightning he'll say, 'Right, right,' and charge us double."

"Oh, I doubt that."

Joe found a pair of blue socks and sat down to put them on. "Don't argue. Just call. Let him take it from there."

"But isn't lightning damage covered by insurance," I persisted, "under an act-of-God clause?"

He stopped, one sock partially on, hanging off his toes like a blue nightcap. Then he shook his head. "I don't think so. You can look, but I doubt it." He pulled the sock on.

The file was way back in the closet, and I poked around till I came up with our homeowner's policy. Sure enough, in the section entitled Perils Insured Against, right between Riot or Civil Commotion and Damage from Self-Propelled Missiles and Spacecraft was Lightning, Thunderstorms, and Hail.

"I'm right," I said. "We're covered for lightning."

"Let me see that." Joe snatched it away from me. He read for a moment, then folded it up. "Tell the man about the lightning."

He mentioned it again at breakfast. It was his last thought before he got on the boat, and once he got to work he called me. "Don't forget, tell him the well or whatever was struck by lightning."

I did, but I needn't have. The electrician said it was evident. Five hundred dollars later the evidence was repaired.

I tried to place the blame on the church, contending it was a heavenly critique of the Easter sermons, but Daddy, Peter Edwards, and Father Barnstable—all of whom had given sermons—denied responsibility. They intimated it was due to the specter of the entire Combs family in church at once. Perhaps it was.

Lately, experience being the teacher it is, we've had fewer and fewer catastrophic mistakes. The septic tank has been behaving itself, the pipes have stayed clear, and it's been six months since a window broke. Of course, last week the handle fell off the oven door, the water pump in the car broke, the vacuum cleaner sucked up a nail and sheared off something, and yesterday when I was scrubbing out the tub Geoffrey came in from playing basketball on the new giant structure Joe and Hal put up.

"Mom," he said, "I don't know what happened. I threw the ball at the hoop, and the hoop fell off."

I thought of Frank Lloyd Wright. "Of course it did," I said, and went back to the tub.

25

But How Do You Stand It?

"**H**ow do you stand it?" Mother stepped over a basketball hoop and carefully placed her foot in the narrow gap between a box of odd sewing remnants and a pie pan full of assorted nuts and bolts. "I couldn't live this way," she said.

I glanced around. The living room looked like a cross between a Rotary Club auction and the aftermath of a garage sale. In the middle stood two upright pianos, back to back and piled high with sheet music, upholstery fabric, the top of an old typewriter case, a wooden sea gull, two vases, and a Chianti bottle. A bare wooden couch and chair Hal had recently finished waited in the comer for bolsters, cushions, and upholstery. The old orange cushions, the carcass of our former couch, lounged in a slovenly pile against the window like a gang sneering, waiting on the comer.

The coffee table, shoved out of the way to make room for the pianos, leaned on wobbly legs against a far wall and panted under a load of paint cans, screwdrivers, saws, drapery rods, a jigsaw puzzle, and the beginnings of Joan's Christmas puppet show. Even the mantel was piled high with trowels, masking tape, and paint rollers, along with the usual assortment of knickknacks and Joan's collection of Christmas candles. (She has a Christmas fetish that knows no season.)

Every chair in the room was heaped with junk, and against the bedroom wall stacks of books, weary from waiting for a shelf, slumped onto the floor—Charlemagne next to Erica Jong, Ben Franklin beside the pharaohs of Egypt.

Mother picked up a bent lampshade off the floor. She held it a moment, searching for a better place to put it, then, finding none, put it back where it was. "Doesn't this drive you crazy?" she asked.

"Oh, a little. But what else can I do? We're doing the library."

Actually it wasn't even one of our more drastic endeavors. No gaping holes to the outside, no wall moving. We were replacing the ceiling and the cardboard walls with Sheetrock, building bookcases, and painting—that's all.

While we talked, Joe, standing on a chair, calmly slapped a strip of tape on the ceiling. He didn't even know we were there. He had the French doors closed and the football game on. Every now and then he waved his putty knife and shouted, "Hot damn!" as someone or other broke loose and ran the length of the field for a touchdown.

Mother shook her head and attempted a retreat. "I just don't see how you stand it," she muttered.

"We're lucky this time," I told her when we were safely back in the kitchen. "This project's going fast."

"I suppose you're right, but I'm glad it's not me." With that she sighed once more, picked up her purse, and left.

Joe hadn't intended to make the library a rush job. It was the next project on the list, that was all. Personally, I dreaded the thought of filling up the living room with debris again, and I complained some.

"Is it going to take long?" I asked.

"As long as it has to."

"Which is about how long?"

"I don't know. I have to finish all the preliminaries and then find a time when Hal and I can build the bookcases."

"As long as that, eh?"

"I'll do it as fast as I can," Joe grumbled. He resents my pressuring him. "However, I'm not going to slap it together."

That's what he thought.

The day we evacuated the library, it was with the usual family effort. We had the same enthusiasm and camaraderie one finds on a chain gang or during a Teamsters strike.

Joan and Robbie were assigned the books from the one shelf we had.

"Take them down and stack them against our bedroom wall," Joe told them.

"But they're heavy."

"Then take a few at a time."

"Why can't Geoffrey do it?"

"Because I have another job for him."

"But—"

"Forget it. Now get going."

Robbie grabbed a stack of war books and staggered out of the room. I found him twenty minutes later leafing through them looking for pictures of disasters. He loves disasters. To him a good day would be one in which he witnessed the bombing of Pearl Harbor, the sinking of the Titanic, two midair collisions, and a nuclear test. It's not that he likes carnage and bloodshed. He likes explosions. I doubt that he realizes people are involved.

Joan was no better. She chose to relocate the back issues of Better Homes and Gardens and consequently found forty-nine pictures of how she wanted her room to look at Christmas.

Joe put Sylvia and Jenny in charge of taking out the rest of the loose stuff, and the results were equally inefficient. Jenny, ever the theatrical entrepreneur, found a carton full of old pictures and slides and wanted to put on a show. Sylvia ran across some of the material I'd brought back from Japan and wanted to make raw silk pants.

David, Geoffrey, Joe, and I moved the pianos.

By dinnertime the living room was almost unnavigable and the library was clear. As we ate, Robbie filled us in on the sinking of the Bismarck and Joan suggested garlands for her door.

Around nine o'clock we crawled into bed.

"That was a good day's work," said Joe, as he settled down to read. He likes to review each day at its end, determining its worth by the amount of work accomplished.

"Sure was."

"Next we'll start ripping the cardboard off the walls."

"OK."

He opened up his book, and I flipped to the magazine section of the paper.

All of a sudden there was a thundering crash of piano chords outside our door. The pictures on the wall trembled slightly and Joe bolted upright.

"My God, what was that?"

"Jenny's practicing, I guess."

"What?" He shook his head as if to drive out the noise.

"I said, I guess Jenny's practicing."

"I realize that, but does she have to practice now?"

I shrugged. "She always practices at night. We just don't hear it in the library with the doors closed."

"Can't she wait till tomorrow?"

"Tomorrow's her lesson, and Mrs. Kaye wants her to work on her fingering."

Jenny ran up and down the scales a few more times, and Joe pulled the covers up trying to keep out the noise.

"Don't worry, honey," I said, chuckling evilly. "It's only till the library's done."

He glared at me over the rims of his glasses. "Very funny." He turned back to his book for a minute, then slammed it shut. "OK, I give up."

With that he struggled to his feet, grabbed a hammer, and marched out of the room.

"Hi, Daddy," Jenny shouted as he went by.

I don't know what he said, but soon I couldn't tell which was Chopin and which was crowbar.

Other projects have been accomplished with less fervor and have taken much longer. Whole sections of the house have stood for months, modestly trying to hide their bare boards. Other piles of books have slid to the floor in utter dejection while the sawdust swirled and the saws chewed eagerly at pristine two-by-fours. And, without fail, somewhere in the middle of each project someone has said, "How do you stand it?"

I'm used to the question. When one has six children, two dogs, two cats, and an assortment of birds, the subject comes up frequently. And though I never have, I'm always tempted to grab the questioner by the shoulders, look deeply into his or her eyes, and say, "Suggest an alternative."

I didn't ask Mother to suggest an alternative. She would have. But it got me to thinking. How do I stand life among the two-by-fours, where plaster dust and sawdust circle endlessly through the house like the volcanic ash from Krakatoa? What keeps me from despairing at the constant mess and upheaval?

It's probably because my housekeeping leaves a lot to be desired anyway. I hate to admit it, but my nesting instincts are few and far between. It must be a genetic flaw, since mothers of large families are supposed to have disinfectant and furniture polish in their veins. But somehow, vacuuming drapery rods and bleaching bathtub stains are not my idea of a burning reason for leaping out of bed in the morning.

I know one thing for certain. My aversion to scrubbing and swabbing isn't due to ignorance. I've read every "helpful hints for harried housekeepers" column there is. I know how to get soot off the fireplace bricks, how to clean grout, and what to do with all the slivers of soap that breed in the soap dish. I know broken walnut halves will erase roller-skate tracks on the grand piano, that nylon net can be used for everything from scrubbing under the water heater to draining spaghetti, and that it's considered chic to put bowl covers on the wheels of your baby buggy when you bring it in the house.

I've read whole books on the subject of keeping a house, hoping to inspire myself. I've drawn charts, kept timetables, and learned mottoes to repeat while dusting the bedsprings.

But somehow when it's oven-cleaning time, I remember a novel I haven't finished, and a voice within me says, The oven will be there tomorrow. The book's due at the library today.

So I read, and later when I turn on the oven to bake the meat loaf and smoke filters out through the burners and follows me around like a pet cloud and the children cough and the cats leave the room and Joe says, "Good Lord, when are you going to get to that oven?" I say, "Tomorrow. I vow I'll do it first thing tomorrow."

With this dilatory outlook, remodeling has only brought me joy and a salve for my conscience.

"Leave the bathroom tiles," Joe tells me. "They have to come out anyway." And I leave them.

"Don't bother scrubbing the wall. We're tearing it down next week." So I drop my sponge and bucket.

"Forget about the wash. Hal and I are moving the pressure tank and the water will be off."

I find that missing out on the Homemaker of the Year award is a small price to pay when I consider the times I've been able to smile and say to relatives, guests, and the refrigerator repairman, " Excuse the mess, but we're remodeling, you know."

There have been times, however, when even I have wondered if it was all worth it—when the well went dry, when we had no heat, when the pipes froze and the roof leaked and the toilet overflowed. I still chafe a bit when I can't make dinner because Joe's painting the kitchen ceiling and has two sawhorses and a plank in front of the stove. I swear when the milk in the refrigerator sours because he and Hal have the power off, when I find drill bits and staples in the washer, or when the vacuum cleaner lets out a shriek which means it's sucked another shingle nail up out of the shag.

When my arms quiver, my hair is full of plaster dust, my back hurts, and my whole right side is bruised from scooching along the roof, I sometimes wonder why we ever decided to buy a home with potential.

Then I look around and I know.

We've created something here—Joe and the children and I—and each one of us recalls the creation and his or her own part of it.

When I look up at the roof, I don't see a roof. I see hot summer days, the children crawling up, down, and over, and shingle hammers bouncing over the edge. I see flashing that I personally put in around the dormers. I can feel how my hands ached as I wielded the heavy tin snips and cut the strips of metal.

The heater isn't a mysterious monster some real-estate salesman assured us was under the house. It's a machine resting in a hole *I* dug. It sends out heat through ducts I whapped together and Joe and David and Geoffrey strung up. It's cobwebs, and nights under the house, and the itch. And it's a glorious click that means I won't have to don three sweaters and thermal underwear.

There isn't a room in this house that doesn't have a history.

"Remember," Joe says when we're sitting around the table after dinner, "the day we bashed in the dining room wall, and the first dinner party we had in here?"

"And the time Joan fell through the ceiling into her own closet and walked funny for a week?"

"And the time," Sylvia bursts in, "Hal threatened to go home and never come back if we didn't stop making so much noise?"

We all have our favorite stories. Jenny remembers how it felt to sleep under the stars when the dormer was nothing but a hole in the sky. David goes on and on about the number of shingles he carried from the front yard up to the roof. He knows how many steps he took, how long it took him, and the approximate weight of each bundle.

I recall a long day on the roof. As I was dragging myself in to go down to get dinner, groaning at the thought of having to cook, I heard Sylvia call, "Dinner's ready! Come and get it."

Geoffrey reminds us that it was he who helped put in the bathroom floor and that he was the first one to go up the stairs. And Joan remembers all the times she kept Joe company when he spackled the upstairs bedrooms.

"Well, I punctured my foot three times on shingle nails," Robbie interrupts, "and I always had to crawl way back under the house to get stuff for Dad."

"Yes, but you didn't have to spend hours in the pump house turning the switch on and off," Geoffrey retorts, "and you didn't have to sit all night under the house, holding the flashlight."

"Yeah, but I held the flashlight for Mom when we were putting in the insulation as a New Year's surprise for Daddy."

"Yeah," they all say, "that was neat. Remember, Daddy? Mom told you to go to the attic for something, and we waited till we heard you get to the top of the ladder. Were you really surprised or did you suspect?"

"I was really surprised," Joe assures them.

And the reminiscences go on.

If we lived in a new house, or one that only needed a coat of paint or a couple of washers for the faucets, our children wouldn't have any "in my day" stories with which to bore their own children. I can hear it now.

"In my day we didn't just move into a room, we had to help build it. We sawed and hammered and painted and worked on the weekends, on vacations, and way into the night, and...

So let the piano stand in the middle of the living room for six weeks or so. And let the books lie there a while longer. Next month, or next year, Jenny will pipe up at dinner and say, "Remember, Daddy, the night we moved the stuff from the library into the living room, and I was practicing, and you came crashing out of your room in your underwear yelling, 'This library's going to be the fastest project the world has ever known'?"

Epilogue

We're almost through now. We don't have a garage yet, or a third bathroom. The kitchen floor needs replacing, and I'm thinking of putting up wallpaper. But I better hurry. Time's running out.

David's graduating from college this spring. Sylvia's on her own and only comes home on weekends. Jenny says she wants a cabin off somewhere in the woods. Geoffrey's building a sailboat and threatens to live in it. And the twins spent a month constructing a clubhouse so they could sleep outside.

Now that each finally has his or her own room, they're leaving. The last time I saw Joe he was at the back door, yelling at a retreating back, "Hey, you, hold it! Where do you think you're going? We're not finished yet."

Post-Epilogue

But they didn't hold it. The emigration continued. When David graduated from college he headed down to Silicon Valley where they appreciate people who, as children, attempted to trisect angles.

The girls got married. First Jenny whose husband, Carlos, spirited her off to California, then Sylvia who with her husband, Roger, fled over the mountains to eastern Washington, and finally Joan whose husband, Doug, though he agreed to stay in the Seattle area goes on at length about a desperate need for sunshine and the day when they both can flee to warmer climes. Geoffrey, also still in Seattle, agrees with Doug and often drones on about plans one day to fly off with Rossana to a not so little grass shack on Maui. Only Robert remains on what island teen agers throughout time have referred to as "The Rock."

Even Joe left. As a result of a brief summer job years before in college when he was with a crew hired to insulate Seattle schools with asbestos, he developed mesothelioma and after a brief three months of agony died short of his 60th birthday.

So, here I am. I have granddaughters, Jenny's Sarah and Emilia and Sylvia's Hannah and Rachel all who have had the audacity to grow up and turn into beautiful young ladies even getting married in Hannah's case. I also have two young grandsons: Geoffrey's Connor and Robert's Joey. But with baseball and grade school and video games they aren't much interested in tales of spackling and clogged drains.

So it is I by myself. The house echoes with forty years of memories: the whine of a skill saw, the pound of a hammer, the drip of a leaky roof. Waking up late at night I can almost hear the girls giggling upstairs or the boys racing their matchbox cars on tracks threaded through bare studs. And at dawn I half expect to see Joe standing by the bed telling me we have to get up and start shingling the roof on the chance it will rain.

But I've given up climbing onto the roof these days. I don't check for leaks. I don't climb out Sylvia's bedroom window in the fall dragging the leaf blower behind me. I don't crawl under the house and, like a beached walrus, inch my way through the dirt to tend to the furnace any more either. I even have left the task of pressurizing the water tank to the professionals, all the while reasoning that this is why God invented the telephone and the yellow pages.

The house is now warm in the winter and cool in the summer. On winter mornings I can watch the sky turn orange and red in the eastern sky as I sip my coffee. In spring I can see the first rays of the sunlight on the tree tops across the bay. The sound of a summer rain still lulls me to sleep at night, and when autumn afternoons are warm and the walnut trees have turned to gold, I'm still glad we bought a house that has windows that swing out.

CPSIA information can be obtained at www.ICGtesting.com
Printed in the USA
BVOW070705100712

294757BV00001B/2/P